Pauline H. Tesler

Jean Shinoda Bolen, MD, is a psychiatrist, a Jungian analyst, and an internationally known author and speaker. Her books include *The Tao of Psychology, Goddesses in Everywoman, Gods in Everyman, Ring of Power, Crossing to Avalon, Close to the Bone, The Millionth Circle, Goddesses in Older Women, Crones Don't Whine, Urgent Message from Mother, Like a Tree,* and *Moving Toward the Millionth Circle.* She is a distinguished life fellow of the American Psychiatric Association, a former clinical professor of psychiatry at the University of California–San Francisco, and a past board member of the Ms. Foundation for Women and the International Transpersonal Association. She lives in Marin County, California.

Goddesses in Everywoman

Also by Jean Shinoda Bolen, MD

The Tao of Psychology
Gods in Everyman
Ring of Power
Crossing to Avalon
The Millionth Circle
Goddesses in Older Women
Crones Don't Whine
Close to the Bone
Urgent Message from Mother
Like a Tree
Moving Toward the Millionth Circle

Goddesses in Everywoman

Powerful Archetypes in Women's Lives

Jean Shinoda Bolen, MD

HARPER

NEW YORK • LONDON • TORONTO • SYDNEY

HARPER

First Harper Colophon edition published 1985.
First Quill edition published 2004.
Thirtieth Anniversary Edition published in Harper paperback in 2014.

The Library of Congress has catalogued the Twentieth Anniversary Edition as follows:
Bolen, Jean Shinoda.
Goddesses in everywoman : powerful archetypes in women's lives / Jean Shinoda Bolen.—20th anniversary ed.
          p. cm.
Originally published: San Francisco : Harper & Row, c1984. With new introd.
          Includes bibliographical references and index.
          ISBN 0-06-057284-1 ISBN 978-0-06-057284-6
          1. Women—Psychology. 2. Archetype (Psychology). 3. Mythology, Greek—Psychology. I. Title.
HQ1206.B54 2004
305.4—dc22
2003063266

ISBN 978-0-06-232112-1 (thirtieth anniversary edition)

21 LSC 20 19 18 17 16 15 14

To my mother, Megumi Yamaguchi Shinoda, M.D.,
who was determined to help me grow up—as she hadn't—
feeling that I was fortunate to be a girl,
and could do whatever I aspired to as a woman.

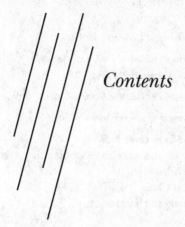

Contents

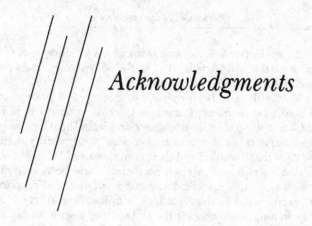

Acknowledgments

Every chapter in this book has many unnamed contributors—patients, friends, colleagues—who exemplified aspects of each goddess archetype, or provided insights into them. Most descriptions are therefore composites of many women, known to me under many circumstances; especially through twenty years of psychiatric practice. It is a privilege to be trusted by people who reveal their depths to me, enabling me to better understand their psychology and through them, the psychology of others, including myself. My patients are my best teachers. To all of them, thank you.

I have been blessed and burdened by many editors, each of whom added to the development of this book and to my growth as a writer during the three years that I worked on the manuscript: editorial direction and comment came from Kirsten Grimstad, Kim Chernin, Marilyn Landau, Jeremy Tarcher, Stephanie Bernstein, and Linda Purrington, to whom I turned for copyediting. And in the midst of their differing perspectives, I also learned to trust my own voice and vision, which was a lesson in itself and led to a change in publishers. In this, Kim Chernin's encouragement was especially valuable.

My thanks go also to Nancy Berry, who worked skillfully and swiftly at the typewriter and computer whenever I called on her for help; to my literary agents, John Brockman and Katinka Matson, who added their expert perspective to a difficult "book birthing" process; and to my publisher, Clayton

Carlson at Harper & Row, who through his intuition and personal regard for my first book, *The Tao of Psychology*, had faith in me and in *Goddesses in Everywoman*.

My family have been stalwart supporters as I labored on this book in their midst. Long ago, I decided that if I were to write, I would do it without withdrawing from them or closing a door between us. I would be available and present, at the same time that I would need their consideration. My husband, Jim, and my children, Melody and Andy, have been with me all the way on this project. In addition to emotional support, Jim has from time to time lent his professional eye as an editor to my writing, encouraging me to trust my own instincts, to leave in examples and images that evoke feelings.

And my heartfelt thanks to many people whose support to finish *Goddesses in Everywoman* came at synchronistic times—whenever I was discouraged and needed to be reminded that this book could be helpful to others. My task was to persevere until the book was finished. Once published, I knew that it would have a life of its own and would find whomever it is supposed to reach.

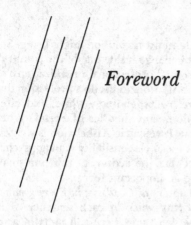

Foreword

I would like to invite you into this book, especially if you are one of those readers who might be, as I was, resistant to its theme. After all, how can mythological goddesses from a patriarchal past help us to analyze our current realities or reach an egalitarian future?

Just as we are most likely to buy books recommended by trusted friends, my inspiration to read this manuscript came from knowing its author.

I met Dr. Jean Shinoda Bolen when she was organizing Psychiatrists for ERA, a group of women and men inside the American Psychiatric Association whose professional experience had led them to believe that equal treatment under the law was crucial to women's mental health. They therefore supported the passage of the Equal Rights Amendment.

All groups are the result of many energies, but Jean was clearly an effective and inspired organizer of this one. She not only envisioned such a group and sparked the imagination of her colleagues; she also followed through on the procedural detail of forging a cohesive, national organization out of busy and disparate people. In that process, she took care to bridge generational, racial, and professional differences, to research accurate, relevant information, and to leave even the most resistant adversary with dignity and some new understanding.

Watching Jean in action left no doubt that she was a practical, expert organizer in the here and now; a gentle revolutionary whose healing calm and accepting spirit were testimony to the better world that a feminist revolution might bring. She helped to create a center of change inside one of the country's most prestigious and influential professional organizations: all this as a woman and a minority woman inside a profession that was 89% male, even more overwhelmingly white, and often still limited by the male-dominant theories of Freud. When the history of the American Psychiatric Association is written, and perhaps the history of social responsibility among psychiatrists in general, I suspect that the actions of this one small, soft-spoken woman will be an important force.

As I read the first chapters of *Goddesses in Everywoman*, I could hear Jean's trustworthy voice in each sentence of its clear, unpretentious prose; yet there were still hints of a romantic or inhibiting predestination in my thoughts about the goddess to come. Because Jung and others who placed such archetypes in the collective unconscious ended with either/or, masculine/feminine polarities—thus inhibiting men as well as women from wholeness, and leaving women at the inevitably less rewarded end of the spectrum—I worried about the way these archetypes might be used by others, or the way women ourselves might be encouraged to imitate and thus accept their limitations.

It was the explanation of the individual goddesses themselves that not only put my worries to rest, but opened new paths to understanding.

For one thing, there are seven complex archetypes to examine and combine in various ways, and each has within herself myriad variations. They take us far beyond the simple-minded dichotomy of virgin/whore, mother/lover that afflicts women in patriarchies. Yes, there are goddesses who identify themselves entirely by their relationship to a powerful man—after all, they lived under patriarchy, as do we—but they also show their power, whether by subterfuge or openly. And there are also models of autonomy that takes many forms, from sexual and intellectual to political and spiritual. Most unusual, there are examples of women rescuing and bonding with each other.

Second, these complex archetypes can be combined and called upon according to the needs of a woman's situation or the undeveloped part of herself. If a glimpse in the media of a female role model can have such important impact on the lives of women, how much more profound might be the activating and calling forth of an archetype within her?

Finally, there is no instruction to stereotype or limit ourselves to one goddess or even several. Together, they make up the full circle of human qualities. Indeed, each of these arose from the fragmentation of the one goddess, Great Goddess, the whole female human being who once lived in prepatriarchal times—at least in religion and imagination. Perhaps then, as now, imagining wholeness was the first step to realizing it.

At a minimum, these archetypal goddesses are a useful shorthand for describing and thus analyzing many behavior patterns and personality traits. At a maximum, they are ways of envisioning and thus calling up needed strengths and qualities within ourselves. As Alice Walker, the poet and novelist, makes so movingly clear in *The Color Purple*, we imagine god and endow her or him with the qualities we need to survive and grow.

The highest value of this book lies in the moments of recognition it provides. The author labels them as moments of "Aha!": that insightful second when we understand and internalize; when we recognize what we ourselves have experienced, feel trust because of that truth, and then are taken one step further to an understanding of, "Yes, that's why."

Each reader will learn something different and that "Aha!" must be our own. For me, the first came from reading of Artemis, who bonded with other women and who rescued her mother while wishing not to be like her. I felt recognition, as well as pride at being cited as an example of this archetype that is rare in a patriarchal society. But I also knew I had not developed the fearlessness of conflict or the real autonomy of Artemis. Persephone mirrors feelings most of us experience as teenagers. Her strength or weakness was another "Aha!": that familiar ability to wait for someone else's image and expectations to be projected onto us, whether a particular man's or that of society; that "trying on" of many identities. So were the constant reading and habit of living inside her head that are typical of Athena; the diffuse and receptive consciousness of Hera, Demeter, and Persephone; and Aphrodite's valuing of intensity and spontaneity over permanence in relationships and in creative work.

Other goddesses are instructive for qualities that we lack

in ourselves and need to develop, or qualities we see in people around us and do not understand. I learned from Hestia's contemplative way of going about daily chores, for instance, that they can be an ordering and sorting of priorities when viewed in a more symbolic and spiritual way. I envied Athena and Artemis for their focused consciousness, and felt more understanding of the many men who have learned not to "notice" or illuminate many things on the periphery of vision. I learned from the example of those two independent goddesses that conflict and hostility may be necessary, even positive, and should not be taken personally.

The author's sensitive analysis of archetypes takes them out of their patriarchal framework of simple exploits and gives them back to us as larger-than-life but believable, real women.

From now on, for instance, when I am longing for one of those magical, spontaneous conversations in which the whole becomes far more than the sum of its parts, with each person improvising as in music, I might think of the qualities of Aphrodite. When I need to retreat to the hearth and contemplation, Hestia could lead the way. When I lack the courage to face conflict on behalf of myself or other women, Artemis is a good woman to remember.

It no longer matters which comes first, the reality or the imagining of reality. As Jean Houston writes in *The Possible Human*, "I have always thought of a myth as something that never was but is always happening."

As we lead ourselves out of unequal societies, gods and goddesses may become one and the same. In the meantime, this book offers us new paths to take: new ways to see and to become.

You may find a myth that will evoke the reality in you.

—GLORIA STEINEM

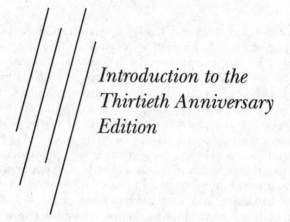

Introduction to the Thirtieth Anniversary Edition

Originally published in 1984, *Goddesses in Everywoman* presented a new psychology of women based on the goddesses of ancient Greece, whose names and mythologies have endured for more than three thousand years. It became a bestseller and then a never-out-of-print classic—like a woman with good bone structure, seemingly ageless.

Goddesses in Everywoman brought together what I knew as a psychiatrist and Jungian analyst, and as a woman in an era of feminism. I saw uniquely female ways of being and behaving that were rewarded or rejected by patriarchal judgments. I also recognized underlying personality patterns that determined how an individual woman responded to unwanted events and opportunities. I found myself turning to the literature of Greek mythology, and there I found remarkable parallels that transformed my thinking. In myths about the Greek goddesses, every goddess has different qualities and values, and as a whole, they include the full panorama of human attributes, including attributes such as competitiveness and intelligence. It was very exciting for me to make this connection. I felt the way an archeologist must feel when a pattern emerges and instead of pottery shards to puzzle over, she now sees a whole vessel, its uses becoming clear in the context of its time. And so it has been for my readers. Over the years, many of them have reported having an *aha!* revelation about themselves in reading these pages and seeing their modern-day experiences through the lens of these goddesses from the past. *Goddesses in Everywoman* has validated their authentic selves and thereby changed their lives.

Goddesses in Everywoman has been spreading its message through translations in Europe, South America, Japan, South Korea, and Taiwan, and most recently Russia and numerous former Soviet republics. It has been secretly translated into Farsi and is being circulated and read underground by Iranian women. That women's rights are human rights and vice versa is not acknowledged in the many parts of the world where women are oppressed and treated as property. There are geographical parallels to the spread of ideas of democracy and human rights, which will naturally and invariably lead to ideas about the empowerment and equality of women. These are ideas whose time has yet to come in some places, but they are on their way. A psychology that supports individual women to make their own choices and see themselves as protagonists in their own life story changes them. And this has a ripple effect across the globe.

There has never been a better time in history for women in the Western-influenced world to live their individual potential in the outer world and to live fulfilling, long, and healthy lives. To live a meaningful life has to do with what matters personally: love of what we do, who we love and are loved by, and living by our values. When those values are courage, kindness, compassion, justice, and service, we help make our world a better place. At a time when humanity could self-destruct and take life on the planet down with us, what we do matters beyond us as well.

Goddesses in Everywoman provides what I called a *binocular* perception of women's psychology. We see through two eyes, and the two images are then merged in the brain into a three-dimensional picture. The equivalent in psychological awareness is realizing that there are two powerful forces that shape every woman's life: the archetypes within us and the outside cultures of family, society, and religion. We each need to become conscious about both in order to make informed choices about what we do with our one precious life.

In *Goddesses in Everywoman*, I describe the qualities that personify each goddess, her symbols, and her lineage, and I retell ancient myths about her. Then I describe the archetype each goddess represents and how these show up in women as personality traits and are expressed through various stages of women's lives. All of the goddess-archetypes have potential shadow qualities, some of which can become symptoms, others of which can cause problems for other people or conflicts with them. Since one-sidedness or identification with a particular archetype may limit or handicap a woman's becoming a whole person and shadow aspects are negative, the last section about each goddess is about "Ways to Grow."

The strength of any particular archetype varies in individuals—in the same way that innate potentials such as musical gifts, types of intelligence, or physical coordination vary among us. Developing or expressing what is deeply within us can be a source of joy. The goddess archetypes are deep desires that vary from woman to woman: for autonomy, creativity, power, intellectual challenge, spirituality, sexuality, or relationships. These urges lead to careers, professions, political action, meditation, or artistic expression; they create the yearnings to have a lover, to be a mother, to be married or alone. Meaning is what we experience subjectively when what we do with our lives engages our archetypal stirrings and yearnings, which are sources of joy and grief.

Five years after *Goddesses in Everywoman, Gods in Everyman* (1989) was published. I had heard from men who asked, "What about us?" after they heard me speak about the goddess archetypes. Many had read *Goddesses in Everywoman* and now better understood the women in their lives. Many men could see that they were attracted to a particular goddess-archetype and were drawn to women who had something about them that hooked this projection. There were even men who said that they had discovered a goddess archetype who lived in and through them. By the time I wrote *Gods in Everyman*, I found myself saying that a more accurate title—and a book twice as long—would have been called *Gods and Goddesses in Everyone.*

Jean Shinoda Bolen, MD
March 2014
Mill Valley, California
www.jeanbolen.com

From the seed grows a root, then a sprout; from the sprout, the seedling leaves; from the leaves, the stem; around the stem, the branches; at the top, the flower. . . . We cannot say that the seed causes the growth, nor that the soil does. We can say that the potentialities for growth lie within the seed, in mysterious life forces, which, when properly fostered, take on certain forms.

M. C. Richards, *Centering in Pottery, Poetry and the Person*

Goddesses in
Everywoman

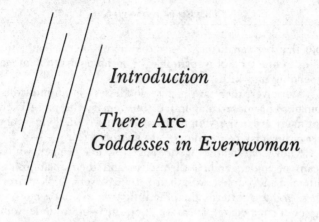

Introduction

There Are Goddesses in Everywoman

Everywoman has the leading role in her own unfolding life story. As a psychiatrist, I have heard hundreds of personal stories, and I realize that there are mythic dimensions in every one. Some women come to see a psychiatrist when they are demoralized or not functioning, others when they wisely perceive that they are caught in a situation they need to understand and change. In either case, it seems to me that women seek the help of a therapist in order to learn how to be better protagonists or heroines in their own life stories. To do so, women need to make conscious choices that will shape their lives. Just as women used to be unconscious of the powerful effects that cultural stereotypes had on them, they may also be unconscious of powerful forces within them that influence what they do and how they feel. These forces I am introducing in this book in the guise of Greek goddesses.

These powerful inner patterns—or archetypes—are responsible for major differences among women. For example, some women need monogamy, marriage, or children to feel fulfilled, and they grieve and rage when the goal is beyond their reach. For them, traditional roles are personally meaningful. Such women differ markedly from another type of woman who most values her independence as she focuses on achieving goals that are important to her, or from still another type who seeks emotional intensity and new experiences and consequently moves from one relationship or one creative effort to the next. Yet another type of woman seeks solitude and

finds that her spirituality means the most to her. What is fulfilling to one type of woman may be meaningless to another,
depending on which "goddess" is active.

Moreover, there are many "goddesses" in an individual
woman. The more complicated the woman, the more likely
that many are active within her. And what is fulfilling to one
part of her may be meaningless to another.

Knowledge of the "goddesses" provides women with a
means of understanding themselves and their relationships
with men and women, with their parents, lovers, and children.
These goddess patterns also offer insights into what is motivating (even compelling), frustrating, or satisfying to some wom-
en and not to others.

Knowledge of the "goddesses" provides useful information for men, too. Men who want to understand women better
can use goddess patterns to learn that there are different types
of women and what to expect from them. They also help men
understand women who are complex or who appear to be
contradictory.

Knowledge of the "goddesses" also provides therapists
who work with women with useful clinical insights into their
patients' interpersonal and intrapsychic conflicts. Goddess patterns help account for differences in personality; they contribute information about the potential for psychological difficulties and psychiatric symptoms. And they indicate the ways a
woman in a particular goddess pattern can grow.

This book describes a new psychological perspective of
women based on images of women—provided by the Greek
goddesses—that have stayed alive in human imagination for
over three thousand years. This psychology of women differs
from all theories that define a "normal" woman as a woman
who conforms to one "correct" model, personality pattern, or
psychological structure. It is a theory based on observing the
diversity of normal variations among women.

Much of what I have learned about women was gained
within a professional context—in my office as a psychiatrist
and Jungian analyst, through supervising trainees and teaching, as Clinical Professor of Psychiatry at the University of
California, and as a supervising analyst at the C. G. Jung Institute in San Francisco. But the female psychology I develop

within these pages comes from more than just professional experience. Much of what I know is derived from being a woman in women's roles—from being a daughter, a wife, a mother of a son and daughter. My knowledge also grew through talks with women friends and in women's groups. Both are situations in which women mirror aspects of themselves to each other—we see ourselves reflected in another woman's experience, and we become conscious of some aspect of ourselves we were not aware of before, or of what we as women have in common.

My knowledge of women's psychology has also grown out of the experience of being a woman at this time in history. In 1963, I began my residency in psychiatry. Two events in that same year led to the women's movement of the 1970s. First, Betty Friedan published *The Feminine Mystique,* articulating the emptiness and dissatisfaction of a generation of women who had lived for and through others. Friedan described the source of this unhappiness as a problem of identity, the core of which was a stunting or an evasion of growth. She maintained that this problem is fostered by our culture, which does not permit women to accept or gratify their basic need to grow and fulfill their potential as human beings. Blowing the whistle on cultural stereotypes, Freudian dogma, and the manipulation of women by the media, her book presented ideas whose time had come—ideas that led to an outpouring of repressed anger, the birth of the women's liberation movement, and later to the formation of NOW, the National Organization for Women.[1]

That same year, 1963, President John F. Kennedy's Commission on the Status of Women published its report, documenting the inequalities in the economic system of the United States. Women were not being paid the same as men for doing the same job; women were being denied employment opportunities and advancement. This glaring unfairness was further evidence of how women's roles were devalued and limited.

I thus entered psychiatry at a time when the United States was on the threshold of the women's movement, and I had my consciousness raised in the 1970s. I became aware of inequalities and discrimination against women and learned that cultural standards determined by men rewarded or punished women for adhering to or rejecting stereotyped roles. As a result, I joined a handful of feminist colleagues in the Northern California Psychiatric Society and in the American Psychiatric Association.

BINOCULAR VISION INTO THE PSYCHOLOGY OF WOMEN

During the same period that I was acquiring a feminist perspective, I was simultaneously becoming a Jungian analyst. After completing my psychiatric residency in 1966, I entered the C. G. Jung Institute of San Francisco as a candidate in the training program and was certified as an analyst in 1976. My perspective on the psychology of women grew steadily over this period, incorporating feminist insights with Jungian archetypal psychology.

It felt as if I were bridging two worlds as I ventured back and forth between Jungian analysts and feminist psychiatrists. My Jungian colleagues didn't bother much with what was going on in the political and social world. Most seemed only vaguely aware of the relevance of the women's movement. My feminist friends in psychiatry, if they thought of me as a Jungian analyst at all, seemed to consider this aspect either an esoteric, mystical interest of mine or a respected subspecialty having little to do with women's issues. In shuttling back and forth, meanwhile, I've discovered that a new depth of understanding results when the two perspectives—Jungian and feminist—are taken together. The two provide binocular vision into the psychology of women.

The Jungian perspective has made me aware that women are influenced by powerful inner forces, or *archetypes,* which can be personified by Greek goddesses. And the feminist perspective has given me an understanding of how outer forces, or *stereotypes*—the roles to which society expects women to conform—reinforce some goddess patterns and repress others. As a result, I see every woman as a "woman-in-between": acted on from within by goddess archetypes and from without by cultural stereotypes.

Once a woman becomes aware of forces that influence

her, she gains the power that knowledge provides. The "goddesses" are powerful, invisible forces that shape behavior and influence emotions. Knowledge about the "goddesses" within women is new territory for consciousness raising about women. When she knows which "goddesses" are dominant forces within her, a woman acquires self-knowledge about the strength of certain instincts, about priorities and abilities, about the possibilities of finding personal meaning through choices others might not encourage.

Goddess patterns also affect relationships with men. They help explain some of the difficulties and affinities certain women have with certain men. Do they choose men who are powerful and successful in the world? Crippled and creative? Boyish? Which "goddess" is the unseen impetus propelling a woman toward a particular type of man? Such patterns influence choices and the stability of relationships.

Relationship patterns also bear the imprint of particular goddesses. Father-daughter, brother-sister, sister-sister, mother-son, lover-lover, or mother-daughter—each pair represents a configuration that is natural for a particular goddess.

Every woman has "goddess-given" gifts to learn about and accept gratefully. Every woman also has "goddess-given" liabilities, which she must recognize and surmount in order to change. She cannot resist living out a pattern determined by an underlying goddess archetype until she is conscious that such a pattern exists and seeks to fulfill itself through her.

MYTHS AS INSIGHT TOOLS

The first important link I saw between mythological patterns and women's psychology was provided by Erich Neumann, a Jungian analyst, in his book *Amor and Psyche*. Neumann used mythology as a means of describing feminine psychology. I found Neumann's combination of myth and psychological commentary to be a powerful "insight tool."

In the Greek myth of Amor and Psyche, for example, Psyche's first task was to sort a huge, disordered heap of seeds, placing each kind of grain in a separate mound. Her initial reaction to this task, as well as to the next three, was despair. I noticed that the myth fit a number of my women patients who were struggling with various important tasks. One was a graduate student who felt overwhelmed by a term paper, not knowing how she could organize the mound of material. Another was a depressed young mother who had to figure out where her time went, sort out her priorities, and find a way to continue to paint. Each woman was, like Psyche, called on to do more than she felt capable of, yet on a course that she herself had chosen. They both took heart from a myth that mirrored their situation, provided them with insight into the way they reacted to new demands, and gave a larger meaning to their struggle.

When a woman senses that there is a mythic dimension to something she is undertaking, that knowledge touches and inspires deep creative centers in her. Myths evoke feeling and imagination and touch on themes that are part of the human collective inheritance. The Greek myths—and all the other fairytales and myths that are still told after thousands of years—remain current and personally relevant because there is a ring of truth in them about shared human experience.

When a myth is interpreted, intellectually or intuitively grasped understanding can result. A myth is like a dream that we recall even when it is not understood, because it is symbolically important. According to mythologist Joseph Campbell, "Dream is the personalized myth, myth the depersonalized dream."[2] No wonder myths invariably seem vaguely familiar.

When a dream is correctly interpreted, the dreamer has a flash of insight—an "Aha!"—as the situation to which the dream refers becomes clear. The dreamer intuitively grasps and keeps the knowledge.

When someone has an "Aha!" response to an interpretation of a myth, the particular myth is symbolically addressing something that is personally important to him or her. The person now grasps something and sees through to a truth. This deeper level of understanding has occurred in audiences I have spoken to when I have told myths and then interpreted their meaning. It is a way of learning that strikes a chord, in which theory about women's psychology becomes either self-knowledge or knowledge about significant women to whom the men and women in the audience relate.

I began using mythology in seminars on the psychology

6

of women toward the end of the 1960s and early 1970s, first at the University of California Medical Center–Langley Porter Psychiatric Institute, then at the University of California at Santa Cruz and the C. G. Jung Institute in San Francisco. In the next decade and a half, lecturing gave me further opportunity to develop my thoughts and get responses from audiences in Seattle, Minneapolis, Denver, Kansas City, Houston, Portland, Fort Wayne, Washington, D.C., Toronto, New York, and in the San Francisco Bay Area, where I live. Wherever I lectured, the response was the same: when I used myths in conjunction with clinical material, personal experiences, and insights from the women's movement, new and deeper understanding resulted.

I had begun with the Psyche myth, a myth that spoke to women who put relationships first. Then I told a second myth, one whose meaning I had developed, that described women who were challenged rather than overwhelmed when there were obstacles to overcome or tasks to master and who consequently could do well in school and out in the world. The mythological heroine was Atalanta, a runner and a hunter who succeeded well at both roles, outdoing men who tried to defeat her. She was a beautiful woman who was compared to Artemis, Greek goddess of the Hunt and the Moon.

This way of teaching naturally invited questions about other goddesses, and I began to read and wonder about their range and what they represented. I began to have my own "Aha!" reactions. For example, a jealous, vindictive woman walked into my office, and I recognized in her the raging, humiliated Hera, Goddess of Marriage and consort of Zeus. Her consort's philandering provoked the goddess into repeated efforts to seek and destroy "the other woman."

This patient was a woman who had just discovered that her husband was having an affair. Since then, she had been obsessed with the other woman. She had vindictive fantasies, was spying on her, and was so caught up with getting even that she felt crazy. As was typical of Hera, her anger was not directed toward her husband, who had been the one who lied to her and been unfaithful. It was very helpful for my patient to see that her husband's infidelity had evoked a Hera response. She now understood why she felt "taken over" by her rage, and how it was destructive to her. She could see that she needed to confront her husband with his behavior and face the marital problems between them, rather than turn into vengeful Hera.

Then a woman colleague unexpectedly spoke out against the Equal Rights Amendment, which I was supporting. In the midst of the anger and hurt I felt, I suddenly had an "Aha!" insight into the situation. It was a clash of types based on the goddesses in our respective psyches. At that moment, over this subject, I was acting and feeling like Artemis, archetypal Big Sister, protector of women. My opponent, in contrast, was like Athena, the daughter who had sprung full grown from Zeus's head, and was thereafter the goddess-patron of heroes, defender of the patriarchy, very much "her father's daughter."

On another occasion I was reading about the kidnapping of Patty Hearst. I realized that the myth of Persephone, the maiden who was abducted, raped, and held captive by Hades, Lord of the Underworld, was being played out once more, this time in newspaper headlines. At the time, Hearst was a student at the University of California, a sheltered daughter of two modern-day affluent Olympians. She was kidnapped—taken into the underworld by the leader of the Symbionese Liberation Army—imprisoned in a dark closet, and repeatedly raped.

Soon I was seeing the "Goddesses in Everywoman." I found that knowing which "goddess" was present deepened my understanding of everyday occurrences as well as of more dramatic events. For instance: which goddess might be showing her influence when a woman prepares meals and does housework?

I realized that there was a simple test: when a woman's husband goes away for a week, what does she do about meals for herself, and what happens to the house? When a Hera woman (shorthand for "this particular goddess is the dominant influence") or an Aphrodite woman has a solitary dinner, it is likely a sorry and dismal affair: cottage cheese out of the carton, perhaps. Whatever is in the refrigerator or cupboard is good enough for her when she's alone, in marked contrast to the elaborate or good meals she provides when her husband is home. She cooks meals for him. She makes what he likes, of course, rather than what she prefers, because she is a good wife who provides good meals (Hera), is motivated by her maternal nature to take care of him (Demeter), does what pleases him (Persephone), or seeks to be attractive to him (Aphrodite). But if Hestia is the goddess who influences her, a woman will set the table and provide a real meal for herself when she is alone. And the house will stay in its usual good order. If the other goddesses provide the housekeeping motivation, it's more likely to be neglected until just before her husband's return. A Hestia woman will bring in fresh flowers for herself that will never be seen by the absent man. Her apartment or house always feels like home because she lives there, not because she makes it that way for someone else.

Next came the question "Would others also find this way of knowing about women's psychology through myths useful and helpful?" The answer came when I lectured on "Goddesses in Everywoman." The audiences were turned on, intrigued, abuzz with the excitement of using mythology as an insight tool. This was a way for people to understand women, a way that was emotionally moving. As I shared these myths, people saw and felt and heard what I was talking about; as I interpreted the myths, people had "Aha!" reactions. Both men and women grasped the meaning of myths as personal truth, verifying something they already knew and were now making conscious.

I also spoke at meetings of professional organizations and discussed my ideas with psychiatrists and psychologists. Parts of this book were first developed as presentations before the International Association for Analytic Psychology, the American Academy of Psychoanalysis, the American Psychiatric Association, the Women's Institute of the American Orthopsychiatric Association, and the Association for Transpersonal Psychology. My colleagues found this approach clinically helpful, and appreciated the insight into character pattern and psychiatric symptoms that an understanding of the "goddesses" can provide. For most of them, this was the first presentation on the psychology of women they had heard given by a Jungian analyst.

Only my Jungian colleagues were aware that I was (and am) advancing new ideas about feminine psychology that differ from some of Jung's concepts, as well as integrating feminist perspectives with archetypal psychology. Although this book is written for a general audience, the sophisticated Jungian reader might note that a psychology of women based on feminine archetypes challenges the general applicability of Jung's anima-animus theory (see Chapter 3, "The Virgin Goddesses"). Many Jungian writers have written about Greek gods and goddesses as archetypal figures. I am indebted to them for contributing their knowledge and insights, and cite their work (see Chapter Notes). However, in selecting seven Greek goddesses, and categorizing them into three specific groups according to how they function psychologically, I have created a new typology as well as a means of understanding intrapsychic conflicts (the whole book). Within this typology, I have added the concept of Aphrodite consciousness as a third mode to the focused consciousness and diffuse awareness that have already been described in Jungian theory (see Chapter 11, "The Alchemical Goddess").

Two additional new psychological concepts are introduced, but not elaborated on, since to have developed them further would have been a diversion from the theme of this book.

First, the "goddesses" provide an explanation for inconsistencies between women's behavior and Jung's theory of psychological types. According to Jung's psychological types, a person is supposed to be either/or: extraverted or introverted in attitude; to use feeling or thinking as an assessing mode; and perceive through intuition or sensation (through the five senses). Moreover, one of these four functions (thinking, feeling, intuition, sensation) is supposed to be the most consciously developed and relied on; whichever it is, the other half of the pair is supposed to be the least reliable or least conscious. Exceptions to Jung's "either/or, and most developed/least conscious" model have been described by Jungian psychologists June Singer and Mary Loomis. I believe that the goddess archetypes provide an explanation for the exceptions in women.

For example, as a woman "shifts gears" and goes from one facet of herself to another, she can shift from one goddess pattern to another: in one setting, for example, she is an extraverted, logical Athena who pays attention to details; in another situation, she is an introverted hearth-keeping Hestia for whom "still waters run deep." This shifting explains the difficulty that a many-sided woman has determining what Jungian type she is. Or she may be keenly aware of aesthetic details (which Aphrodite influences) and not notice that the stove is still on or the gas gauge reads nearly empty (details that Athena would not miss). The prevailing "goddess" explains how one function (in this case, sensation) can paradoxically be both highly developed and unconscious (see Chapter 14, "Which Goddess gets the Golden Apple?").

Second, from clinical observation, I have realized that the power of a goddess archetype to overwhelm a woman's ego and cause psychiatric symptoms parallels the power attributed to that goddess historically—diminishing in influence from the Great Goddess of ancient Europe through stages to the Greek goddesses, who were daughter or maiden goddesses (see Chapter 1, "Goddesses as Inner Images").

While this book advances theory and provides information helpful to therapists, it is written for everyone who wants to understand women better—especially those women who are closest, dearest, or most mystifying to them—and for women to discover the goddesses within themselves.

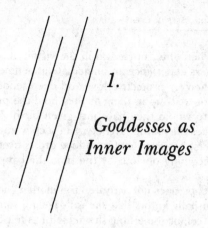

1.

Goddesses as Inner Images

A fragile baby girl was put in my friend Ann's arms, a "blue baby" with a congenital heart defect. Ann was emotionally moved as she held the small infant and looked at her face. She also felt a deep ache in the center of her chest under her breast bone (or sternum). Within moments, she and that baby had forged a bond. After that, Ann visited the child regularly, maintaining contact as long as it was possible. The infant did not survive open-heart surgery. She lived for only a few months, yet she made a profound impression on Ann. At that first meeting, she touched an inner image imbued with emotion that lay deep within Ann's psyche.

In 1966, Anthony Stevens, a psychiatrist and author, studied attachment bonds in infancy at the Metera Babies Centre, near Athens, Greece. What he observed happening between nurses and these orphaned infants paralleled Ann's experience. He found that a special bond was formed between a baby and a specific nurse through mutual delight and attraction, a process that was like falling in love.

Stevens's observations belie the "cupboard love theory," which postulates that bonds gradually form between a mother and a child through caretaking and feeding. He found that no less than a third of the infants became attached to nurses who had done little or no routine caretaking of the child before the bond formed. Afterward, the nurse invariably did much more for the child, usually because she came to reciprocate the attachment but also because the child would often refuse to be tended by any other nurse when "his" nurse was in the vicinity.[1]

Some new mothers experience an immediate attachment to their newborn; a fiercely protective love and deep tenderness toward this infant wells up in them as they hold the precious, helpless baby to whom they have just given birth. We say that the baby evokes the mother archetype in such women. For other new mothers, however, maternal love grows over a period of months, becoming obvious by the time the baby is eight or nine months old.

When having a baby does not activate "the mother" in a woman, the woman usually knows that she isn't feeling something other mothers feel, or something she herself has felt for another child. The child misses a vital connection when "the mother" archetype isn't activated, and keeps yearning for it to occur. (Although, as happened with nurses at the Greek orphanage, the archetypal mother-child pattern can be fulfilled through a woman who is not the biological mother.) And yearning for that missed attachment can continue into adulthood. One forty-nine-year-old woman, who was in a women's group with me, wept as she spoke of her mother's death, because now that her mother was dead that hoped-for connection could never develop.

Just as "the mother" is a deeply felt way of being that a child can activate in a woman, so also each child is "programmed" to seek "the mother." In both mother and child (and therefore in all humans), an image of mother is associated with maternal behavior and emotion. This inner image at work in the psyche—an image that determines behavior and emotional responses unconsciously—is an archetype.

"The Mother" is only one of many archetypes—or latent, internally determined roles—that can become activated in a woman. When we recognize the different archetypes, we can see more clearly what is acting in us and in others. In this book, I will be introducing archetypes that are active in women's psyches and that are personified as Greek goddesses. For example, Demeter, the maternal goddess, is an embodiment of the mother archetype. The others are Persephone (the daughter), Hera (the wife), Aphrodite (the lover), Artemis (the sister and competitor), Athena (the strategist), and Hestia (the hearthkeeper). As names for archetypes, of course, the goddesses are helpful only when the images fit the woman's feelings, for archetypes do not really have names.

C. G. Jung introduced the concept of archetypes into psychology. He saw archetypes as patterns of instinctual behavior that were contained in a collective unconscious. The collective unconscious is the part of the unconscious that is not individual but universal, with contents and modes of behavior that are more or less the same everywhere and in all individuals.[2]

Myths and fairytales are expressions of archetypes, as are many images and themes in dreams. The presence of common archetypal patterns in all people accounts for similarities in the mythologies of many different cultures. As preexistent patterns, they influence how we behave and how we react to others.

THE GODDESSES AS ARCHETYPES

Most of us were taught about the gods and goddesses of Mt. Olympus at some time in school and have seen statues and paintings of them. The Romans worshipped these same deities, addressing them by their Latin names. The Olympians had very human attributes: their behavior, emotional reactions, appearance, and mythology provide us with patterns that parallel human behavior and attitudes. They are also familiar to us because they are archetypal; that is, they represent models of being and behaving we recognize from the collective unconscious we all share.

The most famous of them were the Twelve Olympians: six gods, Zeus, Poseidon, Hades, Apollo, Ares, Hephaestus, and six goddesses, Hestia, Demeter, Hera, Artemis, Athena, and Aphrodite. One of the twelve, Hestia (Goddess of the Hearth) was replaced by Dionysus (God of Wine), thus changing the male/female balance to seven gods and five goddesses. The goddess archetypes I am describing in this book are the six Olympian goddesses—Hestia, Demeter, Hera, Artemis, Athena, and Aphrodite—plus Persephone, whose mythology is inseparable from Demeter's.

I have divided these seven goddesses into three categories: the virgin goddesses, the vulnerable goddesses, and the alchemical (or transformative) goddess. The virgin goddesses were classified together in ancient Greece. The other two categories are my designations. Modes of consciousness, favored roles, and motivating factors are distinguishing characteristics of each group. Attitudes toward others, the need for attachment, and the importance of relationships also are distinctly different in each category. Goddesses representing all three categories need expression somewhere in a woman's life—in order for her to love deeply, work meaningfully, and be sensual and creative.

The first group you will meet in these pages are the virgin goddesses: Artemis, Athena, and Hestia. Artemis (whom the Romans called Diana) was the Goddess of the Hunt and Moon. Her domain was the wilderness. She was the archer with unerring aim and the protector of the young of all living things. Athena (known as Minerva to the Romans) was the Goddess of Wisdom and Handicrafts; patron of her namesake city, Athens; and protector of numerous heroes. She was usually portrayed wearing armor and was known as the best strategist in battle. Hestia, the Goddess of the Hearth (the Roman goddess Vesta), was the least known of all of the Olympians. She was present in homes and temples as the fire at the center of the hearth.

The virgin goddesses represent the independent, self-sufficient quality in women. Unlike the other Olympians, these three were not susceptible to falling in love. Emotional attachments did not divert them from what they considered important. They were not victimized and did not suffer. As archetypes, they express the need in women for autonomy, and the capacity women have to focus their consciousness on what is personally meaningful. Artemis and Athena represent goal-directedness and logical thinking, which make them the achievement-oriented archetypes. Hestia is the archetype that focuses attention inward, to the spiritual center of a woman's personality. These three goddesses are feminine archetypes that actively seek their own goals. They expand our notion of feminine attributes to include competency and self-sufficiency.

The second group—Hera, Demeter, and Persephone—I call the vulnerable goddesses. Hera (known as Juno to the Romans) was the Goddess of Marriage. She was the wife of Zeus, chief god of the Olympians. Demeter (the Roman goddess Ceres) was the Goddess of Grain. In her most important myth, her role as mother was emphasized. Persephone (Proserpina in Latin) was Demeter's daughter. The Greeks also called her the Kore—"the maiden."

The three vulnerable goddesses represent the traditional roles of wife, mother, and daughter. They are the relationship-oriented goddess archetypes, whose identities and well-being depend on having a significant relationship. They express women's needs for affiliation and bonding. They are attuned to others and vulnerable. These three goddesses were raped, abducted, dominated, or humiliated by male gods. Each suffered in her characteristic way when an attachment was broken or dishonored, and showed symptoms that resembled psychological illnesses. Each of them also evolved, and can provide women with an insight into the nature and pattern of their own reactions to loss, and the potential for growth through suffering that is inherent in each of these three goddess archetypes.

Aphrodite, the Goddess of Love and Beauty (best known by her Roman name Venus) is in a third category all her own as the alchemical goddess. She was the most beautiful and irresistible of the goddesses. She had many affairs and many offspring from her numerous liaisons. She generated love and beauty, erotic attraction, sensuality, sexuality, and new life. She entered relationships of her own choosing and was never victimized. Thus she maintained her autonomy, like a virgin goddess, and was in relationships, like a vulnerable goddess. Her consciousness was both focused and receptive, allowing a two-way interchange through which both she and the other were affected. The Aphrodite archetype motivates women to seek intensity in relationships rather than permanence, to value creative process, and be open to change.

THE FAMILY TREE

To better appreciate who the goddesses are and what relationships they had to other deities, let us first put them in mythological context. Here we are indebted to Hesiod (about 700 B.C.), who first tried to organize the numerous traditions concerning the gods into an ordered arrangement. His major work, the *Theogony*, is an account of the origin and descent of the gods.[5]

In the beginning, according to Hesiod, there was Chaos—the starting point. Out of Chaos came Gaea (Earth), dark Tartarus (the lowermost depths of the underworld), and Eros (love).

Gaea, feminine-gendered Earth, gave birth to a son, Uranus, who was also known as Heaven. She then mated with Uranus to create, among others, the twelve Titans—ancient, primeval, nature powers who were worshipped in historical Greece. In Hesiod's genealogy of the gods, the Titans were an early ruling dynasty, the parents and grandparents of the Olympians.

Uranus, the first patriarchal or father figure in Greek mythology, then grew resentful of the children he parented with Gaea, so he buried them in her body as soon as they were born. This caused Gaea great pain and anguish. She called on her Titan children to help her. All were afraid to intervene except the youngest, Cronos (called Saturn by the Romans). He responded to her cry for help and, armed with the sickle she gave him and a plan she devised, lay in wait for his father.

When Uranus came to mate with Gaea, spreading himself on her, Cronos took the sickle, lopped off his father's genitals, and threw them into the sea. Cronos then became the most powerful male god. He and the Titans ruled over the universe and created new deities. Many represented elements present in nature, such as rivers, winds, and the rainbow. Others were monsters, personifying evil or dangers.

Cronos mated with his sister Titan, Rhea. From their union were born the first-generation Olympians—Hestia, Demeter, Hera, Hades, Poseidon, and Zeus.

Once again, the patriarchal progenitor—this time Cronos—tried to eliminate his children. Forewarned that he was destined to be overcome by his own son and determined not to let this happen, he swallowed each child immediately after the birth—not even looking to see if the newborn were a son or a daughter. In all, he consumed three daughters and two sons.

Grief-stricken at the fate of her children, and pregnant again, Rhea appealed to Gaea and Uranus to help her save this last one and to punish Cronos for castrating Uranus and swallowing their five children. Her parents told her to go to Crete when the birth time came and to trick Cronos by wrapping a stone in swaddling clothes. In his hurry, Cronos swallowed the stone, thinking it was the child.

This last, spared child was Zeus, who did indeed later overthrow his father and come to rule over mortals and gods. Raised in secret, he later tricked his father into regurgitating his siblings. With their help, Zeus embarked on a prolonged struggle for supremacy, which ended in the defeat of Cronos and the Titans and their imprisonment in the dungeons of Tartarus.

After their victory, the three brother gods—Zeus, Poseidon, and Hades—drew lots to divide the universe among themselves. Zeus won the sky, Poseidon the sea, and Hades the underworld. Although the earth and Mt. Olympus were supposed to be shared territory, Zeus came to extend his rule over these areas. The three sisters—Hestia, Demeter, and Hera—had no property rights, consistent with the patriarchal nature of the Greek religion.

Through his sexual liaisons, Zeus fathered the next generation of deities: Artemis and Apollo (God of the Sun) were the children of Zeus and Leto, Athena was the daughter of Zeus and Metis, Persephone the daughter of Demeter and Zeus, Hermes (the Messenger God) was the son of Zeus and Maia, while Ares (God of War) and Hephaestus (God of the Forge) were the sons of his royal consort Hera. There are two stories of Aphrodite's origin: in one she is the daughter of Zeus and Dione; in the other, she preceded Zeus. Zeus fathered Dionysus in an affair with a mortal woman, Semele.

At the end of the book, a cast of characters is given: biographical sketches of the gods and goddesses, listed alphabetically for reference, to help keep track of who's who in Greek mythology.

HISTORY AND MYTHOLOGY

The mythology that gave rise to these Greek gods and goddesses emerged from historical events. It is a patriarchal mythology that exalts Zeus and heroes, one that reflects the encounter and subjugation, of peoples who had mother-based religions, by invaders who had warrior gods and father-based theologies.

Marija Gimbutas, a professor of European archaeology at the University of California at Los Angeles, describes "Old Europe," Europe's first civilization.[4] Dating back at least 5000 years (perhaps even 25,000 years) before the rise of male religions, Old Europe was a matrifocal, sedentary, peaceful, art-loving, earth- and sea-bound culture that worshipped the Great Goddess. Evidence gleaned from burial sites show that Old Europe was an unstratified, egalitarian society that was destroyed by an infiltration of seminomadic, horse-riding, Indo-European peoples from the distant north and east. These invaders were patrifocal, mobile, warlike, ideologically sky-oriented, and indifferent to art.

The invaders viewed themselves as a superior people because of their ability to conquer the more culturally developed earlier settlers, who worshipped the Great Goddess. Known by many names—Astarte, Ishtar, Inanna, Nut, Isis, Ashtoreth, Au Set, Hathor, Nina, Nammu, and Ningal, among others—the Great Goddess was worshipped as the feminine life force deeply connected to nature and fertility, responsible both for creating life and for destroying life. The snake, the dove, the tree, and the moon were her sacred symbols. According to historian-mythologist Robert Graves, before the coming of patriarchal religions the Great Goddess was regarded as immortal, changeless, and omnipotent. She took lovers not to provide her children with a father, but for pleasure. Fatherhood had not yet been introduced into religious thought, and there were no (male) gods.[5]

Successive waves of invasions by the Indo-Europeans began the dethronement of the Great Goddess. The dates when these waves began are given by various authorities as between 4500 B.C. and 2400 B.C. The goddesses were not completely suppressed, but were incorporated into the religion of the invaders.

The invaders imposed their patriarchal culture and their warrior religion on the conquered people. The Great Goddess became the subservient consort of the invaders' gods, and attributes or power that originally belonged to a female divinity were expropriated and given to a male deity. Rape appeared in myths for the first time, and myths arose in which the male heroes slew serpents—symbols of the Great Goddess. And, as reflected in Greek mythology, the attributes, symbols, and power that once were invested in one Great Goddess were divided among many goddesses. Mythologist Jane Harrison notes that the Great Mother goddess became fragmented into many lesser goddesses, each receiving attributes that once belonged to her: Hera got the ritual of the sacred marriage, Demeter her mysteries, Athena her snakes, Aphrodite her doves, and Artemis her function as "Lady of the Wild Things" (wildlife).[6]

According to Merlin Stone, author of *When God Was a Woman,* the disenthronement of the Great Goddess, begun by the Indo-European invaders, was finally accomplished by the Hebrew, Christian, and Moslem religions that arose later. The male deity took the prominent place. The female goddesses faded into the background, and women in society followed suit. Stone notes, "We may find ourselves wondering to what degree the suppression of women's rites has actually been the suppression of women's rights."[7]

HISTORICAL GODDESSES AND ARCHETYPES

The Great Goddess was worshipped as the Creator and the Destroyer of Life, responsible for the fertility and destructiveness of nature. And the Great Goddess still exists as an archetype in the collective unconscious. I have often felt the presence of the awesome Great Goddess in my patients. One of my postpartum patients identified with the Great Goddess—in her terrible aspect. Gwen was a young mother who had become psychotic after her baby was born. Convinced that she had consumed the world, she was hallucinating and depressed. She paced the dayroom of the hospital, wretched in her guilt and sorrow. When I fell in step to keep her company, she used to tell me that she had "gobbled up and destroyed the world." During her pregnancy, she had identified with the Great Goddess in her positive aspect as the Creator of Life. Now, after the delivery, she felt herself to be the Great Goddess who had the power to destroy what she created—and who had done so. Her emotional conviction was so intense that she ignored evidence that the world still existed.

The archetype also still lives in its positive aspect. For example, the Great Goddess as life sustainer is the image held by a person who is convinced that his or her life itself depends on maintaining a bond with a particular woman. The woman is "mistaken for" the Great Goddess. This is a fairly common delusion. When the loss of this relationship is so devastating that it leads someone to commit suicide, then life literally did depend on it.

Paralleling the power held by the Great Goddess when she was worshipped, the archetypal Great Goddess has the most powerful effect of any archetype; she is capable of evoking irrational fears and distorting reality. The Greek goddesses were less powerful than the Great Goddess, and more specialized. Each had her own realm and power that was limited to that realm. In women's psyches also, the Greek goddesses are less powerful forces than the Great Goddess; their power to be emotionally overwhelming and distort reality is less.

Of the seven Greek goddesses who represent major, common archetypal patterns in women, Aphrodite, Demeter, and Hera have the most power to dictate behavior. These three are more closely related to the Great Goddess than are the other four. Aphrodite is a lesser version of the Great Goddess in her function as the Goddess of Fertility. Demeter is a lesser version of the Great Goddess in her function as the Great Mother. Hera is a lesser version of the Great Goddess as Queen of Heaven. However, while each one is "lesser" than the Great Goddess, they represent instinctual forces in the psyche that can be compelling when they "demand their due"—as we will see in later chapters.

Women who are acted on by any of these three goddesses must learn to resist, because to blindly do the bidding of Aphrodite, Demeter, or Hera can adversely affect a woman's life. These archetypes—like their counterpart goddesses of ancient Greece—do not look out for the best interests of mortal women, or for their relationships with others. Archetypes exist outside of time, unconcerned with the realities of a woman's life or her needs.

Three of the remaining four archetypes—Artemis, Athena, and Persephone—were "maiden" goddesses, who belonged to the generation of the daughters. These three were one more generation removed from the Great Goddess. As archetypes, they are correspondingly less overwhelming, and chiefly influence character patterns.

And Hestia, the oldest, wisest, and most honored goddess of them all, avoided power altogether. She represents a spiritual component that a woman does well to honor.

GREEK GODDESSES AND
CONTEMPORARY WOMEN

The Greek goddesses are images of women that have lived in the human imagination for over three thousand years. The goddesses are patterns or representations of what women are like—with more power and diversity of behavior than women have historically been allowed to exercise. They are beautiful and strong. They are motivated by what matters to them, and—as I maintain in this book—they represent inherent patterns or archetypes that can shape the course of a woman's life.

These goddesses differ from one another. Each one has both positive and potentially negative traits. Their myths show what is important to them and express in metaphor what a woman who resembles them might do.

I also have come to think of the Greek goddesses of Mt. Olympus—each of whom was unique, some of whom were antagonistic toward each other—as a metaphor for diversity and conflict within women who are complex and many-sided. All the goddesses are potentially present in every woman. When several goddesses compete for dominance in a woman's psyche, she needs to decide which aspect of herself to express and when. Otherwise she will be pulled first in one direction and then another.

The Greek goddesses also lived, as we do, in a patriarchal society. Male gods ruled over the earth, heavens, ocean, and underworld. Each independent goddess adapted to this reality in her own way by separating from men, joining men as one of

2.

Activating the Goddesses

In ancient Greece, women knew that their vocation or their stage in life placed them under the dominion of a particular goddess whom they honored: weavers needed Athena's patronage, young girls were under the protection of Artemis, married women honored Hera. Women worshipped and made offerings at the altars of the goddesses whose help they needed. Women in childbirth prayed to Artemis to deliver them from pain; they invited Hestia onto their hearths to make a house into a home. Goddesses were powerful deities, to whom homage was paid with rituals, worship, offerings, and sacrifices. Women also gave goddesses their due because they feared divine anger and retribution if they did not.

Within contemporary women, the goddesses exist as archetypes and can—as in ancient Greece—extract their due and claim dominion over their subjects. Even without knowing to which goddess she is subject, a woman can nonetheless "give" her allegiance to a particular archetype for either a phase of her life or for a lifetime.

For example, as a teenager a woman may have been boy-crazy and easily infatuated; she may have engaged in early sexuality and been at risk for an unwanted pregnancy—without knowing that she was under the influence of Aphrodite, Goddess of Love, whose drive toward union and procreation may catch an immature girl unaware. Or she may have been under the protection of Artemis, who valued celibacy and loved the wilderness—and may have been a horse-crazy ado-

25

lescent or a backpacking Girl Scout. Or she may have been a young Athena, her nose buried in a book or competing in a science fair, motivated by the Goddess of Wisdom to get recognition and good grades. Or, from the time she first played with dolls, she may have been a budding Demeter, fantasizing about when she could have a baby of her own. Or she may have been like the maiden Persephone gathering flowers in the meadow, a goal-less young woman waiting for something or someone to carry her away.

All the goddesses are potential patterns in the psyches of all women, yet in each individual woman some of these patterns are activated (energized or developed) and others are not. The formation of crystals was an analogy Jung used to help explain the difference between archetypal patterns (which are universal) and activated archetypes (which are functioning in us): an archetype is like the invisible pattern that determines what shape and structure a crystal will take when it does form.[1] Once the crystal actually forms, the now recognizable pattern is analogous to an activated archetype.

Archetypes might also be compared to the "blueprints" contained in seeds. Growth from seeds depends on soil and climate conditions, presence or absence of certain nutrients, loving care or neglect on the part of gardeners, the size and depth of the container, and the hardiness of the variety itself.

Similarly, which goddess or goddesses (several may be present at the same time) become activated in any particular woman at a particular time depends on the combined effect of a variety of interacting elements—the woman's predisposition, family and culture, hormones, other people, unchosen circumstances, chosen activities, and stages of life.

INHERENT PREDISPOSITION

Babies are born with personality traits—energetic, willful, placid, curious, able to spend time alone, sociable—which go along with some goddess archetypes more than with others. By the time a little girl is two or three years old, she already shows qualities typical of particular goddesses. The compliant little girl who is quite content doing whatever her mother wants is very different from the little girl who is ready to take off on her own to explore the neighborhood—as different as Persephone and Artemis.

FAMILY ENVIRONMENT AND GODDESSES

The expectations of the child's family support some goddesses and suppress others. If parents expect daughters to be "sugar and spice and everything nice" or "Mother's little helper," then they are rewarding and reinforcing Persephone and Demeter qualities. A daughter who knows what she wants and expects to have the same privileges and opportunities as her brother might be called "willful" when she is only being her persistent Artemis self, or she may be told to "act like a girl" when she's only being her one-of-the-boys Athena self. Moreover, these days a little girl may find herself in a reverse approval-disapproval pattern: she may be discouraged from staying at home and playing "Mommy" or "house" (which she may want to do). Instead, she is signed up for soccer and early education (on which her parents may want her to thrive).

The child's inherent goddess pattern interacts with family expectations. If the family disapproves of the specific goddess, however, a girl doesn't stop feeling the way she does, although she may learn not to act naturally and her self-esteem suffers. If "her goddess" finds favor with her family, there may also be drawbacks. For example, a girl who tends to follow the lead of others because she is most like Persephone may have difficulties in knowing what she wants after years of being rewarded for pleasing others. And the budding Athena who skips grades has her intellectual abilities reinforced at the expense of friendships with peers. When inherent pattern and family "conspire" to make a woman conform to one goddess, her development becomes one-sided.

If her family rewards and encourages a girl to develop what comes naturally, she feels good about herself as she goes about doing what matters to her. The opposite happens to the girl whose goddess pattern meets family disapproval. Opposition doesn't change the inherent pattern, it just makes the girl feel bad about herself for having the traits and interests she has. And it makes her feel inauthentic if she pretends to be other than she is.

THE EFFECT OF CULTURE ON GODDESSES

Which "goddesses" does the culture support through the roles it allows women to have? Stereotypes of women are positive or negative images of goddess archetypes. In patriarchal societies, the only acceptable roles are often the maiden (Persephone), the wife (Hera), and the mother (Demeter). Aphrodite is condemned as "the whore" or "the temptress," which is a distortion and devaluation of the sensuality and sexuality of this archetype. An assertive or angry Hera becomes "the shrew." And some cultures, past and present, actively deny expression of independence, intelligence, or sexuality in women—so that any signs of Artemis, Athena, and Aphrodite must be quelled.

In ancient China, for example, the custom of binding women's feet meant that women were physically crippled as well as psychologically limited by roles that did not allow independence. Under such conditions, certain goddesses could live only in myths. In her novel *The Woman Warrior*,[2] Maxine Hong Kingston wrote of the devaluation and demeaning of Chinese women, which has persisted into the present. By contrast, she recounted a myth about a strong, Chinese woman-warrior heroine. The myth showed that even if a goddess pattern cannot be lived out in the real life of a woman, that goddess may still find expression in fairytales, myths, and women's dreams.

Women's lives are shaped by the allowable roles and idealized images of the time. These stereotypes favor some goddess patterns over others. In the United States, there have been major shifts in expectations of "what a woman should be" in the past several decades. For example, the baby boom that followed World War II emphasized marriage and motherhood. This was a fulfilling time for women who had Hera's need to be a mate, and for women with Demeter's maternal instinct. It was a difficult time for Athena or Artemis women who were intellectually curious and competitive and wanted to express excellence or achievement at any other task other than raising a family. Women went to college to get their "M.R.S. Degree" and, once married, often dropped out of school. Suburban "togetherness" was the ideal. American women were not stopping at having two children, but were having three, four, five, or six. By 1950 the birthrate in the United States equaled India's for the first and only time.

Twenty years later, the 1970s was the decade of the women's movement—vintage years for Artemis and Athena. Women who were motivated to achieve were now supported by the times. Feminists and career women were in the center of the stage. More women than ever before were now in school, pursuing doctoral, business, medicine, and law degrees. "Until death us do part" marriage vows were increasingly broken, and the birthrate was down. Meanwhile, women motivated by Hera's need to be a mate and Demeter's need to have children were functioning in an increasingly unsupportive climate.

When specific archetypal patterns in some women find favor in the culture, those women can do what is inwardly meaningful to them and can receive outer approval. Institutional support matters greatly. For example, women with Athena's innately logical mind need access to higher education to develop intellectually. Women with Hestia's spiritual focus thrive in religious communities.

THE EFFECT OF HORMONES ON GODDESSES

When hormones shift dramatically—at puberty, during pregnancy, and at menopause—some archetypes are enhanced at the expense of others. The hormones that cause breast and genital development at puberty may stimulate the sensuality and sexuality that are characteristics of Aphrodite. Some girls become young Aphrodite women when they develop physically; others develop breasts and begin menstruating, but do not turn their interest toward boys. Behavior is not determined by hormones alone, but through the interaction of hormones and goddess archetypes.

Pregnancy instigates a massive increase in the hormone progesterone, which sustains the pregnancy physiologically. Again, different women react differently to this increase. Some become emotionally fulfilled as their bodies become large with child, and they feel like the embodiment of Demeter, the mother goddess. Others seem almost oblivious to the pregnancy, missing hardly a day of work.

Menopause—the cessation of menstruation brought about by a drop in estrogen and progesterone—is another time of hormonal change. How a woman responds again depends on which goddess is active. For every grieving Demeter suffering from an empty-nest depression, there seems to be— as anthropologist Margaret Mead remarked—other women with a surge of P.M.Z., or "postmenopausal zest." This upsurge can happen when a newly energized goddess can now have her long-awaited turn.

Even during monthly periods some women experience "a goddess shift," as hormone and archetypes interact and have an impact on their psyches. Women who are sensitive to these changes note that during the first half of the cycle they seem more attuned to the independent goddesses—especially to Artemis or Athena, with their extraverted, go-out-into-the-world focus. Then in the second half of the cycle, as the pregnancy hormone progesterone increases, they note that their "nesting" tendencies seem stronger and their home-body or dependent feelings become more pronounced. Now Demeter, Hera, Persephone, or Hestia becomes the strongest influence.[3]

These hormone and goddess shifts can cause conflict and confusion as first one goddess and then another gains ascendency. A classic pattern is the independent Artemis woman who lives with a marriage-resistant man or with a man she feels isn't husband material. Living together is an arrangement that suits her fine—until the hormonal shift. Somewhere into the second half of the cycle, Hera's need to be a mate receives hormonal support. Not being married now stirs up feelings of resentment or rejection, which leads to a monthly fight or to a minidepression that, just as predictably, passes after she's had her period.

PEOPLE AND EVENTS ACTIVATE GODDESSES

A goddess may become activated and spring to life when the archetype is called forth by a person or an event. For example, one woman finds that another person's helplessness is an irresistible stimulus for her to drop what she's doing and be caretaking Demeter. This shift can have an adverse effect on her job, since that's what she most often drops. She spends too much time on personal telephone calls, listening to the troubles of others. She too often rushes out on an errand of mercy, and is on the verge of being fired. Another woman may find that a feminist rally transforms her into a full-blown Artemis out to avenge intrusions onto women's territory, as she feels a surge of sisterhood and strength. And money matters can turn yet another woman from a casual, people-oriented person into a "bottom-line" Athena, a stickler for contracts concerned with how much is due her.

When a woman falls in love, change threatens former priorities. Inwardly, at the archetypal level, old patterns may no longer hold. When Aphrodite becomes activated, the influence of Athena may wane, making career advancement less important than her new love. Or Hera's pro-marriage values may be overcome, if infidelity results.

Psychiatric symptoms develop if the negative aspect of a goddess becomes activated by circumstance. The loss of a child or a significant relationship can turn a woman into a grieving Demeter mother who stops functioning and just sits, profoundly depressed and unreachable. Or a husband's proximity to an attractive woman—a co-worker, employee, or neighbor—can call forth jealous Hera, causing a woman to become mistrustful and paranoid, seeing deception and infidelity where there are none.

"DOING" ACTIVATES GODDESSES

The saying "Doing is becoming" expresses a way that goddesses can be evoked or developed by a chosen course of action. For example, practicing meditation can gradually activate or strengthen the influence of Hestia, the introverted, inwardly focused goddess. Since the effects of meditation, like meditation itself, are subjective, usually the only person who notices a difference is the woman herself. She may meditate once or twice a day, and then go about her daily routine feeling more "centered," enjoying the times of quiet well-being that are characteristic of Hestia. Sometimes others sense the difference too, as did the office staff of one supervising social worker, who noticed that with meditation she became calmer, less harried, and more compassionate.

In contrast to the gradual effects of meditation, a woman who takes psychedelic drugs may precipitously alter her perception. Although the effect is usually transient, long-term personality changes can result. For example, if a woman who is dominated by Athena—the logic-minded, pragmatic goddess—takes a psychedelic drug, she may find herself enjoying her senses, for a change. What she sees is more intense and beautiful, she becomes completely absorbed in music, feels sensual, sensing she is much more than her mind. She may thus become acquainted with Aphrodite, enjoying intense experiences in the immediate present. Or she may look at the stars and feel one with nature and, for once, be Artemis, Goddess of the Moon, the huntress whose realm was the wilderness. Or the drug experience may take her into "the underworld," where she experiences the intangible and irrational contents of the unconscious. She may become depressed, have hallucinations, or be terrified if her experience parallels Persephone's abduction into the underworld.

A woman who chooses to continue her education beyond high school favors the further development of Athena qualities. Studying, organizing information, taking examinations, and writing papers all require the logic-mindedness of Athena. A woman who chooses to have a baby invites maternal Demeter to be a stronger presence. And signing up for a backpacking trip into the wilderness offers Artemis more expression.

INVOKING THE GODDESSES

Many of the Homeric hymns are invocations to the Greek deities. For example, a Homeric hymn may create an image of a goddess in the mind of the listener by describing her appearance, attributes, and feats. Then she is invited to be present, to enter a home, or provide a blessing. The ancient Greeks knew something we can learn: goddesses can be imagined and then invoked.

In the individual goddess chapters, readers may discover that they are not well acquainted with a particular goddess. They may find that an archetype that they would find extremely helpful is undeveloped or apparently "missing" in themselves. It is possible to "invoke" that goddess, by consciously making an effort to see, feel, or sense her presence—to bring her into focus through the imagination—and then ask for her particular strength. The following invocations are examples.

- Athena, help me to think clearly in this situation.
- Persephone, help me to stay open and receptive.
- Hera, help me to make a commitment and be faithful.
- Demeter, teach me to be patient and generous, help me to be a good mother.
- Artemis, keep me focused on that goal in the distance.
- Aphrodite, help me to love and enjoy my body.
- Hestia, honor me with your presence, bring me peace and serenity.

GODDESSES AND THE STAGES OF LIFE

An individual woman may go through many phases in life. Each stage of her life may have its own most influential goddess or goddesses. Or she may live out one goddess pattern that takes her through successive stages. When women look back on their lives, they often can recognize when one goddess or several goddesses were more important or influential than others.

As a young adult, she may have been focused on her education, as I was in going through medical school. The Artemis archetype kept me focused on the goal. Meanwhile, I called on Athena abilities to learn procedures and facts, which would lead to making diagnoses based on clinical and laboratory findings. In contrast, my college classmates who married shortly after graduation and had children were calling on Hera and Demeter.

Midlife is a time of transition, which often ushers in a changing of the goddesses. Somewhere in the mid-thirties to mid-forties, the prevailing strongest archetype in the previous years now often fades in intensity, allowing other goddesses to emerge. The results of effort put into whatever occupied a woman's early adult years—marriage and children, career, creative effort, a man, or a combination—are evident. More energy becomes available for something else, which is an invitation to another goddess to exert an influence. Will Athena influence her to go to graduate school? Or, will Demeter's desire to have a child prevail—when it is now or never?

Next comes another later-life transition, when the goddesses may shift yet again. The postmenopausal period may herald a shift, as do widowhood, retirement, or feeling like an elder. Will the widowed woman who must manage money for the first time discover a latent Athena and find that she is well able to understand investments? Has unwanted loneliness become comfortable solitude, because Hestia is now known? Or has life now become meaningless and empty, because Demeter has no one to nurture? As in every other stage of life, the outcome for the individual depends on the activated goddesses in her psyche, the realities of her situation, and the choices she makes.

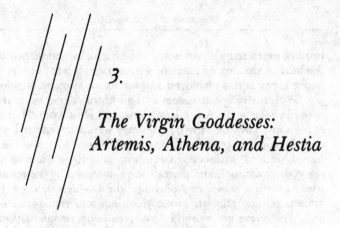

3.

The Virgin Goddesses: Artemis, Athena, and Hestia

The three virgin goddesses of Greek mythology are Artemis, Goddess of the Hunt and of the Moon; Athena, Goddess of Wisdom and Crafts; and Hestia, Goddess of Hearth and Temple. These three goddesses personify the independent, active, nonrelationship aspects of women's psychology. Artemis and Athena are outward- and achievement-oriented archetypes, whereas Hestia is inwardly focused. All three represent inner drives in women to develop talents, pursue interests, solve problems, compete with others, express themselves articulately in words or through art forms, put their surroundings in order, or lead contemplative lives. Every woman who has ever wanted "a room of her own," or feels at home in nature, or delights in figuring out how something works, or appreciates solitude, has a kinship with one of these virgin goddesses.

The virgin goddess aspect is that part of a woman that is unowned by or "unpenetrated" by a man—that is untouched by her need for a man or need to be validated by him, that exists wholly separate from him, in her own right. When a woman is living out a virgin archetype, it means that a significant part of her is psychologically virginal, not that she is physically and literally virginal.

The term *virgin* means undefiled, pure, uncorrupted, unused, untilled, untouched and unworked on "by man," as in *virgin* soil, *virgin* forest; or not previously processed, as in *virgin* wool. *Virgin* oil is oil made from the first pressing of olives or nuts, extracted without heat (metaphorically, untouched by the heat of emotion or passion). *Virgin* metal is what occurs in native form, and is unalloyed and unmixed, as in *virgin* gold.

Within a religious system and an historical period dominated by male gods, Artemis, Athena, and Hestia stand out as exceptions. They never married, never were overpowered, seduced, raped, or humiliated by male deities or mortals; They stayed "intact," inviolate. In addition, only these three of all the gods, goddesses, and mortals were unmoved by the otherwise irresistible power of Aphrodite, the Goddess of Love, to inflame passion and stir erotic yearnings and romantic feelings. They were not moved by love, sexuality, or infatuation.

THE VIRGIN GODDESS ARCHETYPE

When a virgin goddess—Artemis, Athena or Hestia—is a dominant archetype, the woman is (as Jungian analyst Esther Harding wrote in her book *Women's Mysteries*) "one-in-herself." An important part of her psyche "belongs to no man." Consequently, as Harding described it: "A woman who is virgin, one-in-herself, does what she does—not because of any desire to please, not to be liked, or to be approved, even by herself; not because of any desire to gain power over another, to catch his interest or love, but because what she does is true. Her actions may indeed be unconventional. She may have to say no, when it would be easier, as well as more adapted, conventionally speaking, to say yes. But as virgin she is not influenced by the considerations that make the nonvirgin woman, whether married or not, trim her sails and adapt herself to expediency."[1]

If a woman is one-in-herself, she will be motivated by a need to follow her own inner values, to do what has meaning or fulfills herself, apart from what other people think.

Psychologically, the virgin goddess is that part of a woman that has not been worked on, either by the collective (masculine-determined) social and cultural expectations of what a woman should be, or by an individual male's judgment of her. The virgin goddess aspect is a pure essence of who the woman is and of what she values. It remains untarnished and uncontaminated because she does not reveal it, because she keeps it sacred and inviolate, or because she expresses it without modification to meet male standards.

The virgin archetype might manifest as that part of a woman that is secretly or openly a feminist. It may be expressed as an ambition that women are usually discouraged from pursuing—such as aviator Amelia Earhart's desire to fly where no pilot had ever gone before. Or it may be the woman's creativity as poet, painter, musician, making art that grows out of her own experience as a woman—such as Adrienne Rich's poetry, Judy Chicago's paintings, or the ballads Holly Near writes and sings. Or it may be expressed as a meditative practice or as midwifery.

Many women join together to create forms that are "of women." Women's conscious-raising groups, goddess worship on mountaintops, women's self-help medical clinics, and quilting bees are expressions of the virgin goddess archetype manifesting through groups of women.

QUALITY OF CONSCIOUSNESS: LIKE SHARPLY FOCUSED LIGHT

Each of the three goddess categories (virgin, vulnerable, alchemical) has a characteristic quality of consciousness. Focused consciousness typifies the virgin goddesses.[2] Women who are like Artemis, Athena, and Hestia have the ability to concentrate their attention on what matters to them. They have the capacity to become absorbed in what they are doing. In the process of being focused, they can easily exclude everything that is extraneous to the task at hand or to the long-range goal.

I think of focused consciousness as analagous to a sharply focused, willfully directed, intense beam of light that illuminates only what it is focused on, leaving everything outside of its radius in the dark or in the shadows. It has a spotlight quality. In its most concentrated form, focused consciousness can even be like a laser beam, so piercing or dissecting in its ability to analyze that it can be incredibly precise or destructive—depending on the intensity and on what it is focused.

When a woman can focus on solving a problem or achieving a goal, uninterrupted by the needs of those around her, not heeding even her own need for food or sleep, she has a capacity for conscious focus that leads to accomplishments. She gives whatever she is working on her "undivided attention." She has a "one-track mind," which allows her to do what she sets her mind on. When she concentrates on outer goals or whatever the task at hand—as is characteristic of Artemis and Athena—the focus is achievement-oriented.

Danielle Steel, whose seventeen novels have sold more than 45 million copies in eighteen languages, exemplifies this type of focused consciousness. She describes herself as "an overachiever" and says, "It's very intense. I usually work twenty hours a day, sleeping two to four hours. This goes on seven days a week for six weeks" [5] (until the novel is completed).

When the focus is turned inward, toward a spiritual center—which is the directional focus of Hestia—the woman in whom this archetype is strong can meditate for long periods, undistracted by either the world around her, or by the discomforts of maintaining a particular position.

PATTERNS OF BEING AND BEHAVING

Women who follow their own inclinations to become competitive swimmers, active feminists, scientists, statisticians, corporate executives, housekeepers, horsewomen, or who enter convents or ashrams exemplify virgin goddess qualities. In order to develop their talents and focus on pursuing what has personal value, virgin goddess women often avoid fulfilling traditional women's roles. How to do so—that is, how to be true to themselves and adapt to living in "a man's world"—is the challenge.

In mythology, each of the three virgin goddesses faced a similar challenge, and developed a different solution.

Artemis, Goddess of the Hunt, forsook the city, avoided contact with men, and spent her time in the wilderness with her band of nymphs. Her adaption mode was *separation* from men and their influence. This mode is analogous to that of contemporary women who join consciousness-raising groups and become feminists intent on defining themselves and their own priorities, or who work in women-run collectives and businesses that serve womens' needs. Artemis women are also represented by "rugged individualists," who go it alone and do what matters to them, without personal support or approval from men—or from other women, as well.

In contrast, Athena, Goddess of Wisdom, joined men as an equal or as a superior at what they did. She was the coolest head in battle and the best strategist. Her adaptation was *identification* with men—she became like one of them. Athena's way has been taken by many women who have joined the corporate world or who have succeeded at traditionally male occupations.

Finally, Hestia, Goddess of the Hearth, followed an introverted way of adapting by *withdrawal* from men. She withdrew inward, became anonymous in appearance, and was left alone. The woman who adopts this mode downplays her femininity so as not to attract unwanted male interest, avoids competitive situations, and lives quietly, as she values and tends the daily tasks or meditation that give her life meaning.

The three virgin goddesses were unchanged by their experiences with others. They were never overcome by their emotions, nor by any other deities. They were invulnerable to suffering, untouched by relationships, and impervious to change.

Similarly, the more focused on her own course a woman is, the more likely she, too, will not be deeply affected by others. That focus can cut her off from her own emotional and instinctual life, as well as from bonding with others. Psychologically speaking, unless she has been "penetrated," no one has "gotten through to her." No one really matters, and she does not know what emotional intimacy is.

Thus, if a human woman identifies with a virgin goddess pattern, she may lead a one-sided and often lonely life without any truly "significant other." However, although a goddess remains limited to her role, a human woman can grow and change throughout her life. Although she is innately similar to a virgin goddess, she may also discover what Hera has to teach about committed relationships, may feel the stirrings of maternal instinct and learn of Demeter, or may fall in love and unexpectedly discover that Aphrodite is also a part of her.

NEW THEORY

In describing Artemis, Athena, and Hestia as positive, active feminine patterns, I am challenging assumptions traditionally held in psychology. Depending on whether the viewpoint is Freudian or Jungian, qualities that are characteristic of virgin goddesses have been defined as either symptoms or pathology or as expressions of a less than fully conscious masculine element in a woman's psyche. These theories have inhibited behavior and damaged the self-esteem of women who fit virgin goddess patterns. Many women familiar with Freudian theory have thought of themselves as unnatural, for example, because they wanted a career more than they wanted a baby. And many women familiar with Jungian theory have hesitated to voice their ideas, knowing that Jung felt women's capacity to think objectively was inferior and opinionated.

Sigmund Freud's theory of women's psychology was penis-centered. He described women in terms of what they lacked anatomically, rather than in terms of what was present in their bodies or their psyches. In Freud's view,[4] not having penises made women maimed and inferior. As a consequence, he felt, normal women suffered from penis envy, were masochistic and narcissistic, and had poor superego development (that is, an inferior conscience).

Freudian psychoanalytic theory interpreted women's behavior as follows:

- A woman who is competent and self-assured, who accomplishes something in the world, and who appears to be enjoying the opportunity to actualize her intelligence and capabilities is exhibiting a "masculinity complex." According to Freud, she is acting as if she believes that she hasn't been castrated, when of course she has. No woman really wants to excel—the need to excel is a symptom of a masculinity complex, a denial of "reality."
- A woman who wants a baby really wants a penis and sublimates this wish, substituting a wish for the baby in place of her desire for a penis.
- A woman who is sexually attracted to men is so because she discovered her mother doesn't have a penis. (In Freudian theory, a woman's heterosexuality goes back to that traumatic moment when as a little girl, she discovered that she didn't have a penis, and then found out that her mother didn't have one either, and so turned her

libido away from her mother and toward her father, who had one.)
- A woman who is as sexually active as men are supposed to be cannot, in the Freudian view, be enjoying her sexuality and expressing her sensual nature. Instead, she is behaving in a compulsive way, trying to allay anxieties about castration.

C. G. Jung's theory of women's psychology[5] was much "kinder" to women than Freud's in that Jung did not perceive women as just defective men. He hypothesized a psychic structure that corresponded to the different chromosomal makeup of men and women. In his view, women have a feminine conscious personality and a masculine component—called the *animus*—in their unconscious, while men have a masculine conscious personality and a feminine *anima* in their unconscious.

For Jung, receptivity, passivity, nurturing, and subjectivity characterized the feminine personality. Rationality, spirituality, and the capacity to act decisively and impersonally Jung considered masculine attributes. He saw men as being naturally endowed in these areas. Women with similar personality traits, however well developed, were handicapped because they were not men; if a woman thought well or was competent in the world, she only had a well-developed masculine animus that, by definition, was less conscious than and thus inferior to men. The animus could also be hostile, power-driven, and irrationally opinionated, characteristics that Jung (and contemporary Jungians) tend to emphasize when describing how the animus functions.

Although Jung did not see women as inherently defective, he did see them as inherently less creative and less able to be objective or take action than men. In general, Jung tended to see women as they served or related to men, rather than as having independent needs of their own. For example, in regard to creativity, he saw men as the creators and saw women as assistants in men's creative process: "A man brings forth his work as a complete creation out of his inner feminine nature" and "The inner masculine side of a woman brings forth creative seeds which have the power to fertilize the feminine side of the man."[6]

His theoretical position discouraged women's strivings to achieve. He wrote, "By taking up a masculine profession, studying and working like a man, woman is doing something not wholly in accord with, if not directly injurious to, her feminine nature."[7]

GODDESS PATTERNS

When goddesses are seen as patterns of normal feminine behavior, a woman who is naturally more like wise Athena or competitive Artemis than like wifely Hera or motherly Demeter is appreciated as being her feminine self when she is active, objective in her assessments, and achievement-oriented. She is being true to form, like the particular goddess she most resembles. She is not suffering from a masculinity complex, as Freud would diagnose, and is not animus-identified and masculine in her attitude, as Jung would suggest.

When a woman has Athena and Artemis as goddess patterns, "feminine" attributes such as dependency, receptivity, and nurturing may not be facets of her personality. These are the qualities she will need to develop in order to be a person who can form enduring relationships, become vulnerable, give and receive love and comfort, and support growth in others.

Contemplative Hestia's inward focus keeps her at an emotional distance from others. Detached though she is, her quiet warmth is nurturing and supportive. What needs developing that is similar for Artemis and Athena is the capacity for personal intimacy.

These growth tasks differ from the developmental needs of women who resemble Hera, Demeter, Persephone, or Aphrodite. These four goddess patterns predispose women to be in relationships; the personalities of such women fit Jung's description of women. Such women need to learn how to stay focused, objective, and assertive—qualities that are not innately strong in such patterns. These women need to develop the animus or activate the Artemis and Athena archetypes in their lives.

When Hestia is the dominant archetype in a woman, she

shares with these relationship-oriented women a need to develop her animus or have Artemis and Athena as active archetypes in order to be effective in the world.

MASCULINE ANIMUS OR FEMININE ARCHETYPE?

Subjective feelings and dream figures help differentiate whether a woman's active focus is associated with a masculine animus or with a feminine goddess pattern. For example, if a woman feels as if the assertive part of herself is something alien to who she is—that is, like a male in herself on whom she calls in difficult situations requiring her to "be tough" or "think like a man" (neither of which she feels "at home" doing)—then it is her animus that is rising to the occasion and helping her. Much like an auxiliary engine is called on when more power is needed, the animus is held in reserve. This reserve mode is especially true of women in whom Hestia, Hera, Demeter, Persephone, or Aphrodite are the strongest patterns.

But when Athena and Artemis are well-developed aspects of her personality, a woman may *naturally* be assertive, think well, know what she wants to achieve, or compete comfortably. These qualities, far from being alien, feel like inherent expressions of who she is *as a woman,* and not like the qualities of a masculine animus that does it "for her."

Dreams are the second way of differentiating an Artemis or Athena archetype from an animus. They indicate whether these virgin goddesses are the source of a woman's active attitude, or whether qualities such as assertiveness or aiming for goals should be attributed to a masculine aspect of the woman.

When Artemis and Athena are the predominant archetypes, the dreamer is often exploring unfamiliar terrain alone. She is in the role of the protagonist who struggles with obstacles, climbs mountains, or ventures into a foreign country or underground landscape. For example, "I am at the wheel of my convertible, speeding on a country road at night, outrunning whoever is in pursuit"; "I am a stranger in an amazing city that is like the hanging gardens of Babylon"; "It is like being a double agent, I'm not supposed to be there and it would be dangerous if any of the people around me realized who I am."

The difficulties encountered or ease of travel in her dreams bears a correlation to the inner and outer obstacles that the dreamer faces as she attempts to be a self-determined, effective person in the world. As in her dreams, she feels natural as she determines her own path. She is being her active, mind-of-her-own self.

When assertive qualities are in the early stages of developing, a woman dreamer is often accompanied by another figure. This companion can be male or female, an indistinctly seen presence, or a clearly defined, recognizable person. The sex of the companion is a symbolic comment that helps to differentiate whether these emerging capabilities are seen as "masculine" (animus) or "feminine" (virgin goddess).

For example, if the dreamer is developing her Artemis or Athena qualities, and is still in the early stages of her education or career, her most constant dream companion is often a vague, unknown woman, with indistinct features. Later, her companion could be a woman whose education or work path is like the dreamer's, only further along, or a college classmate who went on to make something of herself in the world.

When the companion in a dream adventure is a man or a boy, the dreamer is often a traditional woman, who is identified with the vulnerable goddesses or, as we will see later, with Hestia or Aphrodite. To these women, men symbolize action, and thus they define assertive or competitive qualities as masculine in their dreams.

Thus, when a woman hesitantly enters into the workplace or groves of academia, aided by an animus or masculine aspect of herself, that aspect may be represented in her dreams by a dimly perceived man, perhaps a young boy or an adolescent (still developing), who is with her in an unfamiliar and often dangerous place. After she has received good grades or a promotion and feels more confident of her abilities, the dream terrain becomes more friendly, and the dream symbol is likely to become a familiar man or to seem familiar in the dream. For example, "I am on a long, complicated bus trip with my old boyfriend" or "I am in a car, driven by a man whom I can't place now, but in the dream he is someone I know very well."

The new theory I have elaborated on in this book is based on the existence of archetypal patterns, a concept Jung introduced. I have not discarded the model of women's psychology that Jung described; I see it as fitting some but not all women. The chapters on the vulnerable goddesses and Aphrodite refine Jung's model further, while the three chapters that follow—on Artemis, Athena, and Hestia—provide new patterns that go beyond Jung's concepts.

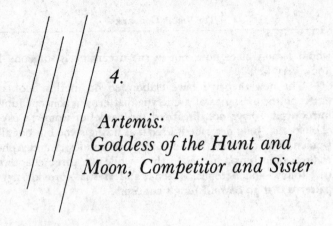

4.

Artemis:
Goddess of the Hunt and
Moon, Competitor and Sister

ARTEMIS THE GODDESS

Artemis, known to the Romans as Diana, was Goddess of the Hunt and Goddess of the Moon. The tall, lovely daughter of Zeus and Leto roamed the wilderness of forest, mountain, meadow, and glade with her band of nymphs and hunting dogs. Dressed in a short tunic, armed with a silver bow, a quiver of arrows on her back, she was the archer with unerring aim. As Goddess of the Moon, she is also shown as a light-bearer, carrying torches in her hands, or with the moon and stars surrounding her head.

As the goddess of wildlife, particularly of young wildlife, she was associated with many undomesticated animals that symbolized her qualities. The stag, doe, hare, and quail all shared her elusive nature. The lioness exemplified her regality and prowess as a hunter, and the fierce boar represented her destructive aspect. The bear was an appropriate symbol for her role as protector of the young (pubescent Greek girls consecrated to Artemis and under her protection were called *arktoi* or "female bears" during a tomboy phase of their lives). Finally, the wild horse roamed widely with companions, as did Artemis with her nymphs.

GENEALOGY AND MYTHOLOGY

Artemis was the first-born twin sister of Apollo, God of the Sun. Their mother, Leto, was a nature deity, the daughter of two Titans; their father was Zeus, chief god of Olympus.

When it was time for Leto to give birth to her children, great obstacles arose. She was unwelcome everywhere she turned, because others feared the vindictive wrath of Hera, the lawful wife of Zeus. Finally, on the barren island of Delos, she found refuge and gave birth to Artemis.

As soon as she was born, Artemis aided Leto during the prolonged labor and difficult delivery of Apollo. For nine days and nine nights, Leto suffered atrocious pain, because of Hera's vengeful efforts. Artemis, who had been a midwife to her mother, was thus also considered a goddess of childbirth. Women addressed her as "helper in pain, whom no pain touches." They prayed to her to end their pain, either through the birth of a baby or through "a kindly death" from her arrows.[1]

When Artemis was three years old, Leto brought her to Olympus, to meet Zeus and her divine relatives. The poet Callimachus, in his "Hymn to Artemis," describes her sitting on the lap of her enchanted father, Zeus, "who leaned down and caressed her, saying, when goddesses bear me children like this, the wrath of jealous Hera troubles me very little. Little daughter, you shall have all you desire."[2]

Artemis asked for a bow and arrows, a pack of hounds to hunt with, nymphs to accompany her, a tunic short enough to run in, mountains and wilderness as her special places, and eternal chastity—all of which her father granted, plus the privilege of making the selections herself.

Artemis then went to the woods and river to choose the most beautiful nymphs. She went beneath the sea to find the Cyclopes, Poseidon's craftsmen, to forge her silver bow and arrows. And finally, with bow in hand, followed by her nymphs, she sought out Pan, the half-man, half-goat, pipe-playing nature deity, and asked for some of his best hounds. As night was coming on, impatient to try out her new gifts, she hunted by torchlight.

In the myths, Artemis acted swiftly and decisively to protect and rescue those who appealed to her for help. She was also quick to punish those who offended her.

Once, when her mother Leto was on her way to Delphi to visit Apollo, the giant Tityus tried to rape her. Artemis came quickly to her mother's aid, took deadly aim with her bow and arrow, and slew him.

Another time, arrogant and unwise Niobe made the mistake of insulting Leto, boasting that she, Niobe, had many beautiful sons and daughters, while Leto had only two. Leto called on Artemis and Apollo to avenge this insult, which they speedily did. With their bows and arrows, Apollo killed her six sons and Artemis slew her six daughters. And Niobe was changed into a weeping pillar of stone.

It is noteworthy that Artemis repeatedly came to her mother's aid. No other goddess is known for this. Other women also successfully appealed to her. The woodland nymph, Arethusa, called to Artemis as she was about to be raped. Arethusa had returned from a hunt, undressed, and was refreshing herself with a swim, when the god of the river became desirous of her and pursued the naked nymph, who fled in terror. Artemis heard her cry, rescued her in a cloud of mist, and transformed her into a spring of water.

Artemis was merciless to those who offended her—as blundering Actaeon discovered. While wandering in the forest, the hunter Actaeon accidently came on the goddess and her nymphs bathing in a hidden pool, and gawked at the sight. Offended by this intrusion, Artemis splashed water into Actaeon's face, which turned him into a stag. He became quarry for his own hunting dogs, who pursued him. In a panic, he tried to flee, but was overtaken and torn to bits.

Artemis also killed another hunter, Orion, whom she loved. This death was inadvertent, provoked by Apollo, who was offended by Artemis's love for Orion. One day, Apollo saw Orion as he waded in the sea, his head just above the water. Apollo then found Artemis some distance away, pointed to a dark object in the ocean, and said she could not hit it. Goaded by her brother's challenge and not knowing that she was aiming at the head of Orion, she let fly an arrow that killed him. Afterward, Artemis placed Orion among the stars and gave him one of her own hounds, Sirius the Dog Star, to accompany him across the heavens. Thus, the one man she loved became a casualty of her competitive nature.

Although she is most known as the Goddess of the Hunt, Artemis was also Goddess of the Moon. She was at home in the night, roaming her wilderness domain by moonlight or torchlight. In her Moon Goddess aspect, Artemis was related to Selene and Hecate. The three have been seen as a moon trinity. Selene ruling in heaven, Artemis on earth, and Hecate in the uncanny and mysterious underworld.

ARTEMIS THE ARCHETYPE

Artemis as Goddess of the Hunt and Goddess of the Moon was a personification of an independent feminine spirit. The archetype she represents enables a woman to seek her own goals on terrain of her own choosing.

VIRGIN GODDESS

As a virgin goddess, Artemis was immune to falling in love. She was not abducted or raped, as were Persephone and Demeter, and was never half of a husband-wife pair. Artemis as a virgin goddess archetype represents a sense of intactness, a one-in-herselfness, an attitude of "I-can-take-care-of-myself" that allows a woman to function on her own with self-confidence and an independent spirit. This archetype enables a woman to feel whole without a man. With it, she can pursue interests and work at what matters to her without needing masculine approval. Her identity and sense of worth is based on who she is and what she does, rather than whether she is married, or to whom. An insistence on being addressed as "Ms." expresses a typically Artemis virgin goddess quality, that emphasizes independence and separateness from men.

THE GOAL-FOCUSED ARCHER

As Goddess of the Hunt in pursuit of her chosen quarry, Artemis the Archer could aim for any target, either near or far away, and could know that her arrows would unerringly reach their marks. The Artemis archetype gives women the innate ability to concentrate intensely on whatever is important to her and to be undistracted from her course, either by the needs of others or by competition from others. If anything, competition heightens the excitment of "the chase."

Goal focus and perseverence despite obstacles in the way or elusiveness of the quarry are Artemis qualities that lead to achievements and accomplishments. This archetype makes it possible to hit a self-chosen mark.

ARCHETYPE OF THE WOMEN'S MOVEMENT

Artemis represents qualities idealized by the women's movement—achievement and competence, independence from men and male opinions, and concern for victimized, powerless women and the young. Artemis the goddess aided her mother Leto in childbirth, rescued Leto and Arethusa from rape, and punished the would-be-rapist Tityus and the intrusive hunter Actaeon. She was the protectress of the young, especially of preadolescent girls.

These concerns of Artemis parallel the concerns of the women's movement that have led to the organization of rape clinics, self-protection classes, help for sexually harassed women, and shelters for battered women. The women's movement has emphasized safe childbirth and midwifery, has been concerned about incest and pornography, and is motivated by a desire to prevent harm to women and children and to punish those who do such harm.

THE SISTER

Artemis the goddess was accompanied by a band of nymphs, minor deities who were associated with mountains, woods, and streams. They traveled with her, exploring and hunting over a wide wilderness terrain. They were unconstrained by domesticity, fashions, or ideas of what women "should" be doing, and were beyond the control of men or of masculine preferences. They were like "sisters," with Artemis as the "Big Sister" who led them and to whom they could appeal for help. Because Artemis is its archetypal inspiration, it is thus no wonder that the women's movement has emphasized the "sisterhood" of women.

Gloria Steinem, a founder and editor of *Ms.* magazine, is a contemporary woman who personifies aspects of the Artemis archetype. Steinem has become a larger-than-life, mythic personality to people who project the goddess image onto her. There in the public eye is Gloria Steinem, a leader of the women's movement, and there in the mind's eye is a tall, graceful Artemis, standing in the midst of her companions.

Women who align themselves with the aims and aspirations of the women's movement often admire and identify with Gloria Steinem as a personification of Artemis. This identification was especially true in the early 1970s, when a great many women wore her trademark aviator glasses and imitated her long, free-flowing hair style, parted in the center. Ten years later, surface emulation has been replaced by efforts to be, like her, attractive women with personal power and independence.

The Artemis mystique surrounding Steinem's role and appearance is enhanced by her single status. Although she has been linked romantically with several men, she has not married—fittingly for a woman who represents a "one-in-herself" virgin goddess, who "belongs to no man."

Steinem is in the tradition of Artemis in that women appeal to her for help, which, big-sister-like, she provides. I felt her support firsthand, when I asked her to come to the American Psychiatric Association annual meetings to help those of us who were trying to get the APA to back the women's movement boycott of states that had not ratified the Equal Rights Amendment (ERA). I was fascinated to see how much power was attributed to Gloria Steinem by many men who "had offended her" and who then reacted as if they might share Actaeon's fate. Some male psychiatrists who opposed her actually expressed (unfounded) fears that they could be financially ruined or could even lose research grant money if this "goddess" were to exercise her power to punish and destroy them.

BACK-TO-NATURE ARTEMIS

In her affinity for the wilderness and undomesticated nature, Artemis is the archetype responsible for the at-oneness with themselves and with nature felt by some women when they backpack into forested mountains, fall asleep under the moon and stars, walk on a deserted beach, or gaze across the desert and feel themselves in spiritual communion with nature.

Lynn Thomas, writing in *The Backpacking Woman*, describes the perceptions of a woman appreciating the wilderness through her Artemis nature:

> There are for starters, grandeur and silence, pure water
> and clean air. There is also the gift of distance . . . the
> chance to stand away from relationships and daily
> ritual . . . and the gift of energy. Wilderness infuses us
> with its own special brand of energy. I remember lying
> by the Snake River in Idaho once and becoming aware
> I could not sleep . . . natures's forces had me in hand. I
> was engulfed by a dance of ions and atoms. My body
> was responding to the pervasive pull of the moon.[3]

"MOONLIGHT VISION"

The eye-on-target clarity of focus of Artemis the Hunter, is one of two modes of "seeing" associated with Artemis. "Moonlight vision" is also characteristic of Artemis as the Moon Goddess. Seen by moonlight, a landscape is muted, details are indistinct, beautiful, and often mysterious. One's vision is drawn upward to the starry heavens or to a vast, panoramic view of nature. In moonlight, a person in touch with Artemis becomes an unself-conscious part of nature, in it and one-with-it for a time.

In her book *Women in the Wilderness,* China Galland emphasizes that when women walk into the wilderness they also walk inward: "Going into the wilderness involves the wilderness within us all. This may be the deepest value of such an experience, the recognition of our kinship with the natural world."[4] Women who follow Artemis into the wilderness characteristically discover themselves becoming more reflective. Often, their dreams are more vivid than usual, which contributes to their looking inward. They see inner terrain and dream symbols by "moonlight," so to speak, in contrast to tangible reality, which is best appreciated in the bright light of day.

CULTIVATING ARTEMIS

Artemis-idenitified women immediately recognize their affinity with this goddess. Other types of women may also become aware of their need to make her acquaintance. And yet other women know that Artemis exists in them and realize the need for her to become a more influential part of themselves. How can we cultivate Artemis? Or strengthen this archetype? And how can we encourage the growth of Artemis in our daughters?

Sometimes the goal of developing Artemis requires drastic measures. For example, one talented woman writer, whose work was significant to her, repeatedly abandoned it whenever a man came into her life. Every man was initially intoxicating. Soon he became a need. Her life would revolve around him, and if he became distant or rejecting she would get increasingly frantic. After a friend commented that she was addicted to men, she saw the pattern and decided that if she were going to take her writing seriously, she would have to go "cold turkey" and "swear off" men for a period of time. She moved out of the city, only occasionally seeing old friends, while she cultivated solitude, work, and Artemis within herself.

A woman who marries young often goes from being a daughter to a wife (archetypally Persephone and then Hera), and may discover and value Artemis qualities only after a divorce, when she lives alone for the first time in her life. Such a woman may go on a vacation by herself and find that she can have a good time; or discover the satisfactions of running several miles each morning; or enjoy being part of a women's support group.

Or a woman may have a series of relationships, may feel worthless in the intervals between men, and may develop Artemis only after she "gives up on men" and seriously concludes that she may never marry. Once she has the courage to face this possibility and to organize her life around her friends and what matters to her, she may feel a one-in-herself sense of wholeness, an unexpected well-being that comes from developing the Artemis archetype.

Wilderness programs for women evoke Artemis, especially

those that combine a group experience with a solo heroic journey. When women go on Outward Bound trips or on vision quests for women, they cultivate the Artemis archetype. Similarly, when our daughters compete in sports, go to all-girl camps, travel to explore new places, live in foreign cultures as exchange students, or join the Peace Corps, they gain experiences that can develop the self-sufficient Artemis.

ARTEMIS THE WOMAN

Artemis qualities appear early. Usually an Artemis baby is the one who looks absorbingly at new objects, who is active rather than passive. People often comment on this capacity to concentrate on a self-selected task: "She has an amazing power of concentration for a two-year-old," or "She's one stubborn kid," or "Be careful what you promise her, she's got a mind like an elephant; she won't forget—she'll hold you to it." The Artemis penchant for exploring new territory usually begins when she manages to get up and over the crib railing, out of the playpen, and into the bigger world.

Artemis has a tendency to feel strongly about her causes and principles. She may have come to the defense of someone smaller or may fervently assert "That's not fair!" before embarking on some campaign to right a wrong. Artemis girls brought up in households that favor sons—giving the boys more privileges or expecting them to do fewer household chores—do not meekly accept this inequity as a "given." The budding feminist is often first glimpsed as the little sister demanding equality.

PARENTS

An Artemis woman who securely pursues her own course, all the while feeling good about who she is as a person, and glad that she is a female, often has had the equivalent of a loving Leto and an approving Zeus to help her "actualize" her Artemis potential. For an Artemis woman to compete and achieve with success and without conflict, paternal approval is highly important.

Many supportive fathers are like Zeus, in providing the

"gifts" that will help her do what she wants to do. Perhaps the gifts are intangible: shared interests or similarities with him that he recognizes and encourages. Or they can be more tangible gifts, such as special lessons and equipment. For example, tennis champion Chris Evert Lloyd was coached by her tennis pro father, Jimmy Evert, who provided her with her own tennis racket when she was only six years old.

When an Artemis daughter has a nontraditional mother and father, however, life no longer resembles Mt. Olympus— there was no equivalent in Greek mythology. When both parents are equals who share childrearing and household chores, and each has a career, the Artemis daughter has a model for growth that allows her to value and develop her Artemis qualities. Moreover, she can do so without considering such qualities incompatible with maternity or relationships.

Problems arise when parents criticize or reject an Artemis daughter for not being the girl they expect her to be. A mother who wants a placid, cuddly baby girl, and who has instead an active, "Don't fence me in" infant, may feel either disappointed in the baby or rejected by her. A mother who expects a daughter to tag along after her, run to her for help, and compliantly concede that "Mother knows best" will not find her expectations fulfilled if she has an Artemis daughter. Even at three years old, "Little Miss Independent" doesn't want to stay home with Mommy; she'd rather play with the bigger kids down the block. And she doesn't like to wear frilly clothes or be cute for her mother's friends.

Later, when Artemis wants to do something requiring parental permission, she may run into opposition. If the boys get to do something and she can't "because she's a girl," she may howl in protest. And she may withdraw resentfully if her protests are to no avail. Opposition and disapproval may harm her self-esteem and self-confidence, especially if her admired father criticizes her for not being ladylike and never treats her like "his special girl," while at the same time being contemptuous or critical of her ideas, abilities, or aspirations.

In my practice, I hear what happened when such fathers opposed their Artemis daughters. Typically, the daughter maintained a defiant pose outwardly but inwardly was wounded. She appeared to be strong, uninfluenced by what he thought, biding her time until she could be on her own. The consequences vary in intensity and severity, but follow a pattern: what results is a woman who feels conflict about her competence and often sabotages herself—her own doubts are her worst enemies. Although on the surface she successfully resisted her father's power to limit her aspirations, she incorporated his critical attitude into her psyche. Deep down, she struggles with feelings that she is not good enough, hesitates when new opportunities are offered, achieves less than she is capable of, and, even when she succeeds, still feels inadequate. This pattern is culturally produced by families and cultures that place a higher value on sons than on daughters and that expect daughters to be stereotypically feminine.

One Artemis woman, who attended a seminar I taught, commented, "My mother wanted a Persephone (a compliant mother's little daughter), and my father wanted a son. What they got was me." Some mothers of Artemis daughters are also rejecting and critical of their daughters for pursuing goals that they do not value. Their daughters usually are not dissuaded by this disapproval, but it nonetheless is undermining. However, the weight of their mothers' negativity usually is less than that of their fathers because of the greater authority fathers carry.

Another common mother-daughter difficulty that Artemis daughters have is with mothers whom they view as passive and weak. Their mothers may have been depressed, victimized by alcohol or a bad marriage, or immature. When they describe their relationships with their mothers, many Artemis daughters in this mother-daughter configuration say, "I was the parent." Talking further brings out their sadness at not having stronger mothers and not being strong enough themselves to change their mothers' lives. While the goddess Artemis was always able to help her mother Leto, the efforts of Artemis daughters to rescue their mothers was often unsuccessful.

Devaluation and lack of respect for their weak mothers strengthens the virgin goddess qualities of Artemis daughters. Determined not to resemble their mothers, they suppress dependency feelings, avoid expressing vulnerability and vow to be independent.

When an Artemis daughter lacks respect for a mother whose major roles have been the traditional ones, she is in a bind. In rejecting identification with her mother, she usually finds herself rejecting what is considered as feminine—softness, receptivity, and stirrings toward marriage and motherhood. She is plagued by inadequacy feelings—this time in the realm of her feminine identification.

ADOLESCENCE AND YOUNG ADULTHOOD

As a girl, the Artemis woman typically is a natural competitor, with perseverance, courage, and will to win. In pursuit of whatever the goal, she will push herself to the limit. She may be a Girl Scout—hiking, climbing, sleeping out of doors, riding a horse, swinging an axe as she chops wood for the campfire, or, like Artemis herself, becoming an expert archer. The unmistakable Artemis teenager is the "horse-crazy" girl, whose world revolves around horses. The heroine of the movie classic *National Velvet* personifies this archetypal adolescent Artemis.

The Artemis teenager is a girl with a streak of independence and a bent for exploration. She ventures into the woods, climbs hills, or wants to see what is in the next block and the block after that. "Don't fence me in" and "Don't tread on me" are her slogans. As a girl, she is less conforming or compromising than many of her peers, because she is less motivated by eagerness to please others and because she usually knows what she wants. This sureness may rebound on her, however: others may consider her "pig-headed," "stubborn," and "unfeminine."

When she leaves home for college, the Artemis woman enjoys the exhilaration of independence and the competitive challenge of whatever interests her. She usually finds a group of like spirits to "run with." If she's political, she may be out running for office.

And, if she's a physical conditioning buff, she may actually be running many miles a day, reveling in her strength and grace, enjoying the reflective state her mind goes into as she runs. (I've yet to meet a woman who has run a marathon who has not had a strong streak of Artemis in her that is responsible for the combination of goal focus, intensity, competitiveness, and will that is required.) Artemis is also found in women skiers, who chart their course down the mountain instinctively, always tilted forward in a physical and psychological attitude that unhesitantly moves forward, challenged by the difficulties.

WORK

The Artemis woman puts effort into work that is of subjective value to her. She is spurred on by competition and undeterred (up to a point) by opposition. The Artemis woman who has entered a helping profession or the legal field usually has an ideal that influenced her choice. If she is in business, she probably started out with a product that she believed in, or perhaps one that helped her to do something she wanted to do. If she is in a creative field, she most likely is expressing a personal vision. If she has entered politics, she is an advocate of a cause, most usually to do with environmental or feminist issues. Worldly success—fame, power, or money—may come to her, if what she excels at is rewarded.

However, the interests pursued by many Artemis women have no commercial value, and do not lead to a career or enhance reputation or pocketbook. Sometimes, on the contrary, that interest is so personal or off the beaten track, so absorbing of time, that *lack* of success in the world and *lack* of relationships are guaranteed. Yet the pursuit is personally fulfilling to the Artemis element in the woman. For example, the advocate of the lost cause, the unappreciated reformer, the "voice crying in the wilderness" that no one seems to heed is most likely an Artemis woman, as may be the artist who continues working with no encouragement or commercial success. (In the artist's case, Aphrodite, with her influence on creativity and emphasis on subjective experience, joins Artemis.)

Because an Artemis woman is nontraditional, conflicts within herself or with others may arise that can hamstring her efforts. What she wants to do may be "off limits" to her, for example, if her family views her aspirations as inappropriate for a daughter. The career choice she wants to follow may

58

have been closed to women until just recently. If she were "born too soon" for the women's movement, she may have been defeated by obstacles and lack of support, and her Artemis spirit may have been broken.

RELATIONSHIP TO WOMEN: SISTERLY

Artemis women have a sense of affiliation with other women. Like the goddess herself, who surrounded herself with nymph-companions, Artemis women usually consider their friendships with other women very important. This pattern goes back to elementary school. They have "best friends" with whom they have shared whatever has been significant in their lives, and their friendships eventually may span decades.

In the work world, Artemis women easily ally themselves with "old girl networks." Support groups, networks with other women, and mentor relationships with younger women in their fields are natural expressions of the sister archetype.

Even Artemis women who are individualists and who avoid groups almost always support women's rights. This stance may reflect an affinity with their mothers through which they developed an awareness and sympathy for women's lot in the world. Or the stance may be related to the unlived-out, frustrated aspirations of their mothers. Many Artemis women in the 1970s were doing and being what their own mothers may have wanted to do or be, but could not. When their mothers were young adults, the post–World War II baby boom years did not allow Artemis much expression. Often a supportive mother can be found somewhere in the background of an Artemis woman, applauding her feminist daughter.

By nature, most Artemis women have feminist leanings—the causes espoused by feminists strike a responsive chord. The Artemis woman usually feels that she is an equal of men; she has competed with them and has often felt that the stereotyped role she was supposed to play was unnatural. Hiding her abilities—"Don't let the man know how smart you are" or "Let the man win (the argument or the tennis game)"—goes against her grain.

SEXUALITY

An Artemis woman may resemble the goddess in maintaining eternal chastity, her sexuality remaining undeveloped and unexpressed. In contemporary times, however, this pattern is rare. More likely, by the time she is an adult an Artemis woman has acquired sexual experience as part of her tendency to explore and try new adventures.

An Artemis woman's sexuality may resemble that of a traditional work-oriented man. For both, relationships are secondary. Involvement in career, creative project, or cause is primary. Sex is, then, a recreational sport or a physical experience—rather than a physical expression of emotional intimacy and commitment (a motivation that Hera provides) or an instinct deeply expressive of her own sensual nature (for which Aphrodite is needed).

If she is a lesbian, an Artemis woman is usually part of a lesbian community or network. Although both heterosexual and homosexual Artemis women have intense and important relationships with women friends, the lesbian Artemis woman may consider sexual intimacy as another dimension of friendship—rather than as the reason for the relationship.

The lesbian Artemis woman may either have a mirror-image lover, an almost identical-twin relationship, or she may be attracted to a nymphlike, softer, more "feminine" person than herself, with a less distinct personality. She, like her heterosexual equivalent, avoids relationships in which she is contained or dominated by a "parental" partner or in which she herself is expected to play the parent role.

MARRIAGE

Marriage is often far from an Artemis woman's mind in the early adult years, when she is engrossed in work or causes. Besides, "settling down" holds no great attraction for an on-the-move Artemis. If she is attractive and popular, chances are that she has played the field, comfortably going out with a variety of men—not just one alone. She may have even lived with a man in preference to marrying him. She may stay unmarried.

When she does marry, her mate is often a fellow class-mate, colleague, or competitor. Usually her marriage has an egalitarian quality. These days, she is likely to keep her own name, and not change to his once she does marry.

RELATIONSHIPS WITH MEN: BROTHERLY

The goddess Artemis had a twin brother, Apollo, the many-faceted God of the Sun. He was her male counterpart: his domain was the city, hers the wilderness; his was the sun, hers the moon; his the domesticated flocks, hers the wild, un-tamed animals; he was the god of music, she was the inspiration for round dances on mountains. As a second-generation Olympian, Apollo was in the generation of the sons, rather than the fathers. On the one hand, he was associated with rationality and laws. On the other, as the God of Prophecy (his priestesses prophesied at Delphi), he was also associated with the irrational. Like his sister, Apollo is androgynous: each had some qualities or interests that are usually linked with the opposite sex.

The Artemis-Apollo twinship is the model most commonly seen in the relationships Artemis women have with men—be they friends, colleagues, or husbands. Moreover, the Artemis woman is often attracted to a man whose personality has an aesthetic, creative, healing, or musical side. His work may be either in the helping professions or in a creative field. He is usually her intellectual equal, with shared or complementary interests. One example of an Artemis-Apollo relationship is that of Jane Fonda (actress, activist, and advocate of physical fitness) and her husband Tom Hayden (liberal politician).

An Artemis woman is not at all charmed by dominating men and "Me Tarzan, you Jane" relationships. Nor is she interested in mother-son relationships. She avoids men who insist on being the center of her life. Standing tall psychologically, as the goddess herself did physically, she feels ridiculous attempting to play the role of "the little woman."

Often an Artemis-Apollo relationship and outdoor interests go hand in hand. Both partners may be skiers or runners and physical fitness buffs. If an Artemis outdoor woman cannot share backpacking, skiing, or whatever she loves to do with a partner, she may feel that an essential element of relationship is missing.

The Artemis-Apollo relationship may result in an asexual, companionable marriage, in which the partners are each other's best friends. Some Artemis women even marry gay men, for instance, and value the companionship and the independence each partner in such a relationship allows the other. An Artemis woman may stay best friends with an ex-husband who left their brother-sister marriage when he fell in love with another woman of a different type.

For an Artemis woman to have a deep and important sexual element in her marriage, another goddess—Aphrodite—must have an influence. And for that marriage to be a monogamous, committed relationship, Hera must also be present in the woman. Without these other two goddesses, an Artemis-Apollo relationship easily becomes a brother-sister one.

Besides the pattern of relationships between equals, the second common relationship pattern for Artemis women is involvement with men who nurture them. Such a man is the person she "comes home to." He teaches her to be considerate and sensitive to feelings. And he is often the one who wants them to have a child.

Less compatible or complementary relationships entered into by Artemis women often recapitulate early father-daughter conflicts. Such a husband does not support her aspirations, and undermines and criticizes her. As with her father, she is defiant and continues with her career. Yet her self-esteem is affected, or else her spirit is beaten down and she finally conforms to his idea of how she should be.

Or, paralleling the myth of Artemis and Orion, an Artemis woman may fall in love with a strong man and may then be unable to keep a competitive element out of the relationship, which kills it. If he achieves some recognition and (rather than be glad for him) she resents his success and finds a way to tarnish it, this competitiveness will erode the love he has for her. Or it may be the man's competitiveness that kills off *her* love. For example, he may react to her achievements as winning or surpassing him. If both are unable to stop competing, challenges of any kind that arise between them, from ski racing to a game of gin rummy, are likely to be taken in deadly earnest.

Men for whom an Artemis is "my kind of woman" are often attracted to her as a twin or kindred spirit—a female counterpart of themselves. Or they may be attracted to her independent, assertive, spirit and strength of will, which may be undeveloped in themselves. Or they may be drawn to her as an image of purity that corresponds to an ideal in themselves.

The twin motif underlies the most common attraction. Here the man is drawn to his female counterpart, an equal with whom he feels natural, someone he can have at his side as he pursues what challenges him.

The man who sees in Artemis admired qualities that are undeveloped in himself is usually drawn to her strength of will and independent spirit. He places her on a pedestal for qualities that are usually thought of as "unfeminine." She is beautiful to him for her strengths. His idealized woman resembles Wonder Woman (who disguised herself as Diana, the Roman name for Artemis).

When my son was eight, I overheard his friend speaking admiringly of a girl's daring exploits. He saw his girlfriend as outspoken and brave, a girl who he could count on to come to his rescue: "If anyone messed with me, I'd call her up and she'd be over in a minute." As a psychiatrist, I've heard that same tone of admiration, that same pride in affiliation, when men who have Artemis as an ideal image speak of the exploits or accomplishments of women they love.

A third kind of man is drawn to the purity of Artemis, her virginity and identification with pristine nature. In Greek mythology, this attraction was personified by Hippolytus, a handsome youth who dedicated himself to the goddess Artemis and to a life of celibacy. His chastity offended Aphrodite, Goddess of Love, who then set in motion a tragic sequence of events—a myth I'll describe in the Aphrodite chapter. Such men—attracted to women who seem to be as pure as Artemis—are offended by earthy sexuality. Like youthful Hippolytus, they may be in late adolescence or early adulthood, and may be virgin themselves.

CHILDREN

The Artemis woman is hardly an Earth-Mother type—and being pregnant or nursing a baby will not fulfill her. In fact, pregnancy may be repugnant to the Artemis woman who likes having an athletic, graceful, or boyish figure. She doesn't feel a strong instinctual pull to be a mother (for this, Demeter must be present). Yet she likes children.

When an Artemis woman has children of her own, she is often a good mother—like the female bear, which is her symbol. She is the kind of mother who fosters independence, who teaches her young how to fend for themselves and yet who can be ferocious in their defense. Some children of Artemis women are convinced that their mothers would fight to the death for them.

Artemis women are comfortable not having children of their own, putting their particular kind of mothering energy—which can be like that of a youthful aunt—to use with other people's children. Being Girl Scout counselors, stepmothers, or members of the "Big Sisters of America" provide such opportunities. In these roles, they resemble the goddess Artemis, who protected girls on the threshhold of being women.

Artemis mothers do not look back with longing to when their children were babies or dependent toddlers. Instead, they look forward to when their children will be more independent. Active boys or girls who like to explore find that their Artemis mothers make enthusiastic companions. An Artemis mother is pleased when a child comes home with a garter snake, and gladly goes camping or skiing with her children.

But trouble brews when an Artemis woman has a dependent, passive child. Trying to foster independence too early may, for such children, worsen matters by increasing the clinging. The child may feel rejected, not good enough to live up to the standards of his or her Artemis mother.

MIDDLE YEARS

An Artemis woman between the ages of thirty-five and fifty-five may find herself in a midlife crisis if she does not have any other goddess aspects in her life. Artemis is a pattern that is very compatible with a goal-oriented young woman who single-mindedly pursues her self-chosen goal. But in her middle years a shift may occur. Now there are fewer "uncharted wildernesses" for her to explore. She has either succeeded in achieving her targeted goals, reached a plateau, or failed.

The midlife of an Artemis woman may also usher in a more reflective time as she turns inward, more influenced by Artemis as Goddess of the Moon than by Artemis as the Goddess of the Hunt. Menopausal fantasies and dreams may stimulate an extroverted Artemis woman to journey inward. On the journey, she confronts "ghosts" from her past, often discovering long-ignored feelings or yearnings. This menopausal impetus toward introversion is related to Hecate, the old crone who was the goddess of the dark moon, ghosts, and the uncanny. Hecate and Artemis were both moon goddesses who roamed on Earth. The connection of the two goddesses is seen in older Artemis women who venture into psychic, psychological, or spiritual realms, with the same sense of exploration they had as younger women in other pursuits.

LATER YEARS

It is not unusual for a woman to have her Artemis qualities persist into old age. Her youthful activeness never ceases. She doesn't settle down; her mind or body—often both—is on the move. She is a traveler exploring new projects or foreign countries. She retains an affinity for the young and an ability to think young, which keeps her from feeling "middle aged" when she is in her middle years, or "old" when she is in her later years.

Two locally known Northern California women personify this aspect of Artemis. One, the naturalist-teacher Elizabeth Terwilliger, now in her seventies, leads bands of schoolchildren into meadows, woods, streams, and mountains. She excitedly spies a rare mushroom half hidden near the roots of a tree, holds up a pretty snake, points to the edible plants on the hillside, and passes the miners' lettuce around to taste. All the while, she is sharing her enthusiasm, turning on successive generations of children, as well as receptive adults, to the wonders of nature.

A second spritely, aged Artemis is Frances Horn, whose explorations led her into human nature. At seventy, she received her doctorate in psychology; at seventy-five, she published *I Want One Thing*,[5] an autobiographical book that charts her explorations and notes what she found that was of lasting value.

Georgia O'Keeffe, the best-known American woman artist, continued to exemplify Artemis when she was in her nineties, as she had done all her life. She had a passion and a spiritual affinity for the untamed Southwest, combined with an intensity of purpose through which she reached her life goals. O'Keeffe is quoted as saying, "I've always known what I've wanted—and most people don't."[6] She mused that her success may have been due to a streak of aggression, which led to her having "taken hold of anything that came along that I wanted." Artemis-like O'Keeffe clearly took unerring aim and achieved what she sought.

In 1979, O'Keeffe at ninety-two was the only living woman to be included in artist Judy Chicago's "The Dinner Party," a tribute in place settings of porcelain and embroidery to thirty-nine important women in history. O'Keeffe's plate rose off the table higher than any other plate—symbolizing, in Chicago's view, O'Keeffe's "almost successful aspiration to be entirely her own woman."[7]

PSYCHOLOGICAL DIFFICULTIES

Artemis the goddess roamed through her chosen terrain with company of her own chosing, doing what pleased her. Unlike goddesses who were victimized, Artemis never suffered. However, she did harm others who offended her, or threatened those under her protection. Similarly, the psychological difficulties that characteristically are associated with Artemis women usually cause others to suffer, rather than bringing pain on themselves.

IDENTIFYING WITH ARTEMIS

To live "as Artemis" in pursuit of a goal or focused on work may be quite satisfactory for an Artemis woman, who characteristically may not feel a lack in her life, especially if she is able to invest her considerable energy in work that has a deep meaning for her. She is likely to have an on-the-move lifestyle, which she enjoys. A "home base" is not important. Nor are marriage and children pressing needs, regardless of pressure from family and society, unless Hera and/or Demeter are also strong archetypes. Although she is missing close and committed emotional intimacy, she has enduring sisterly and brotherly relationships with men and women friends, and can enjoy the company of other people's children.

Identifying with Artemis shapes a woman's character. She then needs to be challenged and involved in interests that are personally rewarding. Otherwise, the archetype is thwarted and unable to find adequate expression, and the Artemis woman herself feels frustrated, and ultimately depressed. This was the situation for many Artemis women in the post–World War II, Baby Boom years, who tried unsuccessfully to adapt to the roles available to them.

Recalling how destructive Artemis the goddess could be toward others, it is not surprising to realize that a woman's unconscious identification with Artemis may be expressed through actions that damage and hurt other people. These negative potentialites are enumerated in the paragraphs that follow.

CONTEMPT FOR VULNERABILITY

As long as there is an element of "pursuit" on her part, an Artemis woman may be interested in a man. But if he moves closer emotionally, wants to marry her, or becomes dependent on her, the excitement of the "hunt" is over. Moreover, she may lose interest or feel contempt for him if he shows "weakness" by needing her. As a result, an Artemis woman may have a series of relationships that go well only as long as the man keeps some emotional distance and is not always available. This pattern can arise if a woman identifies with the "one-in-herself" virgin goddess element and denies her own vulnerability and need for another. To change, she must discover that the love and trust of another special person is very precious to her.

Until then, from the man's vantage point, she is like a

mermaid: half of her is a beautiful woman, half of her is cold and inhuman. Jungian analyst Esther Harding made some observations about this aspect of a virgin goddess woman: "The coldness of the moon and the heartlessness of the Moon Goddess symbolize this aspect of feminine nature. In spite of its lack of warmth and its callousness, partly perhaps because of its very indifference, this impersonal eroticism in a woman often appeals to a man."[8]

And an Artemis woman can be cruel to a man who loves her, once she no longer is interested in him. She may rebuff him and treat him as an unwanted intruder.

DESTRUCTIVE RAGE: THE CALYDON BOAR

The goddess Artemis had a destructive aspect that was symbolized by the wild boar, one of the animals sacred to her. In mythology she unleashed the destructive Calydon Boar on the countryside when she was offended.

As described in *Bullfinch's Mythology*, "The boar's . . . eyes shone with blood and fire, its bristles stood like threatening spears, its tusks were like those of Indian elephants. The growing corn was trampled, the vines and olive trees laid waste, the flocks and herds were driven in wild confusion by the slaughtering foe."[9] This is a vivid picture of rampaging destruction, a metaphor for an Artemis woman on the warpath.

The rage of Artemis is surpassed only by that of Hera. Yet although the intensity of feeling of both goddesses appears similar, the direction of the anger and the provocation differ. A Hera woman rages at "the other woman." An Artemis woman is more likely angry at a man or men in general for depreciating her or for failing to treat with respect something she values.

For example, consciousness raising in the 1970s women's movement usually led to constructive changes. But as many Artemis women became aware of society's unfair limitations and demeaning attitudes toward women in general, they reacted with intense hostility that was often out of proportion to the particular provocation. Prudent bystanders wisely got out of the way when a Calydon Boar met a Male Chauvinist Pig in the early 1970s! Moreover, many women were also wounded and "trashed" by Artemis women who went on a rampage after such consciousness-raising sessions.

In the myth of the Calydon Boar, the same Atalanta who raced Hippomenes faced the charging boar with a spear in her hand. The boar had already gored and killed many famous male heroes who had tried to bring it down. Its hide was tougher than armor. Now it was up to her: either stop the beast or be destroyed. She waited until the boar was almost on her, took careful aim, and then threw the spear through an eye (its only vulnerable spot) to hit the mark.

The destructive rage of an Artemis woman can only be stopped by what Atalanta did. The Artemis woman must confront her own destructiveness directly. She must see it as an aspect of herself that she must stop before it consumes her and devastates her relationships.

It takes courage to confront the inner boar, for doing so means that the woman must see how much damage she has done to herself and others. She can no longer feel righteous and powerful. Humility is the lesson that returns her humanity—she becomes all too aware that she, too, is a flawed human woman, not an avenging goddess.

INACCESSIBILITY

Artemis has been called "the Far-Distant Artemis."[10] Emotional distance is a characteristic of an Artemis woman, who is so focused on her own aims and undistracted that she fails to notice the feelings of others around her. As a consequence of her inattentiveness, people who care about her feel insignificant and excluded, and become hurt or angry at her.

Again, she must achieve conscious awareness before she can change. Here, an Artemis woman needs to hear and heed what others say. They in turn would do best to wait until she isn't concentrating on a pet project and can turn her focus on them. (If they bring it up at the time when she is engrossed in what she is doing, friction is inevitable, unless the Artemis woman is already aware of what she does and appreciates the reminder that she's doing it again.) Artemis was a "now you see her, now you don't" goddess, who could literally disappear into the forest, much as wild animals can sometimes be seen one moment and gone the next. When emotional distance is an inadvertent side affect of intense concentration, a sincere desire to remain in touch and accessible to those who matter can mitigate this tendency. This remedy applies on a day-to-day basis as well as to periodic "disappearing acts."

MERCILESSNESS

Artemis was often merciless. For example, the hunter Actaeon inadvertently intruded on her and lacked the good sense to know that gawking at a naked goddess was a capital offense. So Artemis changed him into a stag that was torn to pieces by his own hounds. And when conceited Niobe demeaned Leto, the mother of Artemis and Apollo, the twins at once defended Leto's honor—without mercy.

Outrage at wrongs done, loyalty to others, strength to express a point of view, and a propensity to take action can be very positive characteristics of Artemis and of Artemis women. But the mercilessness of the punishment they mete out can be appalling: all twelve of Niobe's children were killed by the twin archers so that she would have nothing to brag about.

The lack of mercy often arises when an Artemis woman judges the actions of others in terms of unmitigated black and white. In this perspective, not only is an action either all bad or all good, but the person who does such a thing is too. Thus, an Artemis woman feels justified if she retaliates or punishes.

She needs to develop compassion and empathy, which may come with maturity, in order to change this attitude. Many Artemis women enter adulthood feeling self-confident and invulnerable. With life experience, however, their compassion can grow as they too suffer, are misjudged, or fail at something. If an Artemis woman learns how it feels to be vulnerable and becomes more understanding, if she finds that people are more complex than she thought, and if she forgives others and herself for making mistakes, then these lessons learned from living will make her more merciful.

THE CRUCIAL CHOICE: SACRIFICING OR SAVING IPHIGENIA

One last myth about Artemis speaks to a significant choice for an Artemis woman. This is the myth of Iphigenia, and the choice involves the role of Artemis either as the savior of Iphigenia or as the cause of her death.

In the story of the Trojan War, the Greek ships assembled at the Greek port of Aulis before setting sail for Troy. There the fleet was becalmed; no winds arose to fill the sails. Convinced that the calm was the doing of a god, Agamemnon (the commander of the Greek forces) consulted the expedition's seer. The seer declared that Artemis had been offended and could be appeased only by the sacrifice of Agamemnon's daughter Iphigenia. At first, Agamemnon resisted, but as time passed and the men became more angry and unruly, he tricked his wife Clytemnestra into sending Iphigenia to him, on the pretext that she was to be married to the Greek hero Achilles. Instead, she was prepared for the sacrifice—her life in exchange for fair winds that might carry the fleet to war.

What happened next is told in two versions. According to one, the death of Iphigenia was carried out as demanded by Artemis. According to the other, Artemis interceded just at the point of sacrifice, substituting a stag in her place, and carried her off to Tauris, where Iphigenia became one of Artemis's priestesses.

These two endings can represent the two possible effects of Artemis. On the one hand, she rescues women and feminine values from the patriarchy, which devalues or oppresses both. On the other, with her intense focus on goals she can also require that a woman sacrifice and devalue what has been traditionally considered "feminine"—those receptive, nurturing, related-to-others, willing-to-make-sacrifices-for-the-sake-of-others qualities. Every Artemis woman is likely to have some part of her that is like Iphigenia—a young, trusting, beautiful part that represents her vulnerability, her potentiality for intimacy, and her dependency on others. Will she rescue and protect this aspect of herself so that it can grow, even as she moves through her life, aiming for what matters to her? Or will she require that she kill this Iphigenia part of herself, in order to be as focused, hard, and clear as possible?

WAYS TO GROW

To grow beyond Artemis, a woman must develop her less conscious, receptive, relationship-oriented potential. She needs to become vulnerable, to learn to love and care deeply about another person. If this happens, it may do so within a relationship—usually with a man who loves her, sometimes with another woman, or by having a child.

Often this advance can occur only after an Artemis woman has "run down," after she has aimed for a series of targets and achieved them or failed, after the thrill of the hunt, the race, or the pursuit has grown stale. A man who loves her may need to wait until then, and until he can get some aid from Aphrodite.

THE ATALANTA MYTH: A METAPHOR FOR PSYCHOLOGICAL GROWTH

Atalanta was a heroine whose courage and capabilities as a hunter and runner were equal to any man's.[11] She had been exposed on a mountaintop soon after her birth, was found and nurtured by a bear, and grew to be a beautiful woman. A hunter named Meleager became her lover and companion. The twinlike pair became well-known hunters, famous throughout Greece, especially for their part in the Calydon Boar hunt. Meleager died in her arms shortly thereafter. Atalanta then left the mountain country they had roamed together, to confront her father and be recognized as heir to his throne.

Now many suitors came to win her hand, and she spurned them all. When a clamor arose for her to choose among them, she said that she would marry the man who could beat her at a footrace. If he won, she would marry him; if he lost, he would forfeit his life. Race after race was run, with fleet-footed Atalanta always in the lead.

Finally, unathletic Hippomenes, who truly loved her, decided to enter the race even through it would probably cost him his life. The night before the race he prayed to Aphrodite, Goddess of Love, for help. She heard his plea and gave him three golden apples to use in the race.

Apple 1: Awareness of Time Passing. Early in the race, Hippomenes threw the first golden apple in Atalanta's path. She was drawn to its shining beauty and slowed down to pick it up. Hippomenes pulled ahead in the race as she gazed at the golden apple in her hand. Reflected back to her, she saw her own face, distorted by the curves of the apple: "This is how I will look when I grow old," she thought.

Many active women are unaware of time passing, until sometime in midlife when the challenges of competition or reaching goals wane. For the first time in her life, such a woman may become aware that she is not an eternal youth and reflect about the course she is on, and where it is taking her.

Apple 2: Awareness of the Importance of Love. Then he threw the second apple across her path. Atalanta once more focused on the race and effortlessly gained on Hippomenes. As she stopped to retrieve Aphrodite's second golden apple, memories of Meleager, her dead lover, surged up in her. Yearnings for physical and emotional closeness are stirred by Aphrodite. When this is combined with awareness that time is passing, an Artemis woman's usual focus is diverted by a new receptivity to love and intimacy.

Apple 3: Procreative Instinct and Creativity. The finish line was within sight as Atalanta drew up even with Hippomenes. She was about to pass him, and win, when Hippomenes dropped the third golden apple. For a split second, Atalanta hesitated: should she cross the finish line and win the race, or take the apple and lose? Atalanta chose to reach for the apple just as Hippomenes crossed the finish line to win the race and Atalanta for his wife.

Aphrodite's procreative instinct (aided by Demeter) slows down many active, goal-focused women in the latter part of their thirties. Career-oriented women are often caught by surprise by a compelling urgency to have a child.

This third golden apple may also represent other than biological creativity. Achievement may become less important after midlife. Instead, the generativity represented by Aphrodite is directed toward transforming experience into some form of personal expression.

If knowledge of Aphrodite is brought through the love of another person, then an Artemis woman's one-sidedness, however satisfying it has been, may give way to the possibility of wholeness. She can turn inward to reflect on what is important to her, and be inner-directed as well as outer-focused. She becomes aware that she has needs for intimacy as well as for independence. Once she acknowledges love, she—like Atalanta—will have moments of decision to decide for herself what is most important.

5.

Athena:
Goddess of Wisdom and
Crafts, Strategist and
Father's Daughter

Athena the Goddess

Athena was the Greek Goddess of Wisdom and Crafts, known to the Romans as Minerva. Like Artemis, Athena was a virgin goddess, dedicated to chastity and celibacy. She was the stately, beautiful warrior goddess, protector of her chosen heroes and of her namesake city, Athens. She was the only Olympian goddess portrayed wearing armor—the visor of her helmet pushed back to reveal her beauty, a shield over her arm, and a spear in her hand.

Befitting her role as the goddess who presided over battle strategy in wartime and over domestic arts in peacetime, Athena was also shown with a spear in one hand and a bowl or spindle in the other. She was the protector of cities, patron of military forces, and goddess of weavers, goldsmiths, potters, and dressmakers. Athena was credited by the Greeks with giving humanity the bridle to tame the horse, with inspiring shipbuilders in their craft, and with teaching people how to make the plow, rake, ox yoke, and chariot. The olive tree was her special gift to Athens, a gift that led to the cultivation of olives.

Athena was often depicted with an owl, a bird associated with wisdom and prominent eyes—two of her traits. Intertwined snakes were shown as a design on her shield or on the hem of her robe.

When Athena was pictured with another figure, that other was invariably a male. For example, she was seen next to a seated Zeus, in the stance of a warrior standing guard beside her king; or she was placed behind or beside either Achilles or Odysseus, the major Greek heroes of the *Iliad* and the *Odyssey*.

The martial and domestic skills associated with Athena involve planning and execution, activities that require purposeful thinking. Strategy, practicality, and tangible results are hallmarks of her particular wisdom. Athena values rational thinking and stands for the domination of will and intellect over instinct and nature. Her spirit is found in the city; for Athena (in contrast to Artemis), the wilderness is to be tamed and subdued.

GENEALOGY AND MYTHOLOGY

Athena's entrance into the company of Olympians was dramatic. She sprang out of Zeus's head as a full-grown woman, wearing flashing gold armor, with a sharp spear in one hand, emitting a mighty war cry. In some versions, her delivery resembled a Caesarean operation of sorts—Zeus was plagued by an excruciating headache as "labor" proceeded, and he was aided by Hephaestus, the god of the forge, who struck him on the head with a double-edged axe, opening a way for Athena to emerge.

Athena considered herself as having only one parent, Zeus, with whom she was forever associated. She was her father's right-hand woman, the only Olympian he entrusted with his thunderbolt and aegis, the symbols of his power.

The goddess did not acknowledge her mother, Metis; in fact, Athena seemed unaware she had a mother. As Hesiod recounts, Metis was Zeus's first royal consort, an ocean deity who was known for her wisdom. When Metis was pregnant with Athena, Zeus tricked her into becoming small and swallowed her. It was predicted that Metis would have two very special children: a daughter equal to Zeus in courage and wise counsel, and a son, a boy of all-conquering heart, who would become king of gods and men.[1] By swallowing Metis, Zeus thwarted fate and took over her attributes as his own.

In her mythology, Athena was a protector, advisor, patron, and ally of heroic men. The list of those whom she helped reads like a "Who's Who of Heroes."

Among them was Perseus, who slew the Gorgon Medusa—that female monster with serpents for hair, brazen claws, and staring eyes whose glance turned men into stone. Athena suggested a trick with mirrors by which Perseus could see the Gorgon's reflection in his shield and avoid gazing directly at her. She then guided his sword hand as he decapitated the Medusa.

Athena also helped Jason and the Argonauts build their ship before they set out to capture the Golden Fleece. She gave Bellerophon a golden bridle with which he could tame the winged horse Pegasus, and came to the aid of Heracles (the Roman Hercules) during his twelve tasks.

During the Trojan War, Athena was very active on behalf of the Greeks. She looked after her favorites, especially Achilles, the most formidable and mighty of the Greek warriors. Later, she aided Odysseus (Ulysses) on his long journey home.

Besides championing individual heroes and being the Olympian positioned closest to Zeus, Athena sided with the patriarchy. She cast the deciding vote for Orestes, in the first courtroom scene in Western literature. Orestes had killed his mother (Clytemnestra) to avenge the murder of his father (Agamemnon). Apollo spoke in defense of Orestes: he claimed that the mother was only the nourisher of the seed planted by the father, proclaimed the principle that the male predominates over the female, and cited as proof the birth of Athena, who had not even been born from the womb of a woman. The jury's vote was tied when Athena cast the decisive vote. She sided with Apollo, freed Orestes, and ranked patriarchal principles above maternal bonds.

In Athena's mythology, only one well-known story involves a mortal woman. This is Arachne, whom Athena turned into a spider. Athena, as Goddess of Crafts, was challenged to a contest of skill by a presumptuous weaver named Arachne. Both worked with swiftness and skill. When the tapestries were finished, Athena admired the flawless work of her competitor, but she was furious that Arachne dared to illustrate the amorous deceptions of Zeus. On the tapestry, Leda is caressing a swan—a disguise for Zeus, who had entered the bedchamber of the married queen as a swan in order to make love to her. Another panel was of Danaë, whom Zeus impregnated in the form of a golden shower; a third pictured the maid Europa, kidnapped by Zeus in the guise of a magnificent white bull.

The theme of her tapestry was Arachne's undoing. Athena was so incensed at what Arachne portrayed that she tore the work to pieces and drove Arachne to hang herself. Then, feeling some pity, Athena let Arachne live, but transformed her into a spider, forever condemned to hang by a thread and spin. (In biology, spiders are classified as *arachnids*, after this unfortunate girl.) Note that Athena, very much her father's defender, punished her for making Zeus's deceitful and illicit behavior public, rather than for the impudence of the challenge itself.

ATHENA THE ARCHETYPE

As Goddess of Wisdom, Athena was known for her winning strategies and practical solutions. As an archetype, Athena is the pattern followed by logical women, who are ruled by their heads rather than their hearts.

Athena is a feminine archetype: she shows that thinking well, keeping one's head in the heat of an emotional situation, and developing good tactics in the midst of conflict, are natural traits for some women. Such a woman is being like Athena, not acting "like a man." Her masculine aspect, or animus, is not doing the thinking *for* her—she is thinking clearly and well for herself. The concept of Athena as an archetype for logical thinking challenges the Jungian premise that thinking is done for a woman by her masculine animus, which is presumed to be distinct from her feminine ego. When a woman recognizes the keen way her mind works as a feminine quality related to Athena, she can develop a positive image of herself, instead of fearing that she is mannish (that is, inappropriate).

When Athena represents only one of several archetypes active in a particular woman—rather than a single dominant pattern—then this archetype can be an ally of other goddesses. For example, if she is motivated by Hera to need a mate to feel complete, then Athena can help assess the situation and develop a strategy to get her man. Or, if Artemis is the guiding inspiration for a women's health collective or a women's studies center, the success of the project may depend on the political acumen of Athena. In the midst of an emotional storm, if a woman can call on Athena as an archetype in herself, rationality will help her to find or keep her bearings.

VIRGIN GODDESS

The invulnerable and intact qualities descriptive of Artemis apply to Athena as well. When Athena rules in a woman's psyche, she—like women who resemble either Artemis or Hestia—is motivated by her own priorities. Like the Artemis archetype, Athena predisposes a woman to focus on what matters to her, rather than on the needs of others.

Athena differs from Artemis and Hestia in that she is the virgin goddess who seeks the company of men. Rather than separating or withdrawing, she enjoys being in the midst of male action and power. The virgin goddess element helps her to avoid emotional or sexual entanglements with men, with whom she works closely. She can be companion, colleague, or confidante of men without developing erotic feelings or emotional intimacy.

Athena emerged into the company of the Olympians as a fully grown adult. She was depicted in her mythology as taking an interest in worldly matters of consequence. The Athena archetype thus represents an older, more mature, version of a virgin goddess than does Artemis. Athena's realistic orientation to the world as it is, her pragmatic attitude, her conformity to "adult" (that is, traditionally held) standards, and lack of romanticism or idealism complete this impression of Athena as the epitome of the "sensible adult."

THE STRATEGIST

Athena's wisdom was that of the general deploying forces or of the business magnate outmaneuvering competition. She was the best strategist during the Trojan War. Her tactics and interventions won victories for the Greeks on the battlefield. The Athena archetype thrives in the business, academic, scientific, military, or political arenas.

For example, Athena may be manifested by a woman

with a master's degree in business administration who, allied with a powerful mentor, is making her way up the corporate ladder. Mary Cunningham's rapid ascent to the vice-presidency of Bendix Corporation as the talented protégée of the president and chairman of the board followed an Athena course. When their relationship received unfavorable attention, she resigned to move laterally into an important position with Schenley, another major corporate power. This wise move could be considered the equivalent of a strategic retreat and a decisive action taken under fire.

Athena's acumen enables a woman to make her way effectively in situations wherever political or economic considerations are important. She may use her ability to think strategically to further her own projects, or as companion-advisor to an ambitious man on the rise. In either case, the Athena archetype rules in women who know what the "bottom line" is, whose intelligence is geared to the practical and pragmatic, whose actions are not determined by emotions or swayed by sentiment. With Athena in her psyche, a woman grasps what must be done and figures out how to achieve what she wants.

Diplomacy—which involves strategy, power, and deceptive maneuvers—is a realm in which Athena shines. Clare Booth Luce—a famous beauty, playwright, Congresswoman, ambassador to Italy, and an honorary general in the U.S. Army—had these Athena qualities. She was admired and criticized for her ambition and for using her intelligence and alliances to cut her way through a man's world. (She was married to Henry R. Luce, a founder of *Time* Magazine and a Zeus in his own realm.) In the eyes of her admirers, she deserved praise for her "coolness" under fire, although her critics cited her as a "cold" schemer.[2]

Equally Athena-like is the woman with a doctoral degree who is effective in academia. To achieve tenure requires doing research, getting published, serving on committees, receiving grants—knowing what the game is and scoring points. To get ahead, women as well as men need mentors, sponsors, and allies. Intellectual ability alone is usually not enough; tactical and political considerations are involved. What subject she studies, teaches, or researches; which campus she settles on; and which department chair or mentor she chooses all play a part in deciding if she will get the grants and positions needed in order to do the work.

To accomplish what she has done, Rosalyn Yalow, the Nobel Prize winner in chemistry for her discoveries in radio-immunoassay (the use of radioactive isotopes to measure amounts of hormones and other chemicals in the body) must be a brilliant Athena. She has spoken of the joy of working her hands and her brain (combining the wisdom and handi-craft aspects of Athena). Yalow had to be a keen strategist to devise the laboratory sequences leading to her discoveries, an ability that must also have held her in good stead when career politics were involved.

THE CRAFTSWOMAN

As Goddess of Crafts, Athena was involved with making things that were both useful and esthetically pleasing. She was most noted for her skills as a weaver, in which hands and mind must work together. To make a tapestry or a weaving, a woman must design and plan what she will do and then, row by row, methodically create it. This approach is an expression of the Athena archetype, which emphasizes foresight, planning, mas-tery of a craft, and patience.

Frontier women who spun thread, wove cloth, and made practically everything that was worn by their families embod-ied Athena in her domestic realm. Side by side with their hus-bands, they wrested land from the wilderness, subduing nature as they pushed the frontier west. To survive and suc-ceed required Athena traits.

THE FATHER'S DAUGHTER

As the archetype of "the father's daughter," Athena rep-resents the woman who quite naturally gravitates toward power-ful men who have authority, responsibility, and power—men who fit the archetype of the patriarchal father or "boss man." Athena predisposes woman to form mentor relationships with strong men who share with her mutual interests and similar ways of looking at things. She expects two-way loyalty. Like Athena herself, once she gives him her allegiance, she is his most ardent defender or "right-hand woman," trusted to use his authority well and to guard his prerogatives.

Many dedicated executive secretaries who devote their lives to their bosses are Athena women. Their loyalty to their chosen great man is unwavering. When I think of Rosemary Woods, Richard Nixon's personal secretary, and that 18-minute erasure on the Watergate tapes, I wonder if Athena's hand was present. I know it would have been like Athena to have realized the "wisdom" of getting rid of such evidence and like Athena to have erased it without feeling guilt.

The father's daughter quality may make an Athena woman a defender of patriarchal right and values, which emphasize tradition and the legitimacy of male power. Athena women usually support the status quo and accept the established norms as guidelines of behavior. Such women are usually politically conservative; they resist change. Athena has little sympathy for the unsuccessful, downtrodden, or rebellious.

For example, Phyllis Schlafly—a Phi Beta Kappa with a master's degree from Radcliffe, and an extraordinarily well-organized and articulate woman—led the opposition to the Equal Rights Amendment. Before her leadership of the opposition, ratification seemed inevitable. In the first twelve months of its life, the year before Phyllis Schlafly formed her organization, STOP ERA, in October 1972, the ERA rolled up thirty ratifications. But once she led her troops into battle, the momentum stopped. In the next eight years, only five more states ratified—and five of the thirty-five ratified states voted to rescind their ratification. Schlafly, whose biographer called her *The Sweetheart of the Silent Majority*,[3] is a contemporary Athena in the role of an archetypal father's daughter, defending patriarchal values.

THE GOLDEN MEAN

When the Athena archetype is strong, the woman shows a natural tendency to do everything in moderation, to live within "the Golden Mean"—which was the Athenian ideal. Excesses are usually the result of intense feelings or needs, or of a passionate, righteous, fearful, or greedy nature—all of which are antithetical to rational Athena. The Golden Mean is also supported by the Athena tendency to monitor events, note effects, and change a course of action as soon as it appears unproductive.

ARMORED ATHENA

Athena arrived on the Olympian scene in splendid golden armor. And, in fact, being "armored" is an Athena trait. Intellectual defenses keep such a woman from feeling pain—both her own pain or that of others. In the midst of emotional turmoil or hard infighting, she remains impervious to feeling as she observes, labels, and analyzes what is going on and decides what she will do next.

In the competitive world, the Athena archetype has a decided advantage over Artemis. Artemis aims for goals and competes, but she is unarmored, as was the goddess Artemis, who wore a short tunic. If a woman's archetype is Artemis rather than Athena, she takes personally any unexpected hostility or deception. She may be hurt or outraged and may become emotional and less effective. In the same situation, Athena coolly assesses what is happening.

CULTIVATING ATHENA

Women who are not innately like Athena can cultivate this archetype through education or work. Education requires development of Athena qualities. When a woman takes school seriously, she develops disciplined study habits. Mathematics, science, grammar, research, and writing papers require Athena skills. Work has a similar effect. To behave "professionally" implies that a woman is objective, impersonal, and skillful. A woman who feels deeply for others may enter medicine or nursing, for example, and may find that that she has entered Athena's territory and needs to learn dispassionate observation, logical thinking, and skills.

All education stimulates the development of this archetype. Learning objective facts, thinking clearly, preparing for examinations, and taking the tests themselves are all exercises that evoke Athena.

Athena can also develop out of necessity. A young girl in

an abusive household may learn to hide her feelings and put on protective armor. She may become numb and out of touch with her feelings because otherwise she is not safe. She may learn to observe and strategize in order to survive. Athena becomes activated at any point that a victimized woman begins to plan a means of surviving or getting away.

Walter F. Otto, author of *The Homeric Gods*,[4] called Athena "the ever-near" goddess. She stood immediately behind her heroes and was invisible to others. She whispered advice, counseled restraint, and gave them an edge over their rivals. The "ever-near" Athena archetype needs to be invited "to come closer" whenever a woman needs to think clearly in the midst of an emotional situation, or whenever she competes on the same terms as a man in her particular occupation or educational field.

ATHENA THE WOMAN

There is a certain type of stable and outgoing American woman who seems to best personify Athena in everyday guise. She is practical, uncomplicated, unselfconscious, and confident, someone who gets things done without fuss. Typically the Athena woman is in good health, has no mental conflicts, and is physically active, as befits identification with Athena (who in her aspect of Athena Hygieia was also Goddess of Health). In my mind's eye, I see her as one of those clean-cut, well-scrubbed women who wear the "preppy" look all their lives. An Athena woman's psyche bears a similarity to the no-nonsense look of "preppy" clothes—practical, durable, of lasting quality, and uninfluenced by fashion changes.

The fashionable "preppy" look may be worn by the suburban Athena woman; the "downtown" variation is the tailored suit and blouse worn by the successful working woman in business. Both the suburban casual and the downtown business versions are influenced by Brooks Brothers—that upperclass, English look favored by many businessmen and prep school boys. Rounded Peter Pan collars and button-down shirts are appropriate garb for Athena women, who cultivate an ageless asexuality.

YOUNG ATHENA

An Athena child shares the capacity for concentration of a young Artemis, to which she adds a decidedly intellectual bent. For example, at three Athena may be a self-taught reader. Whatever the age, once she has discovered books she will probably have her nose in one. When she's not reading, she's dogging her father's footsteps, asking "Daddy, why?" or "Daddy, how does this work?" or, most typically, "Daddy, show me!" (She usually does not ask, "Mommy, why?"—unless she happens to have an Athena Mommy, who gives her the logical answers she seeks.) The Athena girl is curious, seeks information, wants to know how things work.

PARENTS

When an Athena daughter grows up as a favorite child of a successful father who is proud that "she takes after him," he helps her develop her natural tendencies. When her role model gives her his blessing, confidence in her abilities is her "birthright." Such a daughter grows up secure and without conflicts about being bright and ambitious. As an adult woman, she then can be comfortable exerting power, wielding authority, and demonstrating her capabilities.

But not all Athena women have Zeus fathers who favor them. When they do not, an essential ingredient for development is missing. Some Athena women have very successful fathers who are too busy to notice them. Other Zeus fathers insist that their daughters behave like traditional girls; they may teasingly say, "Don't fill your pretty head with facts" or chide them by saying, "This isn't what little girls should play with" or "This doesn't concern you, this is business." As a result, she may grow up feeling that she is unacceptable the way she is and often lacks confidence in her abilities even if she was not discouraged from entering the business or professional field.

When an Athena woman has a father who is very unlike Zeus—perhaps a business failure, alcoholic, unsung poet, or unpublished novelist—her Athena development is usually handicapped. She may not aspire to reach goals she could have fulfilled. And even when she appears successful to others, she often feels like an imposter who will be "found out."

Unless they themselves are Athena women, most mothers of Athena daughters feel unappreciated, or feel as if their daughters are from a different species of being altogether. For example, any relationship-oriented woman will likely find herself lacking rapport with her Athena daughter. When she talks about people and feelings, the daughter is uninterested. Instead, her daughter wants to know how something works, and finds her mother hasn't the foggiest notion or desire to know. As a result of their differences, the Athena daughter may treat her mother as an incompetent. One such mother noted that her daughter "was age ten going on thirty." Her daughter's slogan seemed to be, "Oh, mother, be practical!" This mother went on to say that "Sometimes my daughter makes me feel as if she were the adult, and I were a retarded child!"

Equally invalidating may be an Athena daughter's experience with a mother who gives the impression that there is something wrong with her daughter. Such a mother may comment, for example, "You're nothing but a calculating machine!" or "Try pretending that you're a girl."

The woman who develops her Athena qualities and is a high achiever with solid self-esteem usually has had parents in the Zeus-Metis mold[5] (successful father in the foreground, nurturing mother in the background) and has had the position in the family of a first-born son. Often her position in the family came by default. She may have been the only child, or the oldest of several girls. Or her brother may have suffered from a mental or physical impairment, or may have been a grave disappointment to their father. And as a consequence, she was the recipient of her father's aspirations for a son, and the companion with whom he shared his interests.

An Athena with a positive self-image, who has no conflicts about having ambition, might also be the daughter of dual-career parents, or the daughter of a successful mother. She grows up having a mother for a role model and parental support to be herself.

ADOLESCENCE AND YOUNG ADULTHOOD

Athena girls look under car hoods. They are the ones who learn how to fix things. They are the girls in computer classes who immediately and eagerly catch on to how the machines work and have an affinity for computerese. They may take to computer programming like a duck to water, because they think linearly and clearly, with attention to detail. They are the girls who learn about the stock market, who save and invest.

Very often, an Athena girl thinks that "most girls are silly or dumb," expressing much the same attitude that preadolescent boys seem to have. An Athena girl is much more likely to be interested in classifying a strange bug than to be alarmed by it. She is puzzled when other girls have "Little Miss Muffet" responses. As befitting a girl who takes after Athena, who punished Arachne, no spider "who sits down beside her" will scare Miss Athena away.

Young Athena may excel at sewing, weaving, or needlepoint. She may enjoy various crafts and she may share these interests with her mother or other traditionally minded girls with whom she otherwise often feels little in common. She, more than they, may enjoy the challenge of making a pattern and developing a skill, and may not be motivated by being able to make doll clothes or pretty things for herself. She takes pleasure in the workmanship of what results. Practicality and an appreciation for quality motivate her to make her own clothes.

Athena girls are usually not problem daughters, when many others are. Screaming or tearful scenes are notably absent. Hormonal changes hardly seem to affect such a girl's behavior or moods. She may spend her high school days with boys who are her intellectual equals. She may enroll in a chess club, work on the school annual, or compete in the science fair. She may like math and excel in it, or spend time in the chemistry, physics, or computer lab.

Socially aware, extraverted Athena girls use their powers of observation, noting what to wear, or what social alliances she should maintain. They comment on their ability to compete socially and be popular and yet not be emotionally "all that invested."

Athena women plan ahead. Most give considerable thought to what they will do after high school. If such a woman is financially able to go on to college, she will have thought about the colleges available to her and will have chosen wisely for herself. Even if her family cannot help her to go to college, she will usually find a way to work her way through with scholarships or financial aid. The equivalent of a female Horatio Alger is almost always an Athena woman.

Most Athena women find college liberating. Having chosen a school that is right for them because of its educational offerings and the makeup of the student body, they plunge in, freer to be themselves than was possible in high school. Typically, Athena women choose coeducational schools because of their compatibility with and high regard for men.

WORK

The Athena woman intends to make something of herself. She works hard toward that end, accepts reality as it is, and adapts. Thus the adult years are usually productive ones for her. In the world of power and achievement, her use of strategy and logical thinking show her kinship with Athena. In the home, she excels in the domestic arts (also Athena's realm), using her practical mind and aesthetic eye to run an efficient household.

If the Athena girl must go directly from high school to work, she often prepares for this necessity by taking business education courses and summer jobs that present good opportunities. Athena women do not play Cinderella; they do not wait to be rescued through marriage. Fantasizing that "Someday my prince will come" is foreign to an Athena woman's style.

If she marries and runs a household, she is usually an efficient manager. Whether for shopping, laundry, or housekeeping, she has a system that works. In the kitchen, for example, everything is probably in place. No one needs to teach an Athena woman about a flow chart—organization comes naturally to her. She usually plans shopping for the week ahead, and plans meals to make optimal use of bargains. The Athena woman finds challenging the tasks of living within a budget and spending money well.

The Athena woman can be a superb teacher. She explains things clearly and well. If the subject requires precise information, she is likely to have mastered it. Her forte may be to explain complex procedures that progress in a step-by-step fashion. The Athena teacher is likely to be one of the most demanding. She is one of those "no excuses" teachers, who expect and get maximum performance. She doesn't "fall for" sad stories or give unearned grades. She does best with students who challenge her intellectually. She favors the students who do well and spends more time with them than with those that fall behind (unlike a maternal Demeter teacher, who gives more of herself to those who need help the most).

As a craftsperson, an Athena woman makes functional objects that are aesthetically pleasing. She also has a business head, and so concerns herself with showing and selling her work, as well as making it. She works well with her hands, and, whatever her craft, she prides herself on mastering the skill required and on the workmanship of her product. She can do variations of the same object with enjoyment.

An Athena woman in an academic field is likely to be an able researcher. With her logical approach and attention to details, doing experiments or gathering data comes naturally to her. Her fields of interest are usually those which value the clarity of thinking and use of evidence. She tends to be good at math and science, and may go into business, law, engineering, or medicine—traditionally male professions, where she feels quite comfortable being one of the few women in her field.

RELATIONSHIPS WITH WOMEN: DISTANT OR DISMISSED

An Athena woman usually lacks close women friends, a pattern that may have been noticed around puberty when she did not form best-friend bonds, or even before. In adolescence, most friends share their fears, dark secrets, longings, and anxieties about their changing bodies, parental difficulties, and uncertain futures. Concerns about boys, sex, and drugs are the primary anxieties for some girls. Others are in the midst of poetic or creative upheavals or preoccupied with thoughts about death, insanity, mysticism, or religious conflict. All are topics to discuss with friends who have similar concerns, not with an unromantic observer or skeptical rationalist, such as young Athena is.

Moreover, in Greek mythology, Athena once had a friend who was like a sister, called Iodama or Pallas. The two girls were playing a competitive game, which turned deadly when Athena's spear accidentally struck and killed her friend. (One account of the origin of the name "Pallas Athena" was to honor her friend.) As in the myth, if the Athena girl's lack of empathy does not kill her potential for friendship with other girls, her Athena need to win may do so. In real life, a woman friend may become appalled when her Athena companion forgets the importance of their relationship and instead concentrates on winning—sometimes even by deception, revealing a side of her personality that kills the friendship.

A lack of kinship with other women usually began in childhood with their admiration of and affinity to their fathers, and/or with dissimilarity of personality and intellect between themselves and their mothers. This tendency is then compounded by a lack of close female friendships. As a consequence, Athena women don't feel like sisters under the skin with other women. They neither feel themselves akin to traditional women, nor to feminists, whom they may superficially resemble, especially if they are career women. Thus "sisterhood" is a foreign concept to most Athena women.

In mythology, it was Athena who cast the decisive vote for the patriarchy in the trial of Orestes. In contemporary times, it has often been an Athena woman who, by speaking against affirmative action, the Equal Rights Amendment, or abortion rights, was decisive in defeating the feminist position. I recall how effective Athena was when I was an ERA proponent. An Athena woman would rise to speak with a ringing cry of "I am a woman and I am against the ERA!" And the mostly male and mostly silent opposition would rally behind her. Each time, she was a local equivalent of Phyllis Schlafly— both in her role as defender of the patriarchal status quo, and in her customary position as the woman colleague with whom the men felt most comfortable.

The story of Arachne (the weaver who was turned into a spider by Athena for daring to make public Zeus's seductions and rapes) is another myth with contemporary parallels. A student or secretary may file a complaint of sexual harassment against her professor or employer. Or a daughter may uncover incest in the family and draw adverse attention to the behavior of her (often prominent) father. Or a patient may report that her psychiatrist has acted unethically by having sexual relations with her. Such a woman, like Arachne, is a "nobody" who exposes the behavior of a powerful man who in private takes advantage of his dominant position to sexually intimidate, seduce, or overwhelm vulnerable women.

An Athena woman is often angry at the woman who complains, rather that at the man against whom the complaint is made. She may blame the female victim for provoking what happened. Or, more typically, like the goddess herself, she is incensed that the woman would make public an action that subjects the man to criticism.

Feminists react in anger to successful Athena career women who on the one hand take status quo, patriarchal positions on political issues involving women, and who on the other hand appear to derive the most benefits from the women's movements' influence on education, opportunities, and advancement. The first woman to gain entry or recognition in a male-dominated situation often is a woman feminists describe as a "Queen Bee." Such women do not help their "sisters" get ahead. In fact, they may make general advancement more difficult.

RELATIONSHIPS WITH MEN: ONLY HEROES NEED APPLY

The Athena woman gravitates toward successful men. In college, she was drawn to the star in the department. In business, she is attracted to the man on the rise who will one day head the corporation. She has a canny ability to spot winners. She is attracted to power, either seeking it herself—often with the help of a successful older male mentor—or more traditionally, as a companion, wife, executive secretary, or ally of an ambitious and able man. For Athena women (as former Secretary of State Henry Kissinger noted), "power is the best aphrodisiac."

Athena women do not suffer fools lightly. They are impatient with dreamers, are unimpressed with men who are in search of anything otherworldly, and are unsympathetic when men have too much compassion to act decisively. They do not think of poets or artists who starve in garrets as romantic figures, nor are they charmed by eternal adolescents masquerading as men. For an Athena woman, "tender-hearted," "neurotic," or "sensitive" are adjectives to describe "losers." When it comes to men, only heroes need apply.

An Athena woman usually chooses her man. She may do so either by refusing dates or job opportunities with men who do not meet her standards of success or potential for success; or she may set her sights on a particular man, with such subtle strategy that he remains unaware, believing it was he who chose her. With the timing instincts of a sensitive negotiator who knows her man, she may be the one to bring up the subject of marriage or of a working alliance.

If she seeks to become his business protégée or secretary, she finds an opportunity to impress him with her capabilities and hard work. Once in his proximity, she strives to become indispensable to him—a role that, once achieved, gives her both emotional and work satisfaction. To be "an office wife" or a "second in command" gives an Athena woman both a sense of power and affiliation with a chosen "great man," to whom she may give a lifetime loyalty.

An Athena woman loves to discuss strategy and be privy to what goes on behind the scene. Her advice and counsel can be quite perceptive and helpful, as well as potentially ruthless. She values men who go after what they want, who are strong, resourceful, and successful winners of modern power struggles. For some Athena women, the more like the "wily Odysseus" her man turns out to be, the better.

SEXUALITY

An Athena woman lives in her mind and is often out of touch with her body. She considers the body a utilitarian part of herself, of which she is unaware until it gets sick or hurt.

Typically, she is not a sensual or a sexy woman, nor is she flirtatious or romantic.

She likes men as friends or mentors rather than as lovers. Unlike Artemis, she rarely considers sex a recreational sport or adventure. Like an Artemis woman, she needs either Aphrodite or Hera as active archetypes in order for sexuality to become an expression of erotic attraction or emotional commitment. Otherwise, sex is a "part of the agreement" inherent in a particular relationship, or is a calculated act. In either case, once she makes up her mind to be sexually active, she usually learns how to make love skillfully.

An Athena woman often stays celibate for long periods in her adult life, while she focuses her efforts on her career. If she is a devoted executive secretary or an administrative assistant to a chosen great man, she may stay a celibate "office wife."

If a married woman stays identified with Athena, her attitude toward sexuality may be roughly the same as her attitude toward other bodily functions—something that is done regularly and is good for her. It is also part of her role as wife.

Athena seems well represented among lesbian women, contrary to what might be expected (given the Athena woman's patriarchal loyalties, affinity for heroes, and lack of sisterly feelings). The lesbian Athena woman has a tendency to have a partner cast in the same mold as herself. They may both be professional women, high achievers who began as colleagues prior to becoming lovers.

In their relationship, lesbian Athena women may admire the other's "heroic" qualities and success, or may be drawn to the other's intellect. Companionship and loyalty, rather than passion, hold them together; sex between them may dwindle to nothing. They are likely to keep the homosexual nature of their relationship secret from others. Their relationship is often long-lasting, surviving separations caused by career requirements.

MARRIAGE

When women did not have much opportunity to succeed in their own careers, most Athena women made "good marriages." They married hard-working, achievement-oriented men whom they respected. Then as now, an Athena woman's marriage is likely to be more a companionable partnership than a passionate union.

Chances are that she has sized him up quite accurately and that they are quite compatible. She is his ally and helpmate, a wife vitally interested in his career or business, who will map out strategy with him on how to get ahead and who will work at his side if necessary. Like Athena, who held Achilles back as he was about to draw his sword against his leader, Agamemnon, in anger, she may also wisely restrain him from premature or impulsive action.

If her husband is older and well established at the time of the marriage, and involved in very complicated and sophisticated or technical dealings, an Athena wife's main role will be as his social ally. Her task, then, is to be a social asset, to entertain well, to be his right-hand woman in maintaining important social alliances.

Apart from counseling her husband or entertaining to advance his career, she usually runs a household very competently. She finds it easy to keep track of the budget and of tasks, given her attention to detail and practical approach. She also takes on bearing and raising children or heirs as her part of the partnership.

Communication between an Athena wife and her husband about events is usually excellent. But communication about feelings may be practically nonexistent, either because, like her, he disregards feelings, or because he has learned that she does not understand feelings.

Both Hera women and Athena women are drawn to men with power and authority, like Zeus. However, what they expect from him and the nature of the bond that each type of woman has to him are vastly different. A Hera woman makes a man into her personal god, responsible for fulfilling her—the attachment she feels for him is a deep, instinctual connection. When she learns that he is unfaithful, she is wounded to her core and rages at the other woman, who assumes great importance in her eyes.

In contrast, an Athena woman is practically impervious to sexual jealousy. She views her marriage as a mutually advantageous partnership. She usually gives and expects loyalty, which she may not equate with sexual fidelity. Also, she finds it difficult to believe that she will be replaced by a passing attraction.

Jacqueline Kennedy Onassis appears to be an Athena woman. She married Senator John F. Kennedy, who became President of the United States. Later she became the wife of Aristotle Onassis, reputed to be one of the richest, most ruthless, and powerful men in the world. Both men were known to have extramarital affairs. Kennedy was a womanizer, with numerous liaisons, and Onassis had a well-publicized long-term extramarital affair with opera star Maria Callas. Unless Jacqueline Kennedy Onassis was a consummate actress, she seems not to have been vindictive toward the other women. Her apparent lack of jealousy and rage, plus her choice of powerful men, are characteristic of an Athena woman. As long as the marriage itself is not threatened, an Athena woman can rationalize and accept the fact of a mistress.

Sometimes, however, an Athena woman grossly underrates the significance of her husband's interest in another woman. She has a blind spot here—untouched by passion herself, she cannot calculate its importance to someone else. Also, she has a lack of empathy or compassion for vulnerable feelings or spiritual values that may have special meaning for her husband. This lack of understanding may catch her unaware and unprepared when, contrary to her expectations, her husband wants to divorce her and marry the other woman.

When the decision to divorce is made by the Athena woman, she may be able to shed a husband of whom she is "quite fond" with relatively little emotion or grief. This certainly was the impression given by a thirty-one-year-old stockbroker I knew. She was in a dual-career marriage until her advertising executive husband was fired. He moped around the house rather than aggressively seeking work, and she grew increasingly unhappy with and disrespectful of him. After a year, she told him she wanted a divorce. Her attitude was similar to that of a businessman who fires a man unable to carry out the responsibilities of the job or who replaces a worker when a better man for the job comes along. She was sadly reluctant to tell him and found the actual confrontation painful, yet her bottom-line conclusion was that he must go.

And once the unpleasant task was done, she felt a sense of relief.

Whether or not she instigates the divorce, the Athena woman copes competently with the situation. Settlements are usually negotiated without rancor or bitterness. She doesn't feel personally devastated even if he is leaving her for someone else. She may remain on good terms with an ex-husband and may even continue with a business partnership.

The dual-career marriage, where both husband and wife are seriously involved in careers, is a relatively new phenomenon. Athena women may be more successful than most at this type of marriage. It takes the mind of Athena to plan and carry out the logistics of having two working partners with long-term goals, and with schedules that may not conform to a standard 9-to-5 workday, while maintaining the accoutrements and social presence of upwardly mobile or professional-class people. Athena women tend to be more conservative about traditional roles, and are less likely to make egalitarian demands for the sake of principle. Therefore, the Athena woman in a dual-career marriage usually oversees the household, hires efficient help, and gives the impression of being a superwoman as she takes care of her own career and their home, and serves as her husband's ally and valued confidante.

CHILDREN

As a mother, the Athena woman can hardly wait for her kids to grow up to the age when she can talk to them, do projects with them, and take them to see what there is to see. She is the opposite of a Demeter "Earth Mother," who instinctively seeks to be a mother, loves to hold babies, and wishes they would never grow up. An Athena woman, in contrast, would just as soon "rent a womb" whenever that option becomes possible, as long as she could be sure of the parentage of the baby. And she uses surrogate mothers, hiring housekeepers and nannies to care for her children.

The Athena mother shines if she has competitive, extraverted, intellectually curious sons. They are her budding heroes in the making, who draw on her ability to teach, ad-

96

vise, inspire and exhort them to excel. She's apt to reinforce stereotypical male behavior in her sons, early giving them the "Strong men don't cry" message.

Athena mothers also do well with daughters who are like them, the independent ones who share their mothers' logical approach to things. Such women can be role models and mentors for daughters who are like themselves. Some Athena mothers, however, have daughters who are very different from themselves. Such daughters, for example, may be innately more interested in what people feel than in how things work, and may not be assertive or intellectual. With a traditional daughter, an Athena mother does less well. She may be amused, accepting, and tolerant of a daughter who is unlike herself. Or she may discount the daughter and favor a son. Either way, the daughter feels an emotional distance and senses that she is not valued as she is.

The Athena woman finds it difficult to deal with either sons or daughters who are easily moved by feelings. The situation is harder, of course, on the children. If they accept her standards, they are likely to grow up devaluing themselves for being crybabies as children, and for being oversensitive as adults. Her practical-mindedness also makes her impatient with a dreamy child who fantasizes.

An Athena mother expects her children to do what is expected of them, to rise above the emotion-evoking events in their lives, and be "good soldiers"—as she is.

MIDDLE YEARS

The Athena woman often finds the middle years to be the best part of her life. With her ability to see matters as they are, she rarely has illusions to be disillusioned about. If all goes according to plan, her life unfolds in an orderly fashion.

In midlife, an Athena woman usually takes time to assess her situation. She reconsiders all options, and then makes a fairly orderly transition to the next phase. If work is her primary concern, she is in mid-career, and can now see her trajectory: how high she can rise, how secure her situation is, where a relationship with a mentor can take her. If she is a mother, as her children have grown she is likely to have taken on projects to which she can devote more time as the children need her less.

However, midlife for an Athena woman can unexpectedly turn into a crisis. Emotional chaos may intrude on her orderly life. She may find herself in the midst of a midlife marital crisis, which can shake her equanimity and expose her to deeper feelings. Often her husband's crisis instigates hers. The companionable marriage, which has been a successful alliance for both, may now be unsatisfactory for him. He may now feel the lack of passion in his marriage, and may feel himself drawn to another woman who stirs him romantically and erotically. If his wife stays true to her Athena nature, her response will be to cope sensibly. However, at midlife other goddesses are more easily activated, and for the first time in her life she may react unpredictably.

Menopause is not a cause for Athena to grieve, because she never defined herself as primarily a mother. Nor are youth or beauty essential for an Athena woman's self-esteem, which is based on her intelligence, competence, and often indispensability. Hence growing older is not a loss for most Athena women. On the contrary, because she is more powerful, useful, or influential in her middle years than as a young adult, her confidence and well-being may even be enhanced during these years, when other women are anxious about looking older and becoming less desirable.

LATER YEARS

The Athena woman changes very little over the decades. She remains throughout life an energetic, practical woman who pitches in—first at home and work, and then often as a volunteer in the community. She is often a supporter of traditional institutions, most likely fairly conservative ones. The married Athena woman of the middle and upper classes is the backbone of volunteer charities and churches. She helps to run hospital auxiliaries, United Way charities, and the Red Cross, becoming more prominent as she gets older.

When her children grow up and move away, an Athena woman does not mourn an empty nest. Now she has time for more projects, studies, or work that she enjoys. Usually her relationships with her adult children are amiable. Because she has encouraged them to be independent and self-sufficient, and has neither been intrusive nor encouraged dependency, most of her children and grandchildren do not have problems with her. They usually respect her and often like her. Although she often lacks demonstrativeness and does not express much feeling, she maintains family contact and communication about events, as well as keeping up family holidays and traditions.

In their later years, many Athena women become respectable pillars of the community. A few turn out to be "little old ladies in tennis shoes," business-minded women who have been ridiculed for asking pertinent questions at stockholder meetings. They won't be put off by other people's nonsense or muddled thinking, and their persistence is especially annoying to men in authority.

When widowhood comes, an Athena woman has usually anticipated it. An Athena woman knows her life expectancy is longer than a man's and, because she may have married a man older than herself, she is not caught unaware or unprepared by widowhood. She is a widow who manages her own money, who invests in the stock market, or continues the family business or one of her own.

A widowed or spinster Athena woman often lives alone while maintaining an active and busy life. Her one-in-herself virgin goddess quality serves her well in her last years when she is self-sufficient and active, as it did when she was young.

PSYCHOLOGICAL DIFFICULTIES

Rational Athena never lost her head, her heart, or her self-control. She lived within the Golden Mean, and was not overwhelmed by emotion or irrational feelings. Most of the other goddesses (except Hestia) either unleashed their emotions on others and caused suffering, or were victimized and suffered themselves. The women who are like them likewise have the potential to either cause suffering or to suffer. Athena differed: she was invulnerable, unmoved by irrational or overwhelming emotion, and her actions were deliberate rather than impulsive. Since the woman who resembles Athena shares her attributes, she too is neither a victim of others nor of her own emotions. Her problems arise from her own character traits, from wearing the "aegis and armor" psychologically. One-sided development may cut her off from aspects of herself that need to grow.

IDENTIFYING WITH ATHENA

To live "as Athena" means to live in one's head and to act purposefully in the world. A woman who does so leads a one-sided existence—she lives for her work. Although she enjoys the companionship of others, she lacks emotional intensity, erotic attraction, intimacy, passion, or ecstasy. She is also spared the deep despair and suffering that may follow bonding with others or needing them. Exclusive identification with rational Athena cuts a woman off from the full range and intensity of human emotion. Her feelings are well modulated by Athena, limited to the middle range. Thus she cuts herself off from empathizing with anyone else's deep feelings, from being affected by art or music that expresses intense feelings, and from being moved by mystical experience.

Living in her head, the Athena woman misses the experience of being fully in her body. She knows little about sensuality and about what it feels like to push her body to its limits. Athena keeps a woman "above" the instinctual level, so she does not feel the full strength of maternal, sexual, or procreative instincts.

To grow beyond Athena, a woman needs to develop other aspects of herself. She can do so gradually, if she realizes that Athena limits her and if she is receptive to the perspectives of others. When people talk of emotions and experiences that are deeply meaningful to them and unknown to her, she needs to make an effort to imagine what they are talking about. She needs to recognize that her demands for proof and her skepticism distance her from others and from her as-yet undeveloped potential for spiritual or emotional depth.

An Athena woman sometimes grows beyond Athena unexpectedly or traumatically, under the pressure of circumstances that flood her with feelings from the unconscious. For example, her child may be threatened by illness or may be harmed by someone. If a protective instinct comes out of her archetypal depths that is as ferocious as a raging mother bear's, she discovers that this aspect of Artemis is part of her. Or, if her companionable marriage is threatened by another woman, she may be taken over by Hera's wounded and vindictive feelings, instead of staying rational Athena going about business as usual. Or, she may take a psychedelic drug and be plunged into an altered state of consciousness that awes or scares her.

THE MEDUSA EFFECT

An Athena woman has an ability to intimidate others and to take away the spontaneity, vitality, and creativity of people who are not like her. This is her Medusa effect.

On her breastplate, the goddess Athena wore a symbol of her power—the aegis, a goatskin decorated with the Gorgon's head, the head of Medusa. This was a monster with serpents instead of hair, whose terrifying appearance turned to stone anyone who gazed on it. The Gorgon is also an aspect of the Athena woman. Metaphorically, she too has the power to devitalize experience for others, to take the life out of conversation, to turn a relationship into a static tableau. Through her focus on facts and details, her need for logical premises and rationality, she can turn a conversation into a dry recital of details. Or she can be devastatingly insensitive and can thus change the atmosphere dramatically from deeply personal to superficial and distant. With her critical attitude and dissecting questions, an Athena woman can unintentionally and unconsciously demean another person's subjective experience. She can be unempathetic about spiritual or moral issues that others consider of vital importance, intolerant of the problems people have with their relationships, and critical of any weaknesses. Such lack of empathy is killing.

When the occasion is purely social, this devitalizing Medusa effect may merely bore or infuriate. However, when the Athena woman is in a position of authority and judgment, she may turn on the full power of the Gorgon Medusa to terrify and petrify. For example, she may be conducting a crucial interview with serious consequences. When a person is scrutinized by "Gorgon-Eyed Athena," he or she feels under the magnifying gaze of an analytic, impersonal mind whose questions seem relentlessly directed toward uncovering inadequacies. Up against what feels like a dissecting intellect and a stone heart, the person can feel "turned to stone."

A colleague of mine once described the unfortunate experience of meeting the Gorgon Medusa at her advancement evaluation meeting. Now, this colleague is a therapist who works very well with seriously disturbed patients. Intuitively able to understand the symbolic meaning and the emotions that lie behind irrational behavior, she does beautifully with patients. However, describing one interview with an Athena woman, she said, "I felt my mind going blank. I was, for a moment, literally struck dumb, I couldn't think straight or find words. . . . I didn't come off well at all." More often than not, when a person feels turned to stone by the judgmental scrutiny of someone who has the power to destroy career advancement or educational possibility, that someone is a man who carries the Zeus archetype and "wears the aegis." But as women gain more access to power, the aegis may be increasingly worn by women. And if they are acting as Athena, they may well have a Medusa effect.

Often the Athena woman who is having this Medusa effect is unconscious of her negative power. It is not her intent to intimidate and terrify. She is merely doing her job well, as she sees it—gathering the facts, examining the premises, challenging how the material is structured and supported by the evidence. But unknowingly she may be fulfilling Goethe's observation that we murder when we dissect. With her objective attitude and incisive questions, she disregards efforts to create rapport. Thus she kills off the potential of true communication in which the heart of any matter—or the soul of the person—can be shared.

Sometimes I talk with a patient who is purely intellectual in approach, who gives me a factual report about her life, a recital of events without emotion, leaving out the feelings. I find I must make an effort to stay related to her, fighting to overcome the boredom produced when there is no "life"—no intensity of feeling attached to what happened. What is lifeless in her has a numbing effect on me. As I feel myself "turning to stone," I know at once that this is the problem she brings to every relationship. This is why her life lacks intimacy and is often lonely. When a woman is metaphorically wearing Athena's armor with the Medusa aegis on her breastplate, she is not showing any vulnerability. Her well-armored (usually intellectual) defenses are up, and her authority and critical gaze keep others at an emotional distance.

If she is dismayed by the Medusa effect she has on others, an Athena woman would do well to remember that the Gorgon breastplate was something Athena put on and could take off. Likewise, if an Athena woman "takes off her armor and aegis," she will no longer have a Medusa effect. Her Medusa aegis is gone when she no longer sits in judgment on others, inwardly claiming the authority to validate or invalidate the way other people feel or think or live. When she becomes aware that she has something to learn from people and something to share with them, and thus is involved as a peer, she will have shed her Gorgon breastplate and the Medusa effect.

CRAFTINESS: "DO WHATEVER WORKS"

The Athena woman with an objective to reach or a problem to solve is concerned almost exclusively with the questions "How can I do it?" and "Will it work?" She can be "crafty" or unscrupulous in achieving her goals or defeating her rivals.

This craftiness was characteristic of the goddess Athena. For example, in the climactic confrontation of the Trojan War between the Greek hero Achilles and the more noble Trojan hero Hector, Athena used decidedly "dirty tactics" to help Achilles win. She deceived Hector into believing that his brother was at his side as his spear carrier when he faced Achilles. Then, after he had hurled his only spear and had turned to get another from his "brother," Hector discovered that he was alone and knew his end was near.

The goddess did not concern herself with asking "Is this fair?" or "Is this moral?" What mattered was that it was an effective strategy. The dark side of an Athena woman is related to this aspect of Athena.

When she assesses other people's behavior, effectiveness is the main criterion. It is not part of her thinking nature to be concerned with feeling values such as right and wrong, or good and bad. Thus she has difficulty understanding why people become outraged over unethical or immoral behavior, especially when it doesn't affect them personally. She also doesn't understand why anyone would bother to argue about "the principle of the thing," or about the means used to reach a desired end.

Thus if she were a student in the 1970s, when her classmates were taking to the streets in protest against the Vietnam War or the Cambodian invasion, or were outraged by the Watergate revelations, she was probably not involved. Others may have considered her morally indifferent, when she—true to her Athena form—neither was moved by the contagion of others' feelings, nor was upset on her own. Instead, she was in the classroom or laboratory, pursuing her own career goals.

WAYS TO GROW

Growing beyond the confining limitations of one goddess through the cultivation of others is one possibility that all of the goddess types share. But an Athena woman has several specific directions she can consider following, as well.

TURNING INWARD

The Athena woman who is out in the world can get caught up in the power games of business, law, or politics, and can find that she is always working, "talking shop," or bringing work home from her office. She may feel after a while that her mind never rests—"the wheels are always turning." When she realizes how all-consuming her work is and feels a need for more balance, Athena as Goddess of Crafts provides a psychological way to get her mind off business.

Most dear to Athena of all the crafts was weaving. An Athena businesswoman told me when she took up weaving, "It's the most calming activity I can think of—I get into the rhythm of the loom, my mind is absorbed and empty at the same time, my hands are busy, and at the end I have a beautiful wall hanging."

Another Athena woman may find that sewing frees her from her professional concerns. She finds making her own clothes is both practical and creative. It pleases her to use the finest material and to have as a finished product a designer-quality coat or dress that would have cost more than ten times what she paid for the material. She is infinitely patient when she sews and half-seriously calls it "therapy" because it allows her to get away from her work problems and into another state of mind.

Throwing pots on a wheel is yet another way of getting in touch with this aspect of Athena. In fact, all the crafts offer Athena women an inner balance to an outer-world focus.

RECOVERING THE CHILD

The goddess Athena was never a child; she was born as an adult. This metaphor is not far removed from the Athena woman's actual experience. From the earliest time she can remember, she recalls "figuring things out" or "being smart about everything." But a verbal little girl with a matter-of-fact mind often misses whole areas of subjective experience that she may eventually want as an adult. She may need to discover in herself the child she never was, a child who can be confused or delighted by something new.

To recover her child self, an Athena woman must stop approaching new experience as "a sensible adult" would (as she has done since she was a child). Instead, she needs to approach life as if she were a wide-eyed child and everything were new and to be discovered. When a child is fascinated by something new, she takes it all in. Unlike Athena, she doesn't have a preconceived notion of what it should be, isn't skeptical, and doesn't put well-worn, familiar labels on the experience and file it away. When someone is speaking about something she has not experienced, an Athena woman must learn to listen and to imagine as best she can both the scene and the feelings being described. When she is in the midst of an emotional moment, she has to try to stay in it and let others comfort her. To rediscover her lost child, she needs to play and laugh, cry and be hugged.

DISCOVERING HER MOTHER

In mythology, the goddess Athena was a motherless daughter who took pride in having only one parent: her father Zeus. She was unaware of her mother Metis, whom Zeus had swallowed. Metaphorically, Athena women are "motherless" in many ways; they need to discover the mother and value her, to allow themselves to be mothered.

An Athena woman often has depreciated her own mother. She needs to discover her mother's strengths, often before she can value any similarities to her mother in herself. She often lacks connection to a maternal archetype (personified by the goddess Demeter), a connection she must feel in herself in order to experience maternity and motherhood deeply and instinctually. Christine Downing, author of *The Goddess*, calls this task "the re-membering of Athene," which she speaks of as "the rediscovery of her relation to the feminine, to mother, to Metis."[6]

It is helpful for an Athena woman to learn that matriarchal feminine values, which were held before Greek mythology took its present form, were swallowed up by the patriarchal culture that prevails today. Her intellectual curiosity can lead her from history or psychology toward feminist ideas. From this new perspective, she may begin to think differently about her own mother and other women, and then about herself. In this way, many Athena women have come to be feminists. Once an Athena woman changes the way she thinks, her relationship to people can change.

6.

Hestia:
Goddess of the Hearth and
Temple, Wise Woman and
Maiden Aunt

HESTIA THE GODDESS

Hestia was Goddess of the Hearth, or, more specifically, of the fire burning on a round hearth. She is the least known of the Olympians. Hestia and her Roman equivalent, Vesta, were not represented in human form by painters or sculptors. Instead, this goddess was felt to be present in the living flame at the center of the home, temple, and city. Hestia's symbol was a circle. Her first hearths were round, and her temples were also. Neither home nor temple were sanctified until Hestia entered. She made both places holy when she was there. Hestia was apparently a spiritually felt presence as well as a sacred fire that provided illumination, warmth, and heat for food.

GENEALOGY AND MYTHOLOGY

Hestia was the first child born to Rhea and Cronos: she was the oldest sister of the first-generation Olympians, and maiden aunt to the second. By birthright, she was one of the twelve major Olympians, yet she could not be found on Mt. Olympus, and made no protest when Dionysus, God of Wine, grew in prominence and replaced her as one of the twelve. Since she took no part in the love affairs and wars that so occupied Greek mythology, she is the least known of the major Greek gods and goddesses. Yet she was greatly honored, receiving the best offerings made by mortals to the gods.

Hestia's brief mythology is sketched in three Homeric hymns. She is described as "that venerable virgin, Hestia," one of the three that Aphrodite is unable to subdue, persuade, seduce, or even "awaken a pleasant yearning in." [1]

Aphrodite caused Poseidon (God of the Sea) and Apollo (God of the Sun) to fall in love with Hestia. Both wanted her, but Hestia refused them firmly, taking a great oath that she would remain forever a virgin. Then, as "The Hymn to Aphrodite" explained, "Zeus gave her a beautiful privilege instead of a wedding gift: he has her sit in the center of the house to receive the best in offerings. In all temples of the gods she is honored, and among all mortals she is a venerated goddess." [2] The two Homeric hymns to Hestia are invocations, inviting her into the house or temple.

RITUALS AND WORSHIP[3]

Unlike the other gods and goddesses, Hestia was not known through her myths or representations. Instead, Hestia's significance is found in rituals, symbolized by fire. In order for a house to become a home, Hestia's presence was required. When a couple married, the bride's mother lit a torch at her own household fire and carried it before the newly married couple to their new house to light their first household fire. This act consecrated the new home.

After a child was born, a second Hestian ritual took place. When an infant was five days old, it was carried around the hearth to symbolize its admission into the family. A festive, holy banquet then followed.

Similarly, each Greek city-state had a common hearth with a sacred fire in the main hall. Here guests were officially entertained. And every colony took the sacred fire with them from their home city to light the fire of the new city.

Thus, whenever a new couple or a new colony ventured out to establish a new home, Hestia came with them as the sacred fire, linking old home with new, perhaps symbolizing continuity and relatedness, shared consciousness and common identity.

Later, in Rome, Hestia was worshipped as the goddess Vesta. There, Vesta's sacred fire united all the citizens of

Rome into one family. In her temples, the sacred fire was tended by the Vestal Virgins, who were required to embody the virginity and anonymity of the goddess. In a sense, they were human representations of the goddess; they were living images of Hestia, transcending sculpture or painting.

The girls chosen to be Vestal Virgins were taken into the temple when they were quite young, usually not yet six years old. Garbed alike, their hair shorn as new initiates, whatever was distinct and individual about them was submerged. They were set apart from other people, honored, and expected to live like Hestia—with dire consequences if they did not remain virgins.

A Vestal Virgin who had sexual relations with a man had desecrated the goddess. In punishment, she would be buried alive, entombed in a small, airless underground room with light, oil, food, and a place to sleep. The earth above it would then be leveled off, as if nothing were there. Thus a Vestal Virgin's life as an embodiment of Hestia's sacred flame was snuffed out when she ceased to personify the goddess—covered over with earth as one might extinguish smoldering coals on a hearth.

Hestia was often paired with Hermes, the Messenger God, known to the Romans as Mercury. He was an eloquent and crafty deity, the protector and guide of travelers, god of speech, and patron of businessmen and thieves. His early representation was a pillarlike stone called a "herm." In households, the round hearth of Hestia was inside while the phallic pillar of Hermes was at the threshold. Hestia's fire provided warmth and sanctified the home, while Hermes stood at the door to bring fertility in and keep evil out. In temples, these deities were also linked. In Rome, for example, the shrine of Mercury stood on the right of the steps leading to the temple of Vesta.

Thus in households and temples Hestia and Hermes were related, but separated. Each served a separate, valued function. Hestia provided the sanctuary where people bonded together into the family—the place to come home to. Hermes was the protector at the door, and the guide and companion in the world—where communication, knowing one's way around, being clever and having good luck all make a difference.

HESTIA THE ARCHETYPE

The goddess Hestia's presence in house and temple was central to everyday life. As an archetypal presence in a woman's personality, Hestia is similarly important, providing her with a sense of intactness and wholeness.

VIRGIN GODDESS

Hestia was the oldest of the three virgin goddesses. Unlike Artemis and Athena, she did not venture outside into the world to explore the wilderness or establish a city. She stayed inside house or temple, contained within the hearth.

On the surface, anonymous Hestia seems to have little in common with quick-to-act Artemis or with keen-minded, golden-armored Athena. Yet essential intangible qualities were shared by all three virgin goddesses, however different their spheres of interest or modes of action. Each had the one-in-herself quality that characterizes a virgin goddess. None was victimized by male deities or mortals. Each had the ability to focus on what mattered to them and concentrate on that, without being distracted by the needs of others or by the need for others.

INWARD-FOCUSED CONSCIOUSNESS

The Hestia archetype shares focused consciousness with the other two virgin goddesses. (In Latin, the word for "hearth" is *focus*.) However, the inward direction of the focus is different. Externally oriented Artemis or Athena focuses on achieving goals or implementing plans; Hestia concentrates on her inner subjective experience. For example, she is totally absorbed when she meditates.

Hestia's way of perceiving is by looking inward and intuitively sensing what is going on. The Hestian mode allows us to get in touch with our values by bringing into focus what is personally meaningful. Through this inner focusing, we can perceive the essence of a situation. We can also gain insight into other people's character and see the pattern or feel the significance of their actions. This inner perspective provides clarity in the midst of the confusing myriad of details that confront our five senses.

The inward Hestia may also become emotionally detached and perceptually inattentive to others in her surroundings as she attends to her own concerns. Again, this detachment is characteristic of all three virgin goddesses. Moreover, adding to her tendency to withdraw from the company of others, Hestia's "one-in-herselfness" seeks quiet tranquility, which is most easily found in solitude.

THE HEARTHKEEPER

Hestia as Goddess of the Hearth is the archetype active in women who find keeping house a meaningful activity rather than a chore. With Hestia, hearthkeeping is a means through which a woman puts her self and her house in order. A woman who acquires a sense of inner harmony as she accomplishes everyday tasks is in touch with this aspect of the Hestia archetype.

Tending to household details is a centering activity, equivalent to meditation. If she were articulate about her inner process, a Hestia woman could write a book entitled *Zen and the Art of Housekeeping*. She does household tasks because they matter to her in themselves, and because it pleases her to do them. She derives an inner peace from what she is doing, like a woman in a religious order for whom every activity is done "in the service of God." If Hestia is the archetype, when she finishes her tasks she feels good inside. In contrast, Athena has a sense of accomplishment, and Artemis is simply relieved that a chore is finished, freeing her to do something else.

When Hestia is present, a woman goes about her household tasks with a sense that there is plenty of time. She doesn't have one eye on the clock, because she is neither on a schedule nor "putting in time." Consequently, she is in what the Greeks called *kairos* time—she is "participating in time," which is psychologically nourishing (as are almost all experiences in which we lose track of time.) As she sorts and folds laundry, washes dishes, and cleans up the clutter, she feels an unhurried, peaceful absorption in each task.

Hearthkeepers stay in the background maintaining anonymity. They often are taken for granted, and aren't news-worthy or famous personalities.

TEMPLE HEARTHKEEPER

The Hestia archetype thrives in religious communities, especially those that cultivate silence. Contemplative Catholic orders and Eastern religions whose spiritual practice is based on meditation provide good settings for Hestia women.

Vestal virgins and nuns share Hestia's archetypal pattern. Young women who enter convents give up their previous identities. Their first names are changed, and their last names are no longer used. They dress alike, strive to be selfless, live celibate lives, and dedicate those lives to religious service.

As Eastern religions attract more Westerners, women who embody Hestia can be found in ashrams as well as in convents. Both disciplines place a primary inward focus on prayer or meditation. They place a secondary focus on community maintenance (or housekeeping), which is done with the attitude that this task, too, is a form of worship.

Most temple Hestias are also anonymous women who un-obtrusively participate in the daily spiritual and housekeeping rituals of their religious communities. Noteworthy women members of these communities combine Hestia with other strong archetypes. For example, the mystic St. Teresa of Avila, noted for her ecstatic writings, combined an aspect of Aphrodite with Hestia. Nobel Peace Prize recipient Mother Teresa seems a combination of maternal Demeter and Hestia. Mother superiors who are spiritually motivated, effective administrators usually have strong Athena traits in addition to Hestia.

The home and temple aspects of Hestia come together when religious rituals are observed at home. Hestia could be glimpsed, for example, in watching a Jewish woman prepare for the Seder dinner. As she set the table, she was engrossed in sacred work, a ritual ceremony every bit as significant as the silent interchange between altar boy and priest during a Catholic mass.

THE WISE OLD WOMAN

As elder sister of the first-generation Olympians and maiden aunt of the second generation, Hestia occupied the position of an honored elder. She stayed above or out of the intrigues and rivalries of her relatives and avoided being caught up in the passions of the moment. When this archetype is present in a woman, events don't have the same impact on her as on other people.

With Hestia as an inner presence, a woman is not "attached" to people, outcomes, possessions, prestige, or power. She feels whole as she is. Her ego isn't on the line. Because her identity isn't important, it is not tied to external circumstance. Thus she does not become elated or devastated by whatever happens. She has

> The inner freedom from the practical desire,
> The release from action and suffering, release from the
>   inner
> And the outer compulsion, yet surrounded
> By a grace of sense, a white light still and moving.

> T. S. Eliot, *The Four Quartets*[4]

Hestia's detachment gives this archetype a "wise woman" quality. She is like an elder who has seen it all, and has come through with her spirit undampened and her character tempered by experience.

The goddess Hestia was honored in the temples of all the other gods. When Hestia shares the "temple" (or personality) with other deities/archetypes, she provides her wise perspective on their aims and purpose. Thus a Hera woman, who reacts with pain at discovering her mate's infidelity, is not as vulnerable if she also has Hestia as an archetype. The excesses of all the other archetypes are ameliorated by Hestia's wise counsel, a felt presence that conveys a truth, or offers spiritual insight.

THE SELF: INNER CENTEREDNESS, SPIRITUAL ILLUMINATION, AND MEANING

Hestia is an archetype of inner centeredness. She is "the still point" that gives meaning to activity, the inner reference point that allows a woman to be grounded in the midst of outer chaos, disorder, or ordinary, everyday bustle. With Hestia in her personality, a woman's life has meaning.

Hestia's round hearth with a sacred fire at the center is in the shape of a mandala, an image that is used in meditation and that is a symbol of wholeness or totality. Of mandala symbolism, Jung wrote:

> Their basic motif is the premonition of a center of personality, a kind of central point within the psyche, to which everything is related, by which everything is arranged, and which is itself a source of energy. The energy of the central point is manifested in the almost irresistible compulsion and urge to become what one is, just as every organism is driven to assume the form that is characteristic of its nature, no matter what the circumstances. This center is not felt or thought of as the ego, but, if one may so express it, as the self.[5]

The Self is what we experience inwardly when we feel a relationship to oneness that connects us to the essence of everything outside of us. At this spiritual level, "connecting" and "detachment" are, paradoxically, the same. When we feel ourselves in touch with an inner source of warmth and light (metaphorically, warmed and illuminated by a spiritual fire), this "fire" warms those we love in our households and keeps us in touch with others who are far away.

Hestia's sacred fire was found on the family hearth and within temples. The goddess and the fire were one, linking families with families, city-states with colonies. Hestia was the spiritual connecting link among them all. When this archetype provides spiritual centering and connectedness with others, it is an expression of the Self.

HESTIA AND HERMES: ARCHETYPAL DUALITY

The pillar and circle-shaped ring have come to represent male and female principles. In ancient Greece, the pillar was the "herm" that stood outside the door of the home representing Hermes, while the round hearth inside symbolized Hestia. In India and other parts of the East, pillar and circle are "mated." The upright phallic lingam penetrates the female yoni or ring, which lies over it as in a child's ring-toss game. There pillar and circle merged, while the Greek and Roman kept these same two symbols of Hermes and Hestia related but apart. To further emphasize this separation, Hestia is a virgin goddess who will never be penetrated, as well as the oldest Olympian. She is a maiden aunt of Hermes, who was thought of as the youngest Olympian—a most unlikely union.

From Greek times on, Western cultures have emphasized duality, a splitting or differentiation between masculine and feminine, mind and body, logos and eros, active and receptive, which then all became superior and inferior values, respectively. When Hestia and Hermes were both honored in households and temples, Hestian feminine values were, if anything, the more important—she received the highest honors. At that time, there was a complementary duality. Hestia has since then been devalued and forgotten. Her sacred fires are no longer tended, and what she represented is no longer honored.

When Hestia's feminine values are forgotten and dishonored, the importance of inner sanctuary—going inward to find meaning and peace—and of family as sanctuary and source of warmth is diminished or lost. In addition, the sense of an underlying relatedness to others disappears, as does the need for citizens of a city, country, or the Earth to be linked together by a common spiritual bond.

HESTIA AND HERMES: MYSTICALLY RELATED

At a mystical level, the archetypes of Hestia and Hermes are related through the image of sacred fire at the center. Hermes-Mercury was the alchemical spirit Mercurius, who was envisioned as elemental fire. Such fire was considered the source of mystical knowledge, symbolically located at the center of the Earth.

Hestia and Hermes represent archetypal ideas of spirit and soul. Hermes is the spirit that sets the soul on fire. In this context, Hermes is like the wind that blows over smoldering coals at the center of a hearth, causing them to blaze up. In the same way, ideas can ignite deep feelings, or words can make conscious what has so far been inarticulately known, illuminating what has been dimly perceived.

CULTIVATING HESTIA

Hestia can be found in the quiet solitude and sense of order that comes from doing "contemplative housekeeping." In this mode, the woman can be totally absorbed in each task, unhurried in doing it, with time to enjoy the resulting harmony. Even the most un-Hestian housekeeper can usually recollect times in which she was governed by this archetype. For example, a day taken to clean out a closet may involve discarding and keeping clothes, remembering and anticipating events, sorting both belongings and self. In the end, the housekeeper has an orderly closet that reflects who she is, and a day spent well. Or a woman may experience Hestia in the pleasure and satisfaction of going through old photographs, sorting, labeling, and putting them in an album.

Women who are not Hestia women can decide to spend time "with Hestia"—the inward, quiet, centered part of themselves. To do so, they must make the time and find the space—especially if they are other-directed women, whose lives overflow with activity and relationships, who both pride themselves on and complain about the fact that they "never have a moment's peace."

Inviting Hestia to be part of everyday housekeeping when she is not usually present begins with the intent to shift to a Hestian attitude. After deciding on a task, the woman must provide ample time for it. For example, folding laundry is a repetitious chore for many women who hurry through the task feeling hassled. Adopting Hestia's mode, a woman might welcome the opportunity to fold clothes, as a time to quiet her mind. For Hestia to be present, a woman needs to focus on one task at a time, one area or one room at a time, whatever feels easily manageable in the time available. She must become as absorbed in doing the task as if she were performing the Japanese tea ceremony, with a sense of serenity in each movement. Only then will a pervasive inner quiet replace the ordinary chatter of the mind. The standards to be met need to be the woman's own, the way it is done in accordance with what makes sense to her. In this she is a virgin goddess, not servant to another's needs or standards, nor oppressed by the clock.

Meditation activates and strengthens this introverted, inwardly focused archetype. Once begun, meditation often becomes an everyday practice because it provides a sense of wholeness and centeredness, an inner source of peace and illumination, of access to Hestia.

For some women, poetry emerges when Hestia's presence is felt. May Sarton, author and poet, says that for her such writing "is possible only when I am in a state of grace, when the deep channels are open, and when they are, when I am both profoundly stirred and balanced, then poetry comes as a gift beyond my will."[6] She is describing an experience of the archetype of the Self, which always feels beyond ego and effort, a gift of grace.

FINDING HESTIA THROUGH UNCHOSEN SOLITUDE

Almost everyone experiences periods of unchosen solitude during their lives. Such periods usually begin with loss, grief, loneliness, and longing to be with others. For example, free-lance writer Ardis Whitman's husband gave her a quick hug and dashed out the door, was stricken by a heart attack, and never returned home again. Seven years later, she wrote about some of the unexpected rewards of solitude. Her words evoke feelings associated with Hestia:

> Like the first thin sunlight after rain, there is a meager yet growing warmth that is as indigenous to unchosen solitude as sorrow itself is. It is warmed by memory . . . also by a growing sense of our own identity. When we live surrounded by people, some of the passion and insight natural to us leaks away through the sieve of small talk. At your most daring moments you believe that what is going on is the ultimate human work—the shaping of a soul. The power of life comes from within; go there. Pray; meditate. Reach for those luminous places in yourself.[7]

HESTIA THE WOMAN

A Hestia woman shares the attributes of the goddess in being a quiet and unobtrusive person, whose presence creates an atmosphere of warmth and peaceful order. She is usually an introverted woman who enjoys solitude. Recently I visited a Hestia woman at home, and immediately felt the connection between her personality, the ambience, and the Goddess of the Hearth. The house was clean, cheerful, and orderly. Flowers graced the table, and freshly made bread was cooling. Something intangible made the house feel like a quiet sanctuary, a peaceful place, reminding me of the Zen Mountain Center at Tassajara, California, where the outer world drops away and a timeless calm pervades.

EARLY YEARS

Young Hestia looks very much like a young Persephone: both are pleasant, "easy" children. Even the "terrible twos" come and go with hardly a ripple of stubborness or assertion for either of them. There are subtle differences between these little girls, however. Persephone takes her cues from others and is eager to please. Hestia may do what others tell her and appear to be just as compliant, but when left on her own she contentedly plays without direction. Little Hestia has a quiet, self-sufficient quality. If she hurts herself or gets upset, she is as likely to go to her room to find comfort in solitude, as to her mother. Sometimes people are drawn to an inner presence she conveys, an "old soul" quality about the young child that bespeaks wisdom or tranquillity.

A Hestia girl does little to draw attention to herself or to evoke strong reactions from others. When she keeps her room in order, she may receive praise for it. When she keeps to herself, she may be prodded to join the family or to get out in the world.

PARENTS

The goddess Hestia was the first-born child of Rhea and Cronos, the first one to be swallowed by Cronos, and the last one to be regurgitated. Thus she spent the longest time of any of her siblings captive in the dark and oppressive bowels of her father, and the only one to be there alone. Hers was hardly a happy childhood. Cronos was a tyrannical father who had no warm feelings toward his children. Rhea was ineffectual and powerless, and did nothing to stop the abuse of her children until her last child was born. Of all the children, Hestia was the most on her own to cope in whatever manner she could.

Some Hestia women that I have seen in my practice have had early lives that parallel that of the goddess—abusive, tyrannical fathers and ineffectual (often depressed) mothers. Many were psychologically on their own throughout childhood in households where the needs of the children were discounted and where any individual expression was "swallowed up" by the need of the father to dominate. In this kind of environment, most children emulate their parents: the stronger, especially the boys, may abuse or tyrannize the younger and smaller, or may run away from home or take to the streets. Among the daughters, a powerless but maternal sibling may follow a Demeter pattern and try to look out for her younger siblings, or she may follow a Hera pattern and attach herself to a boyfriend as soon as she is old enough.

A Hestia daughter, however, is likely to withdraw emotionally, retreating inward for solace in the midst of a painful, conflicted family life or a school environment that feels foreign to her. She often feels as alienated or isolated from her siblings as she does from her parents—and she truly is different from them. She tries not to be noticed, has a surface passivity, and an inner sense of certainty that she is different from those around her. She tries to be unobtrusive in all situations and cultivates solitude in the midst of others. Hence she becomes virtually "persona-less," like the goddess herself.

In contrast, a Hestia daughter from an ordinary middle-class family with supportive parents may not appear to be all that Hestian. From nursery school on, she is helped to "get over her shyness or timidity"—which is how others often label her inwardness. Thus she does develop a socially adaptable persona, a way of being pleasant and sociable. She is encouraged to do well in school, to participate in everything from ballet to girls' soccer, to be maternal toward little children, and go out on dates when she is in high school. Yet, however she appears on the surface, she is inwardly true to Hestia; she has a quality of independence and detachment, an emotional evenness that comes from being centered.

ADOLESCENCE AND EARLY ADULTHOOD

Teenager Hestia absents herself from the social dramas, high passions, and shifting alliances of her peers. In this she resembles the goddess Hestia, who took no part in the romantic intrigues or the wars that occupied the other Olympians. As a result, she may be a social isolate who stays on the periphery of activity, a nonparticipant who appears to others to be self-sufficient and isolated by choice. Or, if she has developed other facets of her personality, she may have friends and be involved in school and social activities. Her friends like her quiet warmth and steadiness, although they sometimes are exasperated with her for not taking sides in a controversy or wish she'd be more competitive.

Adolescence may be a time of deepening religious conviction for Hestia. It may lead to her only direct conflict with her parents, if she wants to follow a religious vocation. Although some Catholic families are delighted when a daughter feels called to be a nun, many others are appalled if she takes her faith this seriously. More recently, Hestias have been attracted to various Eastern religions that have flourished in the United States since the 1970s. When Hestia daughters are drawn to ashrams, chant in foreign languages, and take on new names, many parents react in alarm and mistakenly assume that it will be easy to make their quiet, docile Hestia daughters change their convictions. Instead, with the certainty and focus of a virgin goddess, Hestia daughters usually do what matters to them rather than comply with their parents' wishes.

The Hestia woman who goes to college often appreciates the anonymity of a large university and the opportunity to have a place of her own. A woman who is solely Hestia is unlikely to have a personal reason to go to college, however, because intellectual challenge, looking for a husband, or preparing for a profession are not Hestian concerns. For these motivations, other goddesses need to be present. Most Hestia women who attend college do so because other archetypes are also important or because others expect them to do so.

WORK

The competitive workplace does not reward Hestia women. A Hestia woman lacks ambition and drive; she does not want recognition, she does not value power, and strategies to get ahead are foreign to her. As a result, a Hestia woman is likely be found holding a traditional woman's job in an office, where she is either unseen and taken for granted, or appreciated as "a jewel" who works steadily and dependably, stays out of office politics and gossip, and provides an ambience of order and warmth. A Hestia woman enjoys serving coffee and adding a woman's touch to the office.

Hestia women may excel in professions where stillness and patience are required. For example, a photographer's favorite model is a Hestia woman, because there is something "inward-looking" about her eyes, as well as an unself-conscious gracefulness and a stillness reminiscent of "a self-possessed cat," completely absorbed in her pose.

Many Hestia women also do well on the other side of the lens. Hestia's patience and stillness are qualities that reward a photographer who must wait for the right moment, the expressive gesture, or the spontaneous composition. Hestia may "team up" with other archetypes within a woman, thus adding a Hestian quality to her work. For example, the best nursery school teacher I have heard of seemed to be a combination of maternal Demeter and Hestia. Her collegues marvel at the underlying order she effortlessly seems to create around her: "She's never frazzled. Maybe the kids catch serenity from her—all I know is that she somehow transforms a roomful of kids who are competing for attention into a lively, warm group. She never seems hurried, as she gives her full attention here, a hug there, suggests a game or a book, and the kids settle down."

RELATIONSHIP WITH WOMEN

Hestia women often have a few good friends who appreciate being with them from time to time. Chances are these women have some Hestia qualities themselves and look to their Hestia friend as a sanctuary where their own Hestian side can come out. A Hestia woman won't engage in gossip or in intellectual or political discussions. Her gift is to listen with a compassionate heart, staying centered in the midst of whatever turmoil a friend brings to her, providing a warm place by her hearth.

SEXUALITY

When a woman has Hestia as the dominant archetype, sexuality is not very important to her. Interestingly, this seems true even if she is orgasmic. Both Hestia women and their husbands have described how dormant sexuality is for them until sexual intercourse is initiated. Then, said one husband, "She's wildly responsive." One Hestia woman was married to a man who initiates sex "once a month if he's active and once every two months otherwise"; she found that she was orgasmic even with very little foreplay. She enjoyed sex "when it happened" and "was perfectly contented" in its absence. In such women, the Hestia pattern prevails. Aphrodite's sexuality is accessible when evoked during lovemaking but is otherwise absent.

The nonorgasmic Hestia woman views sexuality as "a nice, warm experience" that she enjoys providing for her husband: "It feels good when he comes inside of me. I feel close to him and glad for him." For her husband, sex with her is "like coming home" or "a sanctuary."

A Hestia woman in a lesbian relationship follows the same pattern. Sex isn't very important. If her partner is also more receptive than active sexually, and each waits for the other to initiate sex, their relationship can go for months or even years without sexual expression.

MARRIAGE

A Hestia woman fits the old-fashioned idea of "a good wife." She looks after the home well. She is not ambitious for herself or for her husband—so she neither competes with him nor nags him. She is not a flirt and isn't promiscuous. Although his fidelity isn't of crucial importance to her as it is for Hera, she is like Hera in being faithful herself. There is no temptation to be unfaithful—as long as she is unaffected by Aphrodite.

A Hestia wife may look like a dependent wife, comfortably living out the traditional role. Her appearance may be misleading however, for she maintains an inner autonomy. Part of her quietly remains a one-in-herself virgin goddess. She does not need a man to feel emotionally fulfilled. Without him, life for her would be different but would not lose its meaning or purpose.

The "job description" of traditional married women seems to differ, depending on which goddess is the most active. Hera's emphasis is on "wife," Demeter's is on "mother," Athena's on maintaining an efficient and smooth-running household, which makes "housewife" her designation. Hestia would list her own occupation as "homemaker."

RELATIONSHIPS WITH MEN

Hestia women attract men who are drawn toward quiet, unassertive, self-sufficient women who will be good wives. Such men see themselves in the traditional role of head of household and breadwinner. Men who want sexy women, women who will mother or inspire them, or be their upwardly mobile partners look elsewhere.

Often a Hestia woman attracts men who view women as either madonnas or whores. These men classify women as "good" if they are sexually inexperienced, uninterested in sex, and thus "saintly." They classify women as "bad" or "loose" if they are attracted to men and sexually responsive. This kind of man marries the former and has affairs with the latter. Married to this kind of man, a Hestia woman could stay unenlightened about the pleasures of sexuality because her husband doesn't want a sexually responsive wife with desires of her own.

Many contented traditional marriages are unions of a Hermes husband, who is a businessman-traveler-communicator-entrepreneur agilely negotiating the outside world, and a Hestia wife, who keeps the home fires burning. Often this arrangement works very well for both. Each finds great personal satisfaction in what he and she are doing as individuals, and this satisfaction indirectly supports the activities of the other. He appreciates not having to concern himself with the home front, because she takes care of it very well, isn't doing it for him, and always provides a warm and peaceful home for him between his forays into the world. He likes her combination of homebody and independent spirit.

She, in turn, appreciates the autonomy to decide how their home will be and likes the economic support that allows her the time and space to do whatever matters to her. Also, a Hermes husband is by nature always on the move, creating new proposals, making deals, trying new avenues, trusting his own acumen and instincts—and in general relying mostly on himself in the world. He doesn't need or want a Hera or Athena wife to help provide either an image or a strategy. Thus, he often doesn't expect his wife to come along on business trips or to endure cocktail parties, which suits his Hestia wife quite well.

She prefers to entertain at home, where she provides the atmosphere, prepares the house for company, makes the food, and stays in the background—while her more extraverted husband may take the conversational lead and relate to their guests directly. Her hours of work spent in preparation may be taken for granted, and the value of her contribution to the pleasantness of an evening may remain unappreciated. Like the goddess, it seems to be a Hestia woman's lot to remain anonymous, although she is central.

CHILDREN

A Hestia woman can be an excellent mother, especially if she has some Demeter in her psyche as well. She can be a little too detached when she goes inward, and her love may be a shade too impersonal and undemonstrative. But usually she attends to children with loving and accepting attention. She doesn't have great ambitions for her children and thus she allows them to be themselves. She takes good care of them as a matter of course, and provides a home ambience that is warm and secure. Hestia's children do not have to break away or rebel. As adults in therapy, they do not have major mother problems to work through.

When it comes to helping her children cope with social nuances or competitive situations, however, she is not much use. The same is true for helping with ambitions or career development.

MIDDLE YEARS

By midlife, the course of a Hestia woman's life often seems set. If she married, she is a homemaker who is content in this role. If she didn't marry, she may have the aura of "spinster" or "old maid" because she doesn't mind her single status and isn't out to catch a man. If she's working in an office, or living in a convent or ashram, she's a "fixture" there, who quietly does her part.

Midlife may be the time that a Hestia woman formally enters a convent or ashram, changes her name, and devotes her life to a particular spiritual path. For her it is a natural transition, a deepening commitment to a devotion already practiced. For relatives, the decision may be totally unexpected, because quiet Hestia never broadcasted the importance of this aspect of her life to them.

LATER YEARS

There is always something "old and wise" about a Hestia woman, she has the capacity to grow old gracefully. She is well suited to live alone, and she may have done so all her life. In the role of the archetypal spinster aunt, she may be called on by other family members to help out when needed.

The two major emotional crises that face traditional women are the empty nest and widowhood. But although most Hestia women are wives and mothers, they do not have a deep need to be in either role. Consequently, the loss of these roles does not result in depression for Hestia, as it might for Demeter or Hera women. Coping with the outer world is what is difficult for Hestia women. If they become "displaced homemakers" through divorce or widowhood, and are not provided for economically, they are usually ill prepared by nature and by experience to go out and be successful in the world. Thus they may join the ranks of the genteel poor.

An elderly Hestia woman may have to eke out a living on Social Security, but she is far from impoverished in spirit. Often she lives alone in her last years, with no regrets about life and no fears about death.

PSYCHOLOGICAL DIFFICULTIES

As an archetype of inner wisdom, Hestia lacks negativity. Thus it is not surprising that Hestia doesn't present the usual potential patterns of pathology. She was not involved with other deities and mortals, a pattern of detachment that may cause a woman to be lonely and isolated. The main difficulties for Hestia women, however, are related to what was missing in Hestia. Of all the gods and goddesses of Mt. Olympus, she was not represented in human form—she lacked an image or a persona. And she was not involved in romantic intrigues or conflict—she lacked practice and skills at making her way in these areas.

IDENTIFYING WITH HESTIA

To live "as Hestia" means to be self-effacing, anonymous, a nonentity who nonetheless has a central position in the household. Many women know the drawbacks of this role. Their work is often taken for granted, while their feelings are not taken into consideration. A Hestia woman characteristically lacks assertiveness and doesn't speak up if she feels discounted or devalued. The housework that can be a source of quiet pleasure and inner order loses this meaning if as soon as it is done others disrupt the order and produce disarray. The hearthkeeping Hestia can become burnt out, when her efforts feel meaningless and ineffectual to her.

Identification with emotionally detached Hestia stifles a woman's direct expression of feelings. A Hestia woman indirectly expresses her love and concern for others through thoughtful acts. The saying "Still waters run deep" describes Hestia's introverted feelings, which lie below the surface. Because a Hestia woman is undemonstrative, people who are very important to her may not know that they are. Solitude, which Hestia values, can turn lonely if the people she cares deeply for are unaware of how she feels and leave her alone. It is also sad when someone who wants to be loved by a Hestia woman is loved by her, but never knows so for sure. Her warmth seems impersonal and detached as long as it is not expressed in words or hugs, and may not be specifically directed toward the people she loves. To grow beyond Hestia, a woman must learn to express her feelings, so that people who are special to her can know it.

DEVALUATION OF HESTIA

Within a convent or the institution of marriage—when both existed as lifetime commitments, there was a secure place for Hestia's spirit to thrive. But without the security and stability of lifetime institutions, a Hestia woman may be at a decided disadvantage. She feels herself to be like a turtle without a shell, expected to compete in a rat race. By nature, Hestia is not a joiner or a social climber, isn't moved by political causes and lacks ambition. She isn't out in the world trying to put her mark on it, and doesn't care to be. Thus she is easily overlooked and devalued by achievers, do-gooders, and social arbiters, who measure people by tangible standards and find her lacking.

Devaluation has a negative effect on a Hestia woman's self-esteem. She may feel out of step, maladjusted, and incompetent if she adopts the standards of others and applies them to herself.

WAYS TO GROW

A Hestia woman's difficulties arise when she ventures out of the sanctuary of home or temple to make her way in the world. As an introverted person confronted with the faster, often competitive pace of others, she will be out of place until she develops other aspects of her personality.

FASHIONING A SOCIALLY ADAPTABLE PERSONA

The word *persona* (which means "mask" in Latin) once referred to the masks that were worn onstage to identify immediately the role that actor was to play. In Jungian psychology, the persona is the mask of social adaptation that a person presents to the world. It is the way we present ourselves to others and how we are seen by them. A person with a well-functioning persona is like a woman with a large wardrobe from which she can choose something to wear that is appropriate to the occasion and to her personality, position, and age. How we behave, what we say, how we interact with others, how we identify ourselves are all parts of our persona.

A Hestia woman is by nature uninterested in persona-level concerns, in who's who and how to make a good or appropriate impression. Unless she retreats into a convent and never ventures out again, however, she will have to interact with others, make small talk, and be interviewed and assessed—like everyone else in a competitive culture. She doesn't come by these skills naturally and must learn them. Often the process is very painful. On having to go to a large gathering, she feels inadequate, awkward, shy, and inept; she feels herself without an adequate persona, as if she has "nothing to wear." This distress is reflected in bad dreams in which she finds herself naked or only partially dressed. Sometimes, in metaphorical correspondence to her dream, she presents herself as too naked—she reveals too much, is too honest, allowing people to see what others would keep covered up in the same situation.

A Hestia woman who must appear for an interview or evaluation must fashion a persona consciously, putting as much thought into it as she would into a resume (which could be considered an "on-paper" persona). She needs to have as clear a picture as she can of "who" she is supposed to be in each particular setting, and she must be prepared to try on a number of personas, until she discovers a style that will feel natural to her, once she has "worn" it enough.

ACQUIRING ASSERTIVENESS:
VIA ARTEMIS, ATHENA, OR AN ANIMUS

Besides a persona, a Hestia woman needs to acquire an ability to be assertive; she needs to have an active aspect to her personality if she is going to interact with others, or take care of herself in the world. The goddess Hestia did not jostle for power or compete for golden apples. She stayed out of relationships, avoided Mt. Olympus, was not in the background of the Trojan War, and did not sponsor, rescue, punish, or come to the aid of any mortals. Unlike the goddess, a Hestia woman is a person among people, who must venture outside the walls of house or temple, and who is ill prepared for the experience, unless other parts of her psyche can help her to be active, expressive, and assertive. Artemis and Athena, the active feminine archetypes, can provide access to these abilities, as can the woman's animus, or masculine part of her personality.

Artemis and Athena qualities may have developed if the Hestia woman participated in competitive activities, summer camps, women's groups, outdoor sports, or did well in school. A girl who is archetypally Hestia finds early in life that she must adapt to being in the midst of people and meet extraverted expectations. In the process, she may evoke and cultivate other archetypes. As a result, she can incorporate Artemis or Athena qualities into her personality.

A Hestia woman may feel that the core of her being—feminine, homebody, quiet inward Hestia—remains unaffected by her outer experiences. She may feel, instead, that in the process of adapting to a competitive and social world she develops a masculine attitude or animus. A well-developed animus is like an inner male whom she can summon to speak for her when she needs to be articulate or assertive. However competent he is, though, he feels "foreign" (or "not I") to her.

A Hestia woman's relationship to her animus is often like an inner Hestia-Hermes relationship, paralleling their significance and placement in Greek households. Hestia was represented by the round hearth at the center of the home, while the "herm" or pillar that represented Hermes stood outside the door. Hermes was the protective god at the threshold as well as the god who accompanied travelers. When both Hestia and Hermes are inner aspects of a woman, Hestia can provide an inner private way of being, and her Hermes animus provides an outer way of dealing effectively with the world.

A woman who feels that a Hermes animus in her is interceding with the world has a sense of having a masculine aspect in herself that she uses when she ventures out into the world, through which she can be assertive and articulate. The animus also does sentry duty, assertively guarding her privacy and keeping out unwanted intrusions. With a Hermes animus, she can be quite effective and canny, able to take care of herself in competitive situations. However, when the animus is responsible for a woman's assertiveness, it ("he") is not always present and available. For example, she might answer the phone, anticipating a friend, and instead may hear an aggressive salesperson who asks intrusive questions or an insistent do-gooder who expects her to volunteer her time. Then her animus is caught off guard, and she muddles about ineffectively.

Susan Griffin, Emmy-award-winning playwright, poet, and author of *Woman and Nature*, finds that the Hermes-Hestia alliance explains two very disparate sides of her. At home, she is a soft presence, a Hestia puttering around her kitchen, who makes her house a haven. This very private Susan Griffin contrasts with the sharply articulate, quick-minded, politically savvy ex-*Ramparts* editor, who in the public aspect can be "mercurial"—clever as well as volatile.

HOLDING ONTO ONE'S CENTER: STAYING TRUE TO HESTIA

Apollo and Poseidon both tried to take Hestia's virginity, her one-in-herself intactness. Rather than succumbing to their desires, however, she swore an oath of eternal chastity. What Hestia resisted by rejecting Apollo and Poseidon is metaphorically significant, corresponding to the intellectual and emotional forces that can pull a woman away from her center.

Hestia represents the Self, an intuitively known spiritual center of a woman's personality that gives meaning to her life. This Hestian centeredness may be invalidated if she "gives in to Apollo." Apollo was God of the Sun, and *Apollonian* has become equated with logos, the intellectual life, the primacy of logic and reasoning. If Apollo persuades a woman to give up her Hestian virginity, she will subject her inner, intuitively felt experience to the scrutiny of scientific inquiry. What she feels but cannot express in words is thus invalidated; what she knows as an inner wise woman is thus discounted unless it is supported by hard evidence. When "male" scientific skepticism is allowed to penetrate spiritual experience and to demand "proof," the invasion invariably violates a woman's sense of intactness and meaning.

Alternately, if a Hestia woman is "carried away by Poseidon," she is being overwhelmed by the God of the Sea. Poseidon represents the danger of being flooded by oceanic feelings or by contents that well up from the unconscious. When this flood threatens her, she may dream that a huge wave is bearing down on her. In waking life, preoccupation with an emotional situation may keep her from feeling centered. If the turmoil leads to depression, Poseidon's watery influence can temporarily "put out the fire at the center of Hestia's hearth."

When threatened by either Apollo or Poseidon, a Hestia woman needs to seek her one-in-herselfness in solitude. In quiet tranquility, she can once again intuitively find her way back to center.

7.

The Vulnerable Goddesses: Hera, Demeter, and Persephone

The three vulnerable goddesses are Hera, Goddess of Marriage; Demeter, Goddess of Grain; and Persephone, known as the Kore, or Maiden, and as Queen of the Underworld. These three goddesses personify archetypes that represent the traditional roles of women—wife, mother, and daughter. They are the relationship-oriented goddesses, whose identity and well-being depend on having a significant relationship. They express the needs in women for affiliation.

In their mythologies, these three goddesses were raped, abducted, dominated, or humiliated by male gods. Each suffered when an attachment was broken or dishonored. Each experienced powerlessness. And each responded characteristically—Hera with rage and jealousy, Demeter and Persephone with depression. Each showed symptoms that resembled psychological illnesses. Women in whom these goddesses exist as archetypes are likewise vulnerable. Knowledge of Hera, Demeter, and Persephone can provide women with insights into the nature of their need for relationships and into the pattern of their reaction to loss.

When Hera, Demeter, or Persephone are dominant archetypes, the motivational pull is relationship, rather than achievement and autonomy or new experience. The focus of attention is on others, not on an outer goal or an inner state. Consequently, women identified with these goddesses are attentive and receptive to others. They are motivated by the rewards of relationship—approval, love, attention, and by the need of the archetype to mate (Hera), to nurture (Demeter), or to be dependent (Persephone as the Kore). For these women, fulfilling traditional women's roles can be personally meaningful.

QUALITY OF CONSCIOUSNESS: LIKE DIFFUSELY RADIATING LIGHT

Each of the three goddess categories has a characteristic quality of consciousness. The quality associated with the vulnerable goddess archetypes is "diffuse awareness." Irene Claremont de Castillejo, a Jungian analyst, described this awareness (in her book *Knowing Woman*) as "an attitude of acceptance, an awareness of the unity of all life, and a readiness for relationship." [1] This quality of consciousness typifies relationship-oriented people of both sexes.

I think of this kind of consciousness as analogous to light from a living room lamp, which illuminates and casts a warm glow on everything within its radius. It is a generalized attentiveness that allows a person to notice feeling nuances, a receptivity to the emotional tone in a situation, an awareness of the background sounds as well as whatever is the center of attention in the foreground. Diffuse awareness explains the scanning consciousness that allows a parent to hear a child whimper through the din of conversation, or that enables a wife to know that her husband is upset, feeling ill, or under pressure when he walks in the door (sometimes even before he may be aware of it himself). This receptive, diffuse kind of consciousness can take in the whole or "gestalt" of a situation. (In contrast, the "focused consciousness" characteristic of Artemis, Athena, and Hestia—the three virgin goddesses—concentrates on one element to the exclusion of everything else.)

When I had two children barely out of diapers, I realized how mothers' behavior may be modified by their children to keep them in a state of diffuse awareness. Most of the time when I was around my children, I was attuned to them, in a receptive mental state in which my mind was not focused. I discovered that when I changed modes and concentrated intently on something other than them, they invariably interrupted me.

For example, if they were playing together quietly in the next room, and I busied myself cleaning the sink, sorting clothes, or even doing some light reading, chances were that I could continue doing any "mindless" activity for some time. But if I decided to take advantage of the quiet playtime, to read a journal or study something that required my focused attention, it seemed that about a minute or two later little feet always came running in to interrupt. It seemed as if the kids had ESP when my attentive-to-them, scanning-for-details mental state was replaced by focused attention, which "tuned them out." Trying to focus in the midst of continual interruptions is frustrating. The net effect was to discourage focused consciousness—thus modifying my mental behavior.

When the situation dawned on me, I tried an experiment that others might also try. Wait for one of those calm times when a preschool child is content and awake doing something without you. Note that you can busy yourself with something that does not require concentration. Then check the clock and switch from diffuse awareness to focused consciousness on another type of task. See how long you can focus on this task before the child interrupts you.

Not only little children react thus when the important woman in their lives tunes them out to focus on some concern of her own. My women patients have also described countless incidents with other people. For example, when a relationship-oriented woman enrolls in a course or returns to college as a graduate student, one inevitable source of friction between her and those who live with her—husband, lover, older children—are their intrusions and interruptions when she studies. She herself often has trouble concentrating on her work: the receptive, diffuse state of mind that allows a woman to attend to others also allows them to distract her easily.

And when she does concentrate, the man in her life may unconsciously react to her work as if it were a rival taking her away from him. His reaction is to the loss of her attentiveness, which has until then been part of his home environment. He may be reacting to the temporary absence of Hera or Demeter in the woman, who is herself not responding as usual to him.

It is as if an unseen warm light has been turned off, making him feel vaguely anxious and insecure—that something is wrong. And matters get worse after he intrudes "for no good reason," because the usual response to interruptions of focus is irritation. So she is likely to react with annoyance or anger, thus apparently substantiating his feelings of rejection. Every couple I have known about—where the man really does support the woman's academic or career aspirations and where he is really loved by and important to her—has found it helpful to recognize this friction-creating pattern. As soon as he does not take personally her change from diffuse awareness to focused consciousness, the pattern of his unwarranted interruptions and her consequent anger and resentment shifts, and the tension dissolves.

VULNERABILITY, VICTIMIZATION, AND DIFFUSE AWARENESS

The vulnerable goddesses were victimized. Hera was humiliated and abused by her husband, Zeus, who discounted her need for fidelity. Demeter's bond to her daughter was ignored, as was her suffering when Persephone was abducted and kept prisoner in the underworld. Both Demeter and Persephone were raped. Like human women in one-down, suffer-and-be-powerless situations, all three vulnerable goddesses also showed psychiatric symptoms.

The women who resemble these goddesses inwardly and who have diffuse awareness as a mode of consciousness are also susceptible to victimization. In contrast, the goddesses associated with the capacity to define boundaries and aim for goals (Artemis) or think through problems and devise strategies (Athena) that require focused consciousness are the virginal, invulnerable goddesses. The women who are like them are less likely to be victims.

To avoid being victimized, a woman needs to look focused and confident. She must walk briskly as if in a hurry to get somewhere—appearing aimless or absent-minded invites trouble. Although a receptive and approachable woman helps make relationships and homes warm, taking these same qualities out into the world can lead to uninvited intrusions. Any woman standing alone and waiting, or sitting alone at a restaurant or in a lobby, can expect to be approached by men who assume that any woman who is not clearly attached is fair game for comments or attention. If she is receptive and approachable, then her friendliness may invite assumptions that she is a readily available sex object. Thus she may receive unwanted sexual overtures and may become a victim of sexual harassment or of anger when she refuses. Two factors predispose her to victimization: the man's misreading of receptiveness or friendliness as sexual invitation, and the general assumption that any solitary woman can be approached and is potentially available. Another contributing factor is the underlying social assumption that women are property. This assumption forbids men to make comments, speak to, or even "look over" an escorted woman, as men are free to do otherwise.

Women who are like Demeter and Persephone, who feel vulnerable or unprotected, often have anxiety dreams. They may dream that men are breaking into their bedrooms or houses, that lurking or aggressive men are threatening or following them. Sometimes the hostile men in their dreams are familiar: men whose criticism they fear, men who intimidate them by abusive physical threats or by outbursts of anger. If in childhood a woman felt unprotected or was actually abused, the figures that attack her in dreams are often from childhood, or they take place in familiar surroundings from childhood.

Not all women who are relationship-oriented, vulnerable goddess-type women have victim dreams. Like the phases of the goddesses themselves, women who resemble these goddesses can go through a period of life during which they feel safe and unthreatened. Their dream life may be similarly pleasant. However, some women have victim dreams in good times, as if to remind them of their vulnerability. In any case, the dreams of vulnerable women are filled with people and often take place inside buildings; and they evoke memories of past emotional ties as well as describe present relationships in symbolic terms.

PATTERNS OF BEING AND BEHAVING

Each of the three vulnerable goddesses has within her mythology a happy or fulfilled phase; a phase during which she was victimized, suffered, and was symptomatic; and a phase of restoration or transformation. Each represents a stage in a woman's life through which she may pass quickly or in which she may stay for a while.

A woman who discovers that she is like Hera, Demeter, or Persephone can learn more about herself, about her strengths, susceptibilities, and negative potentialities, by understanding the parallels between herself and these archetypal goddesses. If she can learn to predict her own problems, she can save herself some suffering. For example, a Hera woman can avoid a lot of grief by not allowing herself to be propelled unwisely and prematurely into marriage. She needs to learn how to judge a man's character and capacity to love before she marries, because her fate will be determined by her husband. Similarly, a Demeter woman must be clear under what circumstances she would become pregnant and must take precautions before then, because the goddess in her—felt as a compelling maternal instinct—has no concern for the consequences. And a young Persephone woman would do well to move away from home for college or work, so that she has a chance to grow beyond being a compliant mother's daughter.

GROWING BEYOND THE VULNERABLE GODDESSES

While the vulnerable goddesses do not personify qualities that lead to achievement, the woman in whom these archetypes live may grow beyond them. She may discover either her Athena or Artemis qualities, or she may find that competence and competition in the world come through development of what feels to her like the "masculine" part of herself. And she may explore the spiritual and sensual dimensions associated with Hestia, Goddess of the Hearth, and with Aphrodite, Goddess of Love.

The next three chapters delve into the mythology and

characteristics of Hera, Demeter, and Persephone. Each chapter describes the archetypal patterns one goddess personifies, and each shows how a goddess influences the lives of women in whom she lives, as well as how she affects others who are related to such women as spouses, parents, friends, lovers, or children.

Every woman who has ever felt an urge to marry, or have a child, or felt she was waiting for something to happen to change her life—which must include just about every woman—will find herself akin to one of the vulnerable goddesses at some point in her life.

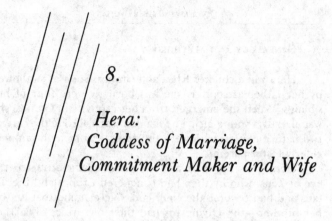

8.

Hera:
Goddess of Marriage,
Commitment Maker and Wife

HERA THE GODDESS

Stately, regal, beautiful Hera, whom the Romans knew as Juno, was Goddess of Marriage. She was the consort of Zeus (Jupiter), the supreme god of the Olympians, who ruled over the heavens and earth. Her name is thought to mean "Great Lady," the feminine form of the greek word *hero*. Greek poets referred her to as "cow-eyed"—to compliment her large and beautiful eyes. Her symbols were the cow, the Milky Way, the lily, and the peacock's iridescent tailfeather "eyes" that symbolized Hera's watchfulness. The sacred cow was an image long associated with the Great Mother Goddesses as provider of nourishment, while the Milky Way—our galaxy, from the Greek *gala*, "mother's milk"—reflects the belief, predating the Olympian deities, that the Milky Way came from the breasts of the Great Goddess as Queen of Heaven. This then became part of Hera's mythology: when milk spurted from her breasts, the Milky Way was formed. The drops that fell to the ground became lilies, flowers symbolizing another pre-Hellenic belief in the self-fertilizing power of the female genitals. Hera's symbols (and her conflicts with Zeus) reflect the power she once held as a Great Goddess whose worship preceded Zeus. In Greek mythology, Hera had two contrasting aspects: she was solemnly revered and worshipped in rituals as a powerful goddess of marriage, and was denigrated by Homer as a vindictive, quarrelsome, jealous shrew.

GENEALOGY AND MYTHOLOGY

Hera was a child of Rhea and Cronos. She was swallowed by her father as soon as she was born, as were four of her siblings. When she emerged from her captivity in Cronos, she was already a young girl. The maiden was placed in the care of two nature deities, who were the equivalent of high-ranking, elderly foster parents.

Hera grew up to be a lovely goddess. She attracted the eye of Zeus, who by then had conquered Cronos and the Titans and had become the chief god. (Never mind that he was her brother—the Olympians had their own rules or lack of them, when it came to relationships.) To get close to the virginal maiden, Zeus changed himself into a shivering, pathetic little bird, on which Hera took pity. To warm the chilled creature, Hera held it to her breast. Then Zeus shed his disguise, resumed his manly appearance, and tried to force himself on her. His efforts were not successful. She resisted his amorous efforts until he promised to marry her. The honeymoon that followed was said to have lasted three hundred years.

When the honeymoon was over, it was really over. Zeus reverted to his premarital promiscuous ways (he had had six different consorts and many offspring before he married Hera). Time and time again, Zeus was unfaithful, evoking vindictive jealousy in his betrayed wife. Hera's rage was not aimed at her unfaithful husband; rather, it was directed at "the other woman" (who more often than not had been seduced, raped, or deceived by Zeus), at children conceived by Zeus, or at innocent bystanders.

There are numerous stories of Hera's wrath. When Zeus carried Aegina off to an island to ravish her, Hera let loose a monstrous dragon—which destroyed most of the populace. And when she became enraged at Dionysus's birth, she drove his foster parents mad in an unsuccessful effort to destroy him.

Callisto was another unfortunate who got caught in the Zeus-Hera crossfire. Zeus deceived Callisto by taking on the appearance of Artemis, Goddess of the Hunt, and then seducing her. Hera reacted to this affair by changing Callisto into a bear and would have had Callisto's son unknowingly kill her.

But Zeus placed both mother and son in the sky as the constellations of Ursa Major and Ursa Minor (the Big Bear and the Little Bear, also known as the Big and Little Dippers).

Hera was humiliated by Zeus's many affairs. He dishonored their marriage, which was sacred to her, and caused her further grief by favoring his children by other women. To add insult to injury, he himself gave birth to his daughter Athena, Goddess of Wisdom—demonstrating that he did not need his wife even for this function.

Hera had several children. In a tit-for-tat reaction to Athena's birth, Hera decided to be the sole parent of a son. She conceived Hephaestus, God of the Forge. When he was born with a clubfoot—a defective child, unlike perfect Athena—Hera rejected him and threw him out from Mt. Olympus.

Hera was also, by some accounts, the sole parent of Typhaon, an inhuman, destructive, "dreadful and baneful" monster. And Ares, God of War, was the son of Hera and Zeus (Zeus held Ares in contempt for losing his head in the heat of battle). Hera also had two colorless daughters: Hebe, an adolescent cupbearer, and Eileithyria, a goddess of childbirth, who shared this role with Artemis (women in labor appealed to her as Artemis Eileithyria).

Hera usually reacted to each new humiliation by taking action. But rage and vindictiveness were not her only responses. At other times, she withdrew. Myths tell of Hera's wanderings to the ends of the earth and the sea, during which she wrapped herself in deepest darkness, separating herself from Zeus and the other Olympians. In one myth, Hera returned to the mountains where she had spent her youthful, happy days. When Zeus saw that she did not intend to return, he tried to stir her jealousy by announcing that he was about to marry a local princess. Then he arranged a mock ceremony with a statue of a woman. This prank amused Hera, who forgave him and came back to Mt. Olympus.

Although Greek mythology emphasizes Hera's humiliations and vindictiveness, in her worship—by contrast—she was greatly revered.

In her rituals, Hera had three epithets and three corresponding sanctuaries where she was worshipped during the year. In the spring, she was Hera *Parthenos* (Hera the Maiden, or Hera the Virgin). She was celebrated as Hera *Teleia* in the summer and autumn (Hera the Perfected One, or Hera the Fulfilled One), and became Hera *Chera* (Hera the Widow) in the winter.[1]

These three aspects of Hera represented the three states of a woman's life, symbolically reenacted in various rites. In the spring, an image representing Hera was immersed in a bath, symbolically restoring her virginity. In summer, she achieved perfection in a ritual wedding. In winter, another ritual emphasized a dispute with and separation from Zeus, which ushered in the phase of Hera the Widow, during which she was in hiding.

HERA THE ARCHETYPE

Hera, as Goddess of Marriage, was revered and reviled, honored and humiliated. She, more than any other goddess, has markedly positive and negative attributes. The same is true for the Hera archetype, an intensely powerful force for joy or pain in a woman's personality.

THE WIFE

The Hera archetype first and foremost represents a woman's yearning to be a wife. A woman with a strong Hera archetype feels fundamentally incomplete without a partner. She is motivated by a "goddess-given" instinct toward marriage. Her grief at being without a mate can be as deep and wounding an inner experience as being childless is for a woman whose strongest urge is to have a baby.

As a psychiatrist, I am well aware of the suffering a Hera woman feels when she has no significant man in her life. Many women have shared their private grief with me. One attorney sobbed, "I'm thirty-nine years old and I don't have a husband, and I'm so ashamed." An attractive nurse, divorced, age thirty-two, said mournfully, "I feel like I have a big hole in my psyche, or maybe it's a wound that never quite heals. God, I'm lonely by myself. I go out enough, I suppose, but none of the men I meet want to get serious."

When a woman with a compelling need to be a mate

becomes involved in a committed relationship, most of the yearning created by the Hera archetype to be a wife is met. But she still feels a pressing desire for marriage itself. She needs the prestige, respect, and honor that marriage connotes for her, and she wants to be recognized as "Mrs. Somebody." She does not want to merely live together, even in an age when such arrangements are not stigmatized. Thus she presses for outer acknowledgment; she finds the big church wedding infinitely preferable to flying to Reno or going down to City Hall.

When Hera is her archetype, a bride may feel like a goddess on her wedding day. For her, impending marriage evokes the anticipation of fulfillment and completeness, which fills her with joy. This is the radiant bride, full of Hera.

The current First Lady, Nancy Reagan, embodies the archetype of the wife. Mrs. Reagan has made it clear that being Ronald Reagan's wife is her most important priority. When she describes the importance of her marriage, she is speaking for all women who embody Hera within a happy marriage:

> As far as I am concerned, I never really lived until I met Ronnie. Oh, I know that this is not the popular admission these days. You are supposed to be totally independent, perhaps having your husband around as something of a convenience. But I cannot help the way I feel. Ronnie is my reason for being happy. Without him, I'd be quite miserable and have no real purpose or direction in life.[2]

Ours is a culture that until very recently echoed Nancy Reagan's point of view: "getting married" was considered a woman's chief accomplishment. Even now, when education and career goals are important, most women cannot escape feeling pressured by cultural expectations to "settle down and get married." Thus the Hera archetype receives enormous support. Moreover, a "Noah's Ark" mentality prevails: people are expected to come in pairs, like shoes or socks. With this as a social norm, single women are made to feel that they are missing the boat. Thus the Hera archetype gets reinforced by negative consequences when she does not conform to Hera, as well as by positive validation if she does.

Evidence that Hera might not be solely a creation of a patriarchal culture—a culture that devalues a woman unless she has been chosen by a man (the more powerful the man the better)—is suggested by a similar drive in many lesbian women. Many lesbians feel the same urge to have a mate, the same need for fidelity, the same expectation that fulfillment will come through her partner, and the same pressing desire for a ritual ceremony that will provide an outer acknowledgment of being paired. Most certainly, the lesbian woman who personifies Hera is not responding to cultural pressure or family expectations, both of which tend to condemn the relationship rather than support it.

CAPACITY FOR COMMITMENT

The Hera archetype provides the capacity to bond, to be loyal and faithful, to endure and go through difficulties with a partner. When Hera is a motivating force, a woman's commitment is not conditional. Once married, she means to stay so, "for better or worse."

Without Hera, a woman may go through a series of short-lived relationships, moving on when the inevitable difficulties arise or the initial magic of falling in love wears off. She may never marry and may feel quite fine about her unmarried state. Or she may go through the motions—big church wedding and all—yet not feel connected, in the vital, Hera way, to the man she has married.

When women marry without Hera, "Something's missing." These were the exact words used by a patient of mine, a forty-five-year-old photographer who lacked a sense of deep connection with her husband. "I like him fine and have been a good wife," she said, "yet I often think living by myself would suit me better. If women flirt with him when I'm around, he sometimes encourages them—for my benefit, I think. He hopes I'll get jealous and then gets upset because I don't get upset. I suppose he suspects that he's not essential to me— which is true. In my bones, I'm really not a devoted wife at all, though my behavior as a wife is beyond criticism." Sadly for them both, even after twenty years of marriage, Hera was not an active archetype.

THE SACRED MARRIAGE

Two of the three meanings of marriage are as fulfillment of an inner need to be a mate and as an outer recognition of husband and wife. The marriage archetype also is expressed on a third, mystical level as a striving for wholeness through a "sacred marriage." Religious wedding ceremonies that emphasize the sacred nature of marriage—characterizing it as a spiritual union or a sacrament through which grace can be channeled—are contemporary reenactments of Hera's sacred rituals.

An insight into this sacred aspect of the Hera archetype came to me from direct experience. I was brought up as a middle-of-the-road Protestant. No mystery or magic accompanied our religious rituals. The communion sacrament was a commemoration that used Welch's grape juice. Thus it was both unexpected and deeply moving for me to find that my marriage ceremony in San Francisco's Grace Cathedral was an awesome inner experience. I felt I was participating in a powerful ritual that invoked the sacred. I had a sense of experiencing something beyond ordinary reality, something numinous—which is a characteristic of an archetypal experience. As I recited my vows, I felt as if I were participating in holy rites.

When the sacred marriage occurs in a dream, there is a similar shift in intensity. What is remembered is the awesomeness of the experience. People often use electrical or energy field metaphors to try to explain what they felt as they connected with the person who was a sacred partner in their dreams. Symbolizing an intrapsychic union between masculine and feminine, the dream is an experience of wholeness. As the dreamer is embraced by her sacred partner, there is a mixture of erotic feeling, bliss, and union. The dream is "numinous" (meaning that it has an inexpressible, mysterious, and divine emotional effect on the dreamer). The dreamer awakens shaken and moved: "It was a dream that was more real to me than how I felt when I woke up. I'll never forget it. When he held me, I felt wonderful. It was like a mystical reunion. I can't explain it: there was a deep sense of peace at the same time that it was electrifying. This dream was a major event in my life."

In this purely inner experience of the sacred marriage, the dreamer experiences herself as Hera the Perfected or Fulfilled One. This often has a quieting effect on the drive to be a mate and the need to be married.

THE SPURNED WOMAN: THE NEGATIVE HERA PATTERN

The goddess Hera did not express anger at Zeus for his public infidelities. The pain she felt at being rejected by him and at being humiliated by his affairs she channeled into vindictive rage directed at the other woman or at children fathered by Zeus. The Hera archetype predisposes women to displace blame from her mate—on whom she is emotionally dependent—onto others. And Hera women react to loss and pain with rage and activity (rather than with depression, as is typical of Demeter and Persephone). In my analytic work, I've found that vindictiveness is a mental sleight of hand, which makes a Hera woman feel powerful rather than rejected.

Jean Harris is a contemporary personification of the spurned Hera. The haughty headmistress of the exclusive Madeira School was convicted of murdering her longtime lover, the developer of the Scarsdale Diet, Dr. Herman Tarnover. Harris was known to have been in a jealous rage over Tarnover's preference for a younger rival, whom she judged as having less breeding, education, and class than herself. She was convicted of the murder after her raw hatred toward the other woman was revealed, in a lengthy letter written to Tarnover just before his death. She wrote,

> You have been the most important thing in my life, the most important human being in my life, and that will never change. You keep me in control by threatening me with banishment—an easy threat which you know I couldn't live with—and so I stay home alone while you

make love to someone who has almost totally destroyed me. I have been publicly humiliated again and again.[3]

In spite of her accomplishments and prestige, Harris was convinced that she was worthless without Tarnover. She had steadfastly maintained that the killing was accidental. Spoken as Hera, who never held Zeus accountable for all his philanderings, this statement could indeed be true, for Harris could not imagine living without him.

CULTIVATING HERA

The need to be more like Hera comes as a realization to some women early in midlife; by then they have had a series of relationships, or they have been so focused on their careers that marriage has not been a priority. Up to this point, they have heeded Aphrodite's inclination to move from one relationship to another, or Persephone's tendency to avoid commitments, or Artemis and Athena's focus on achieving goals. Or the goddesses have been at cross purposes, and Hera's urge to be a mate has been thwarted by the choice of men a woman has made, a choice influenced by other goddesses.

When bonding as a mate is not a strong instinct, it will need to be consciously cultivated. This is usually possible only when a woman sees the need to make a commitment and has the will to keep it, and when the opportunity exists for her to do so. If she loves a man who needs or requires her fidelity, she must make a choice between monagamy or him. She must decide to curb the promiscuity of Aphrodite, or the independence of Artemis and favor Hera. A conscious decision to be a Hera wife can strengthen a woman's connection to the archetype.

If involvement with nonmarrying men prevents a woman from becoming a wife, she needs to become disenchanted by the type of men she has been attracted to and the treatment she has received from them. She also needs to reassess her attitude toward men who have traditional values, because she may have been prejudiced against those very men who want to marry and have families. When her image of a desirable man changes to conform to a type of man who can make a commitment, then fulfilling Hera's urge to be a wife may be possible.

HERA THE WOMAN

The modern Hera is easily recognizable. As the radiant bride walking down the aisle toward her waiting groom, she is the joyful Hera, anticipating her fulfillment. As the betrayed wife, who discovers her husband is having an affair and rages at the other woman, she is Hera the shrew. The Hera woman is embodied by countless women who have been "the Missus"—typically virginal before marriage or at least until the engagement, then the loyal wife for decades, until she becomes the widow living on Social Security.

A Hera woman takes pleasure in making her husband the center of her life. Everyone knows that her husband comes first. The children of a Hera woman realize well the order of her universe: the best is always saved for him. Other people quickly get the picture, too: she puts them "on hold" until she checks with him.

Many women who are cast in the mold of Hera have a matronly quality, and are perceived by everyone as "very much married." And many other women have Hera as one of several aspects of their personalities. On the surface, they may not seem to be Hera women, but as they learn about her they recognize that Hera is a very familiar inner figure.

EARLY YEARS

At age four or five, young Hera can be found playing house—saying, "You be the Daddy, and go to work," as she shows her playmate to the door. Bustling about like a "big person," she sweeps up and puts a dinner of grass salad and mud pies on the table, anticipating the highlight of Hera's day, which is when he comes home and sits down for dinner. (In contrast, the young Demeter, for whom being Mommy is the main event, wheels her doll in a carriage and spends hours dressing, feeding, and putting her "baby" to bed.)

But by age six or seven, when the sexes separate into their own play groups and most little girls think most little boys are "yucky," finding boys to "play house" gets near to impossible. Here and there, even in first grade, some pairing off happens, but for the most part the next glimpse of Hera comes later when kids "go steady."

PARENTS

Hera's parents were Cronos and Rhea—a distant father who swallowed his children, threatened by the possibility that one would overthrow him, and a powerless mother who could not protect her children from him. Cronos and Rhea provide us with a negative and exaggerated picture of a patriarchal marriage: the husband is a powerful, dominating man who will not tolerate competition from his children or allow his wife to have any new interests. The wife passively resists by keeping secrets from him and by using deception. Hera was the only one of her swallowed siblings who had two sets of parents. Once freed from her father, she was raised in an idyllic situation with two nature deities as foster parents.

The theme of two sets of parents—or two models of marriage—is a familiar one to many Hera women. In the midst of a less than ideal family situation that makes other children pessimistic or cynical about marriage, a young Hera holds to an idealized image of marriage, and seeks it for herself as a way out of a bad family situation. In happier circumstances, a Hera daughter sees in her parents' stable marriage what she wants for herself.

ADOLESCENCE AND EARLY ADULTHOOD

The adolescent Hera is most content if she's in a steady relationship. She's the girl who proudly wears her boyfriend's ring on a chain around her neck, daydreams about a big wedding, and keeps trying on his name—writing "Mrs. Bob Smith," "Mrs. Robert Smith," "Mrs. Robert Edwin Smith," in her notebook.

Having a steady feels crucially important to her. If she attends a status-conscious, affluent suburban high school, then it matters who he is—class officer, varsity football player, member of the "in" club. If she's in an inner-city school, what constitutes status may differ, but the pattern is the same. She seeks to be coupled with a high-status young man and yearns for the emotional security she derives from the relationship. Once she is half of an "in" couple, she arranges double dates and parties, looking down on unpaired mortals from her Olympian Hera heights. This same pattern holds through college and afterward.

Some Hera women do marry in high school or right after, in order to "play house" as soon as possible. But most high school romances break up, and the ending of this first serious relationship is usually also the first serious emotional wound for a young Hera woman.

Hera looks at college as the time and place to find a mate. If she is bright and capable, she often does well in college, only to disappoint teachers who assumed that she took her ability seriously. For a Hera woman, education is not important in itself. It may only be part of her expected social background.

Since marriage is what she came to college for, her anxiety grows with the passage of time if a husband does not materialize. As a college student in the mid-1950s, I recall the "unpinned" Hera women who as juniors became increasingly anxious, and as unengaged seniors had an air of desperation, thinking themselves doomed to be old maids. Untactful questions from relatives who asked, "When are you going to get married?" were inordinately painful, since an unmarried Hera woman feels an inner emptiness and lack of meaning that becomes magnified by the expectations of others who also emphasize marriage.

WORK

For the Hera woman, work is a secondary aspect of life, just as going to college is. Whatever her education, career, profession, or title, when Hera is a strong force in a woman's psyche, her work is something she does, rather than an important part of who she is.

A Hera woman may be very good at what she does and may achieve recognition and advancement. If she is not married, however, none of this seems to count for much with her.

On the one scale that counts, she has failed (in her own eyes) regardless of her achievements.

Other goddesses usually are present in a woman who does well in the work world. Yet if Hera is the overriding pattern, she does not feel her work is of major significance. If she is married, she will naturally subordinate her career to her husband's and will gear her work hours and chances for promotion to his needs. Only on the surface will it look as if a Hera woman were in a dual-career marriage: her career is really her marriage.

In this age of dual careers, where two paychecks are often needed, many working wives are Hera women. However, the Hera woman always says, "Whither thou goest, I will go." She will not propose a temporary geographical separation, with one or the other commuting to be together on weekends. Nor will she insist that her career is just as important as his. For that, another goddess must play a part.

RELATIONSHIPS WITH WOMEN:
THE DEVALUED SPECIES

A Hera woman doesn't usually place much importance on friendships with other women and generally does not have a best friend. She prefers being with her husband and doing things with him. If she does have a close and enduring friendship with a woman, other goddesses are responsible.

If she is unmarried, she feels that meeting eligible men is of prime importance. She may pair up with another woman to go with to places where a woman alone would not be comfortable, such as bars. But once in a steady relationship she has little time for her single women friends and usually drops them.

A Hera woman naturally maintains a social custom, common among certain women, of canceling previously made plans to see women friends if she is asked out by a man. Once she is married, this arrangement extends to canceling friendships with women.

A married Hera woman relates to other married women as half of a couple. Either she finds unattached women potentially threatening if her husband shows the least bit of attention, or she discounts them—as merely women without men. After marriage, she does almost all socializing as part of a couple. When a married Hera woman does things with other women, the activity characteristically is related to her husband's profession or his activities. Women's auxiliaries institutionalize this tendency. In such organizations, the husband's position usually determines his wife's elective position. In voting for officers of such an organization, Hera women inevitably consider the status of a woman's husband.

For a Hera woman, when contact with other women is made in the context of couples, the bond between the women is often more like a friendly alliance than a personal friendship. Therefore, a Hera woman easily drops the divorced or widowed "friend," often after years of frequent socialization, when the friend no longer is coupled. Hera women drop each other, reinforcing their inner conviction that a woman is nothing without a husband. Many bitter widows have moved to sunnier climates—not for the weather, but out of anger and pride on finding that there no longer was a place for them in their circle of formerly close friends.

RELATIONSHIPS WITH MEN: EXPECTATIONS OF FULFILLMENT

When the goddess Hera was worshipped in Greek temples and the marriage of Zeus and Hera was ritually enacted, Zeus was called *Zeus Teleios,* meaning "Zeus, Bringer to Fulfillment." A contemporary Hera woman places on a husband the archetypal expectation that he will fulfill her.

A Hera woman is attracted to a competent, successful man—a definition that usually depends on her social class and family. Starving artists, sensitive poets, and genius scholars are not for her. Hera women are not intrigued by men who suffer for their art or political principles.

Sometimes, however, Hera women do seem particularly susceptible to the combination that won Hera herself. Zeus first got close to Hera by changing himself into a shivering bird before revealing himself as chief god. All too often a Hera woman marries this combination of poor little creature in need of warmth (which she provides) and big powerful man. Many men who are highly successful in the world often have, as with Zeus, an appealing, emotionally immature little-boy element that can touch the Hera woman when combined with the power she finds so attractive. He may lack close friends, may not have been privy to the private grief of others, and may not have developed a capacity for empathy.

The man's emotional immaturity is also responsible for his seeking variety rather than depth with women and for his consequent tendency to have affairs, which the Hera woman cannot tolerate. He may be a businessman who enjoys pleasant one-night stands when he goes out of town on business. He enjoys the conquest and the excitement of sex for the first time with a new woman, figuring that what his wife doesn't know won't hurt her. He hates having talks about the relationship or having confrontations about his behavior—so a Hera woman avoids both.

If a Hera woman marries a man who turns out to be a philanderer and a liar, like Zeus, and if she takes him at his word—fairly characteristic of Hera women who want to be reassured—then she will be repeatedly wounded. Many Hera women are handicapped because they have difficulty in assessing underlying character or in realizing patterns of behavior. When sizing up people, such women perceive surfaces rather than possibilities (like looking at a house for sale and seeing just what is there, not what it used to be or what it could become). Finally, the Hera woman's disappointment and pain are proportional to the discrepancy between her archetypal expectations of fulfillment and reality, and the gap may be great.

SEXUALITY

A Hera woman assumes that sexuality and marriage go together. Thus she may have stayed virginal until she was engaged or married. Inexperienced before marriage, she depends on her husband to arouse her sexually. If he does not, she will nonetheless regularly have intercourse as part of her deeply felt role of wife. The idea of dutiful sex probably first arose with Hera women.

It is not unusual for a Hera woman to be inorgasmic in

the beginning of her marriage. Whether or not this situation stays unchanged over the years depends on whether the Aphrodite archetype is activated within the marriage.

MARRIAGE

The Hera woman considers her wedding day the most significant in her life. On that day, she acquires a new name. (She never keeps her own name—she considers it strictly her "maiden name.") She now becomes the wife, which fulfills a drive she has felt as long as she can remember.

Middle America is a setting in which many Hera women thrive. Husbands and wives spend weekends and vacations together. The husband leaves for work and comes home for dinner at a regular time. His friends are men, with whom he may spend time. He respects his wife, expects her to do her job as wife well, and assumes he is married for life. The routine, the togetherness of their social life, and the roles each maintain contribute to the stability of the marriage and to the satisfaction it provides a Hera woman.

Corporate life is another setting that can suit a Hera woman. She can move up the corporate ladder with her husband, relocate geographically or go up another rung and easily leave behind those whose ascent was not so swift. Because the bond to her husband is her major source of meaning, and because her relationships with others are weak, it is easy for her to relocate with him. In contrast, women with strong friendship bonds suffer loss and loneliness with each move, as do those women whose own work is important and who must start anew at each relocation.

A Hera woman's state of happiness depends on her husband's devotion to her, on the importance he places on the marriage, and on his appreciation of her as his wife. But she is drawn toward successful men, many of whom are successful because they are devoted to work or wedded to the job. Therefore, she may find that she's unhappy in spite of being married and even if sexual infidelity never arises. Marriage may not be fulfilling to a Hera woman when it's not very important to her husband.

A contemporary Zeus-like husband often uses marriage

mostly as a part of his social facade. He has wedded a woman of his own social class or higher and can appear with her at his side when that is called for. This arrangement may be a utilitarian marriage for him and a personal disaster for her. If any other archetype were dominant in her, she might be able to accept a marriage that has form without much content. But a Hera woman is wounded by his lack of involvement. He is often engrossed in other interests, usually involving power—such as business transactions and political alliances—and does not share his major concerns with her. She consequently feels an emotional void at her center.

She may try to compensate for (or bury) this feeling of emptiness by a flurry of social activity intended to present a public image of the perfect couple. This picture fits a number of socially prominent couples who put in appearances at such events as the opening night of the opera or the hospital auxiliary-sponsored cotillion. But the togetherness that characterizes them in public is missing in private. Such utilitarian marriages are not limited to any particular class, of course; they can be found at all social levels.

Regardless of the dissatisfactions of her marriage, a Hera woman is the least likely, of all of the goddess types, to seek divorce. Like the goddess Hera, who was humiliated and abused, a Hera woman can endure bad treatment. She feels married at her core. She finds divorce inconceivable—even when it happens to her.

If her husband wants to leave her for someone else and tells her so, a Hera woman deeply resists hearing what he is saying. Marriage is an archetypal experience for her—in her mind, she will always be the wife. Even after a divorce has occurred, a Hera woman may still think of herself as married and may suffer anew each time she is reminded that she's not. This reaction creates problems for others, as well as pain for herself.

She may spend many psychiatric hours struggling with difficulties that can be traced to the archetypal hold on a woman that marriage (or Hera) has, even after the marriage has ended. In my practice, I've seen the effect of Hera on all concerned. For example, the patient may be the divorced Hera woman, who fluctuates between pain and rage, feeling that that she is still the legitimate wife. Or the patient may be the ex-husband, who feels harassed by daily calls from his ex-wife. Or the patient may be the resentful new wife, angry at his ex-wife's intrusion into their life together or at the confusion created by the ex-wife if she insists on using her ex-husband's name on charge accounts and other documents.

CHILDREN

A Hera woman usually has children because this function is part of the role of being a wife. She will not have much maternal instinct, however, unless Demeter is also an important archetype. Nor will she enjoy doing things with her children unless Artemis or Athena are also present.

If a Hera woman has children and can't form an archetypal mother-child bond, her children will sense her failure as a lack of love and protection. Even if she is a full-time wife and mother and is physically very much present in their lives, they will feel a lack of closeness and will sense some emotional abandonment.

When a Hera woman must decide between her husband or her children, she will usually sacrifice the children's best interests in order to keep her husband. I often see adults in my practice who were raised in traditionally structured families, where the father was the head of the household, breadwinner, and petty tyrant. Such patients experienced the mother as supportive and nurturing, but she never acted as a buffer between her husband and the children. The children were always on their own in confrontations with their father, no matter how unreasonable or out of hand he got.

At first in their analysis, such patients feel that the difficulty with the father is in the forefront as they recall the painful parts of their childhood. Sometimes they feel a need to confront their fathers in the present and, if possible, get some acknowledgment or apology for events in the past. At this point, the part played by their mothers comes into awareness.

One patient, a professional woman in her late thirties, who had running battles with her father all through her adolescence, said, "Nothing I ever did was good enough. In his eyes, I was either crazy for thinking about it, or too incompetent to do it—whatever 'it' was, he put me down. He mocked what was important to me, and several times even destroyed something I valued." Now she wanted some acknowledgment from him for her accomplishments—she had a professional degree and a career. She also wanted to let him know how damaging his behavior had been.

One day, she called her parents—who always were together. As usual, they were on separate phone extensions (she can't recall ever talking to one without the other). She addressed her comments to him, specifically saying that she had "something important" to tell him and that she wanted him to listen without interrupting her. She detailed past grievances without getting upset or angry. He surprised her by doing what she asked—simply listening. However, her mother reacted as if the daughter were being abusive: "You have no right to talk to your father that way!" When the mother intervened thus, she provided her daughter with an insight into the role her mother had played all along.

The mother's reaction was typical Hera. Her loyalty was with her husband. How dare a child confront him! He is Zeus, the absolute ruler. How dare a child make him feel bad! He is too vulnerable, as was the shivering bird in need of Hera's warmth and protection.

MIDDLE YEARS

Whether or not her middle years are fulfilling ones depends on whether the Hera woman is married, and whom she married. These are the best years for Hera women who are in stable marriages to men who achieve a measure of success and position and appreciate their wives. In contrast, an unmarried, divorced, or widowed Hera woman is miserable.

In midlife, marriages often undergo stress, which a Hera woman usually does not handle well. When her marriage is in trouble, a Hera woman often makes the situation worse by her possessiveness and jealousy. If for the first time in her married life she knows or suspects the importance of another woman, a vindictiveness never before seen may emerge in all its ugliness, further endangering the marriage that is so important to her.

LATER YEARS

For the Hera woman who went from being Hera the Maiden to Hera the Perfected One, becoming Hera the Widow is the hardest period of her life. Millions of women who outlive their husbands are in this position. On becoming widowed, Hera women not only lose their husbands, they also lose the role of wife, which provided their sense of meaning and identity. They feel insignificant.

At her husband's death, a Hera woman who has not developed other aspects of her herself may go from mourning into a chronic depression, adrift and lonely. This reaction is the consequence of her previous limited attitude and action. A Hera woman is usually not especially close to her children, having always put her husband first. She does not have good friends, having geared her social life to doing everything as a member of a couple. And, as noted earlier, she may find herself dropped from her social circle, just as she herself tended to drop other single women.

The quality of a widowed Hera's life now depends on the presence of other goddesses and on how well she was financially provided for. Some Hera women never recover from the loss of their husbands.

Fortunate Hera women enter old age with their husbands, celebrating their golden wedding anniversary together. They are among the blessed of women; they have been able to fulfill the particular archetype that gives their lives meaning.

PSYCHOLOGICAL DIFFICULTIES

Hera is an undeniable influence in many women's lives. Some other goddesses may be less fulfilling when positively manifested in life, but all are also less destructive than Hera in their negative aspects. Thus, it is especially important for a Hera woman to understand the difficulties of handling the archetype because Hera can be a compelling force.

IDENTIFYING WITH HERA

For a woman to live "as Hera" is the same as identifying with the role of wife. Whether that role will provide meaning and satisfaction or will result in pain and rage depends on the quality of the marriage and on the man's fidelity.

When her instinctual drive is unmet, getting a man is a Hera woman's chief preoccupation and not having a mate her main source of grief. While she seeks her mate, she is often engaged in school or work, has friends, and goes places—all the while hoping to find a husband.

Once married, a Hera woman often constricts her life and conforms to her role and to her husband's interests. If he needs her economic support while he finishes school, she will go to work. If he wants a full-time wife, she will quit her job or not complete her education. If she also works, she's willing to relocate if he wants to move. Often she does not maintain friendships made before marriage and interests that she had prior to meeting her husband.

A man who marries a Hera woman may find that after the wedding she no longer is the woman he married. Before she constricted herself to fit the role of wife, she had broader interests. Even premarital sex may have been much better. The change in sexuality is not uncommon and may date to the wedding night. The influence of all the other goddesses may dramatically diminish when a Hera woman marries.

Hera women also bloom after marriage. The radiant bride becomes the happy wife. If her husband is a devoted Zeus who loves her, the marriage will be a deeply meaningful center of her life. Other goddess aspects may find expression, although always secondary to her role as wife.

Whether or not a Hera woman restricts her activities after marriage and limits her role to being Hera depends on the strength of the archetype, on how well developed other facets of her personality were before marriage, and on the support or lack thereof her husband gives her to grow beyond Hera. Possessive and jealous husbands who expect their wives to conform to their demands act in concert with the Hera archetype to reduce a woman to being only Hera.

DISAPPOINTED EXPECTATIONS

When a woman identifies with Hera, she often assumes that she and her husband will be transformed by marriage, unconsciously expecting her husband to become *Zeus Teleios,* or Zeus who fulfills. After the ceremony, she may be deeply and irrationally disappointed and may feel that he deceived her, as if he had implicitly promised something that he didn't deliver. In fact, however, the culprit was not he, but the archetypal expectation of *Zeus Teleios* that she projected onto him.

Many Hera women project an image of an idealized husband onto a man and then become critical and angry when he does not live up to expectations. Such a woman then may become "shrewish" (Homer's view of the goddess Hera) as she urges him to change. Another type of woman might see the man more clearly in the first place, might not expect that marriage would transform him, or might be able to leave him.

CAUGHT BETWEEN ARCHETYPE AND CULTURE

Hera women can be propelled into marriage as well as be kept trapped there, by archetypal and cultural forces acting together. The archetype is supported by the feminine mystique or "fulfillment through others" that Betty Friedan described. Both forces implicitly promise the fairytale ending "And they lived happily ever after." Once she is married, a Hera woman (more than any other type of woman) feels bonded—for better or worse. When it is "for worse," the Hera archetype, often with the support of the culture, opposes her getting out of a bad marriage. Religious beliefs and family expectations can "conspire" to keep a woman bonded to an alcoholic or to a wife beater.

OPPRESSED OR OPPRESSOR

It is clear, given the consequences of identifying with Hera, that this archetype can oppress women. An unmarried Hera woman may feel that she is incomplete and a failure, or she may be propelled into a bad marriage. A married woman may be unable to leave a bad marriage and may be negatively affected. She may turn into a nagging, dissatisfied woman who feels embittered when her husband fails to live up to Hera expectations. Or she may turn into a raging, wounded, jealous wife if her husband is unfaithful or if she imagines him to be.

Or she may be unable to move out of a marriage that is exceedingly damaging to her.

The goddess Hera suffered more than any other goddess, except Demeter (whose suffering was of a different kind). But she also persecuted others vindictively and thus was the most destructive of all the goddesses. As expressed by contemporary women, Hera's oppressiveness varies from having a judgmental attitude toward others to behaving in an overtly destructive way.

Hera women judge other women and punish them—usually by excluding or ostracizing them and their children—for not meeting Hera's standards. Such women are the social arbiters. They are especially inimical to Aphrodite. Whenever they can, they exclude attractive, sensual women whom men gather around, divorced women, and sexually active single women—all who might be attractive to their partners and are thus threatening. But their judgmentalism also extends toward women who are not personally threatening—for example, they are more critical than sympathetic toward unmarried mothers on welfare and toward rape victims. For Hera, the only truly acceptable role is as a wife of a successful man.

Long after I began to consider myself a feminist, I discovered within myself an unconscious Hera pattern of devaluing other women when I was at an event with my husband. The "click" of recognition came when I realized that I sought out the company of couples when I was at meetings with him, avoiding "unattached women" whom I very much enjoyed when I was alone. When I saw this particular Hera pattern, I was ashamed of my nonfeminist behavior. At the same time, I was humbled to realize that I had previously felt superior to Hera women, when in fact a negative aspect of Hera was part of me, too. After that, I had a full choice of whom to spend time with. And after I discovered that I had something in common with the "Mrs. Him's" that I'd previously put down, I also lost a judgmental attitude that I was well rid of.

THE MEDEA SYNDROME

The term "Medea Syndrome" aptly describes the vindictive Hera woman who feels betrayed and discarded and who goes to extremes for revenge. The Medea myth is a metaphor that describes the Hera woman's capacity to put her commitment to a man ahead of everything else, and her capacity for revenge when she finds that her commitment counts for nothing in his eyes.

In Greek mythology, Medea was the mortal woman who murdered her own children to revenge herself on her man for leaving her. She is "a clinical case" of a woman who was possessed by the destructive aspect of Hera.

Medea was the priestess-daughter of the king of Colchis. The Golden Fleece, which Jason and the Argonauts sought, belonged to this kingdom. Jason needed help if he was to take it, for the fleece was well guarded. Hera and Athena, his patron goddesses, prevailed on Aphrodite to make Medea fall in love with Jason, and help him steal the Golden Fleece. Jason begged Medea to help him, promised he would marry her, and pledged to be with her "till the doom of death fold us around." So, out of her passion for and loyalty to Jason, Medea helped him steal the fleece. By doing so, she betrayed her father and her country, and brought about her brother's death.

Jason and Medea settled in Corinth and had two young sons. As a foreigner, Medea's position was similar to that of a common-law wife. Then opportunistic Jason seized the chance to marry Glauce, the daughter of Creon, King of Corinth. As a condition for the marriage, Jason agreed that Medea and their children would be exiled.

Wounded by his perfidy and humiliated at having all her sacrifices and crimes for him come to nothing, Medea became homicidal. First she gave her rival a poisoned robe. When Glauce put it on, the effect was like a coat of napalm, which burned and destroyed her flesh. Next, Medea was in conflict between her love for her children and her desire for revenge. Fury and pride won out, and to avenge herself against Jason she murdered their children.

Medea behaved monstrously, yet she was clearly the victim of her compelling love for Jason. While some women might get depressed and even suicidal after being rejected and spurned, Medea actively plotted and carried out revenge. Her relationship to Jason was the center of her life. Everything she did was a result either of loving or of losing him. Medea was obsessed, possessed, and driven mad by her need to be Jason's mate. Her pathology stemmed from the intensity of the Hera instinct and from being thwarted.

Although literal reenactments of the Medea myth fortunately are rare, on a metaphoric level they are fairly common. When a woman becomes bonded to a man through the double intervention of Hera and Aphrodite, as happened to Medea, then her instinct to mate and her passion for him force her to put that relationship above everything. She will leave her family, betray its values, and "kill off" family ties if necessary. Many women, like Medea, believe in marital promises of eternal devotion and make tremendous sacrifices for their man, only to be used and left by unscrupulous, ambitious Jasons.

When a couple lives out the drama of Medea and Jason, she may not literally burn and rend the other woman for whom he leaves her, but she often fantasizes or attempts the emotional equivalent. For example, "Medea" may try to destroy the reputation of the other woman with lies or even literally try to harm her.

And if—again paralleling the myth of Medea and Jason—her vindictiveness is greater than is her love for her children and what is best for them, she may try to destroy their relationship to him. She may take the children away, so that he can't see them. Or she may turn his visits with the children into such traumatic events that he gives up his efforts to stay related to them.

Note that, true to Hera at her most destructive, Medea did not murder Jason. Likewise, the hostile, spurned Hera often harms others far more than she harms the man who left her. She especially harms their children.

WAYS TO GROW

Recognizing Hera's influence and understanding her susceptibilities is the first step to growth beyond her. Many women can look back to previous relationships and realize in retrospect that they were too willing to get married. Had "Hera" prevailed and had she had the opportunity, such a woman would have married her high school steady, or a summer romance, or, for that matter, any number of men she did not know very well.

When a woman is under the influence of Hera, she is likely to marry the first respectable man who asks her, or any eligible man she goes out with, without stopping to consider what would be best for her. She would do well to resist marriage until she knows a good deal about her husband-to-be. What kind of character does he have? How emotionally mature is he? How ready is he to settle down? How important is fidelity to him? What does she really feel about him as a person? How compatible are they? Answering these questions honestly is crucial to a Hera woman's future happiness. Once married, she will be dependent on the character of the man she marries and on his capacity to love her. He will decide who she will be—a fulfilled Hera or a rageful, disillusioned Hera.

EXPANDING BEYOND HERA

While a good marriage is the major source of meaning in a Hera woman's life, to limit herself to being a wife means that she may limit her growth and her ability to adapt if death or divorce brings this role to an end. She may unconsciously defer to her husband's choice of activities and friends, and may allow him to decide how she will spend her life. However, she can also become aware of her pattern and can realize that she has neglected other facets of herself, which might enrich her own life as well as her marriage.

In a traditional marriage, the husband and wife are halves of a whole; each fulfills a culturally determined role. This specialization of tasks discourages wholeness within each person. Whatever the culture considers "masculine" is not developed in the woman. A Hera woman easily falls into this pattern. She might even take perverse pride in not knowing anything about cars or numbers, or in not knowing how to deal with people in the business world—because her husband does all these tasks for both of them. Thus, if allowed to do so, Hera also restricts a woman's competence. But a woman can stop reacting and start reflecting about the pattern of her marriage. She can see that she is cast in a role that at best limits her, and at worst is destructive to her. This consciousness is the first step that makes it possible for her to resist Hera and to grow beyond this one pattern. A Hera woman must consciously and repeatedly align herself with other goddesses who allow her to grow beyond the role of wife.

MARRIAGE AS A GROWTH EXPERIENCE

An insecure Hera woman is highly susceptible to jealousy. With very little provocation, she suspects infidelity and feels slighted and humiliated in public by her husband's inattention. If her reactions are not justified, she either alienates him with her accusations or tries to make him more sensitive to the effect he has on her. And the marriage either deteriorates, confirming her fears, or both husband and wife grow closer together.

For example, her husband may learn to respond with compassion to her need to know where he is, rather than with resentment and withholding information. If he can respond thus, her trust will grow. One such husband said, "Now I let her know when to expect me, and if there is a hitch in the plans I telephone rather than leave her at the mercy of the jealous demons that torment her imagination." The Hera woman must decide over and over again whom to trust—that suspicious Hera within or her husband. To grow, she must resist Hera and must give her husband credit for support and fidelity.

TRANSFORMING RAGE AND PAIN INTO CREATIVE WORK: THE HEPHAESTUS SOLUTION

When a Hera woman is in a bad marriage or must struggle to get free of being vindictive, victimized Hera herself, one possible solution is suggested by the myth of Hera's son Hephaestus, God of the Forge. He symbolizes a potential inner strength, which the goddess herself rejected but which is still available to Hera women. (Hera favored her other son, Ares, God of War. "Like mother, like son"—Ares's uncontrolled fury on the battlefield mirrored Hera's out-of-control vindictiveness.)

Hephaestus—known as Vulcan to the Romans—had his forge inside a volcano. Symbolically, he represents the possibility that volcanic rage can be contained and changed into creative energy to make armor and works of art.

A spurned and angry Hera woman can choose between being consumed by her rage or containing her hostile impulses and reflecting on her available choices. If she can see that she is becoming crippled and limited by her rage and jealousy, she could channel her anger into work. She might literally follow the example of Hephaestus (whose wife Aphrodite was repeatedly unfaithful to him) and become a craftswoman. She could work with clay, firing what she makes in the kiln, and in the process become changed herself—metaphorically transformed by the fire of her emotions into an artisan rather than being consumed and destroyed. Or she might channel the intensity of her feelings into painting or writing. Work of any kind, mental or manual, can serve as a means of sublimating rage. And sublimation is much more healthy than allowing rage to feed on itself and destroy her.

ASSESSING THE POSSIBILITY OF A RECONCILIATION: REALITY VERSUS MYTH

A Hera woman needs to know that, once a man has left her, she will have difficulty believing the loss. In this type of situation, she has trouble accepting reality and is likely to believe in a mythic ending—that he, like Zeus, will miss her and come back. A Hera woman cannot afford to disregard the evidence, she needs to accept reality instead of deny it. Only when she stops hoping for eventual reconciliation can she mourn, recover, and go on with her life.

Many Hera women hope that a husband who has left for another woman may come back. In one myth about Hera, this reconciliation does occur, but only after she is able to leave Zeus. In the myth, as noted earlier, Zeus then went to her mountain retreat and took part in a wedding ceremony to a statue disguised as a woman. Hera was amused at this scene, and a reconciliation followed.

Several important psychological elements are present here. First of all, to be reconciled Hera let go of more than

Zeus. She also let go of her hopes that he would change, and let go of the role of victimized, vindictive Hera. Zeus, in turn, discovered that Hera was truly important to him and conveyed this message to her. Perhaps only then could Hera be amused—because she finally recognized that no other woman really had mattered to him all along. Each of his affairs (like the statue) had been a symbol to him, rather than an important relationship.

Life sometimes imitates this mythic happy ending, but not usually. A woman may see that separation has not changed her husband's heart, that he hasn't returned but instead is obviously deeply involved with someone else or is relieved to be away from her. Then she needs to heed reality. Only then can she grieve and go on with her life.

RECYCLING ONESELF

The possibility of completing a cycle and beginning anew is inherent in the mythology of Hera. As noted earlier, in the yearly worship cycle the goddess was Hera the Maiden in the spring, Hera the Fulfilled One in the summer and fall, and Hera the Widow each winter. Every spring she was returned to virginity, and the cycle began again. By understanding this archetypal possibility, a Hera woman in a bad marriage can emotionally "widow" herself by leaving a relationship that offers only emptiness, abuse, or infidelity. She can then start anew and this time can choose wisely. In a new marriage, her drive to be a wife can be fulfilled in a positive way.

The cycle may also be lived out as an inner experience if a woman lets go of the need to be a wife or the expectation that she will be fulfilled through the role of wife. A widowed grandmother, for example, dreamed that she had begun menstruating again—ten years after her menopause—and realized that the dream was an accurate symbolic statement. Feeling whole and on the threshhold of a new phase of her life, she was psychologically the Maiden once more.

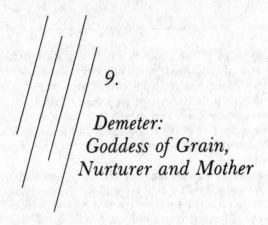

9.

Demeter: Goddess of Grain, Nurturer and Mother

DEMETER THE GODDESS

Demeter, Goddess of Grain, presided over bountiful harvests. The Romans knew her as Ceres—to which our word *cereal* is related. She was described in the Homeric "Hymn to Demeter" as "that awesome goddess, with her beautiful hair . . . and her gold sword"[1] (probably poetic license for a sheaf of ripe wheat, which was her main symbol). She was portrayed as a beautiful woman with golden hair and dressed in a blue robe, or (most commonly in sculpture) as a matronly, seated figure.

Part of Demeter's name, *meter*, seems to mean "mother," but it is not altogether clear what the "de-" or earlier "da-" refers to. She was worshipped as a mother goddess, specifically as mother of the grain, and mother of the maiden Persephone (the Roman Proserpina).

Demeter's life began in the same dismal fashion as Hera's. She was the second child born to Rhea and Cronos, and the second to be swallowed by him. Demeter was the fourth royal consort of Zeus (Jupiter) who was also her brother. She preceded Hera, who was number seven and the last. Out of this union came Zeus and Demeter's only child, their daughter Persephone, with whom Demeter was linked in myth and worship.

The story of Demeter and Persephone—beautifully told in the long Homeric "Hymn to Demeter," centers around

168

Demeter's response to the abduction of Persephone by Demeter's brother Hades, God of the Underworld. This myth became the basis for the Eleusinian Mysteries, the most sacred and important religious rituals of ancient Greece for over two thousand years.[2] This worship was brought to an end in the fifth century A.D., by the destruction of the sanctuary at Eleusus by the invading Goths.

THE ABDUCTION OF PERSEPHONE

Persephone was gathering flowers in a meadow with her companions, and was attracted to an astonishingly beautiful narcissus. As she reached out to pick it, the ground split open before her. From deep within the earth, Hades emerged in his gold chariot pulled by black horses, grabbed her, and plunged back through the abyss just as swiftly as he had come. Persephone struggled and screamed for help from Zeus, but no help came.

Demeter heard the echoes of Persephone's cries and rushed to find her. She searched for nine days and nine nights for her abducted daughter, over the entire land and sea. She did not stop to eat, sleep, or bathe in her frantic search.

(Another myth adds that when Demeter was fruitlessly searching for her abducted daughter, she was seen and desired by Poseidon [Neptune], god of the sea, who pursued her. She tried to avoid him by changing herself into a mare and mingling with a herd of horses. Poseidon, not fooled by this disguise, turned himself into a stallion, found her in the midst of the herd, and raped her.)

At dawn on the tenth day, Demeter met Hecate, Goddess of the Dark Moon and of the Crossroads, who suggested that they go together to Helios, God of the Sun (a nature deity who shared this title with Apollo). Helios told them that Hades had kidnapped Persephone and taken her to the underworld to be his unwilling bride. Furthermore, he said that the abduction and rape of Persephone had been sanctioned by Zeus. He told Demeter to stop weeping and accept what had happened; Hades was after all "not an unworthy son-in-law."

Demeter refused his advice. She now felt outrage and betrayal by Zeus, as well as grief. She withdrew from Mt.

Olympus, disguised herself as an old woman, and wandered unrecognized through the cities and countryside. One day she reached Eleusis, sat down near the well, and was found by the daughters of Celeus, the ruler of Eleusis. Something about her bearing and her beauty drew them to her. When Demeter told them that she was looking for work as a nursemaid, they brought her home to their mother Metanira, for they had a late-born, much-loved baby brother named Demophoön.

Under Demeter's care, Demophoön grew up like a god. She fed him ambrosia and secretly held him in a fire, which would have made him immortal had not Metanira come on the scene and screamed in fear for her son. Demeter reacted with fury, berated Metanira for her stupidity, and revealed her true identity. On saying that she was Demeter, the goddess changed in size and shape and revealed her divine beauty. Her golden hair fell to her shoulders, her fragrance and brightness filled the house with light.

Now Demeter commanded that a temple be built for her. There she installed herself, sat alone with her grief for her abducted daughter, and refused to function. As a consequence, nothing could grow and nothing could be born. Famine threatened to destroy the human race, depriving the Olympian gods and goddesses of their offerings and sacrifices.

Finally, Zeus took notice. First he sent his messenger, Iris, to implore Demeter to come back. Then, since Demeter remained unmoved, every Olympian deity in turn came bearing gifts and honors. To each, the furious Demeter made it known that she would not set foot on Mt. Olympus or allow anything to grow, until Persephone was returned to her.

Finally Zeus responded. He sent Hermes, the Messenger God, to Hades, commanding him to bring Persephone back in order "that her mother on seeing her with her own eyes, would abandon her anger." Hermes went to the underworld and found Hades sitting on a couch next to a depressed Persephone.

On hearing she was free to go, Persephone rejoiced and jumped up with joy to accompany Hermes. But first Hades gave her some sweet pomegranate seeds, which she ate.

Hermes borrowed Hades's chariot to take Persephone home. The horses flew quickly from underworld to upper world, stopping in front of the temple where Demeter waited. When she saw them, Demeter came running, her arms outstretched to embrace her daughter, who herself ran with equal joy into her mother's arms. Then Demeter anxiously inquired whether Persephone had eaten anything in the underworld. If she had not, Persephone would have been completely restored to her. But, because she had eaten the pomegranate seeds, she would spend two-thirds of the year with Demeter and the remainder of the year in the underworld with Hades.

After mother and daughter were reunited, Demeter restored fertility and growth to the earth. She then provided the Eleusinian Mysteries. These were awesome religious ceremonies that initiates were forbidden to reveal. Through the mysteries, people gained a reason to live in joy and die without fearing death.

DEMETER THE ARCHETYPE

Demeter is the maternal archetype. She represents maternal instinct fulfilled through pregnancy or through providing physical, psychological, or spiritual nourishment to others. This powerful archetype can dictate the course a woman's life will take, can have a significant impact on others in her life, and can predispose her to depression if her need to nurture is rejected or thwarted.

THE MOTHER

The mother archetype was represented on Mt. Olympus by Demeter, whose most important roles were as mother (of Persephone) and as provider of food (as Goddess of Grain) and spiritual sustenance (the Eleusinian Mysteries). Although other goddesses were also mothers (Hera and Aphrodite), her daughter was Demeter's most significant relationship. She was also the most nurturing of the goddesses.

A woman with a strong Demeter archetype longs to be a mother. Once she becomes a mother, she finds it a fulfilling role. When Demeter is the strongest archetype in a woman's psyche, being a mother is the most important role and function in her life. The image of mother and child—most often represented in Western art as the Madonna and child—corresponds to an inner picture that deeply moves her.

The mother archetype motivates women to nurture others, to be generous and giving, and to find satisfaction as caretakers and providers. Thus the nurturing aspect of the Demeter archetype can be expressed through the helping professions—teaching, nursing, counseling, in any job in which helping others is part of the role—and in any relationship in which she can be a nurturing person. The archetype is not restricted to being a mother.

MATERNAL INSTINCT

On the biological level, Demeter represents maternal instinct—the desire to become pregnant and have a baby—which some women have yearned to do as long as they can remember.

The Demeter archetype is a compelling force toward getting pregnant. A woman may be quite conscious of how strong the instinct is and may be able to decide when she will fulfill this deep desire. But if unconsciously motivated by Demeter, she may find herself "accidentally" pregnant.

What happens after she discovers an unplanned pregnancy indicates how strong this archetype is in a particular woman. When an abortion is clearly the most sensible or responsible course of action, a non-Demeter woman can arrange to have the abortion and can feel relieved afterward. And from that point on she will take great care never to accidently get pregnant again. In contrast, when Demeter is a strong influence abortion may be in the woman's best interest, but she may find herself unable to have one. Abortion goes against a deep inner imperative in her to have a child. As a consequence, she may have the baby rather than the abortion, thus altering the entire course of her life.

If she does decide to have an abortion, she will feel conflict and turmoil during and after the choice-making process and the procedure. She will feel grief rather than relief, or a mixture of such feelings. Finally, one would think that having gone through so much unhappiness, this type of woman would make sure it would not happen again. But often the opposite is true—she goes through cycles of pregnancy, turmoil, abortion, and depression, because the drive to become pregnant, once thwarted, becomes even stronger.

Demeter's maternal instinct is not restricted to being a biological mother or to nurturing only her own children. Being a foster parent or babysitter allows many women to continue expressing maternal love after their own children have grown or gone. The goddess herself had this role with Demophoön. Emilie Applegate, a San Diego woman who has received recognition as a special foster mother, personifies this aspect of Demeter.[3] She cares for Mexican babies who are so malnourished or ill that their survival is threatened, taking them into her home, where they become part of her own family of three sons and one adopted daughter. She's described as a "Mama Segunda"—a second mother. Applegate—as well as the more celebrated DeBolts, who have adopted handicapped children of many races—have an abundance of maternal instinct and ability to nurture and foster growth that is typically Demeter.

FOOD PROVIDER

Feeding others is another satisfaction for a Demeter woman. She finds nursing her own child tremendously satisfying. It gives her pleasure to provide ample meals for family and guests. If they enjoy her food, she basks in the warmth of feeling like a good mother (rather than—as Athena might— like a gourmet chef). If she works in an office, she enjoys serving others coffee (in marked contrast to an Artemis woman, who feels demeaned and refuses to do so unless the men also take turns).

Demeter, as Goddess of Grain, provided humanity with the ability to cultivate crops and was responsible for the fruitfulness of nature. Similarly, women who move to the country to grow their own food, bake bread, can fruits, and share their bounty with others are expressing the Mother Nature aspect of Demeter.

PERSISTENT MOTHER

Maternal persistence is another Demeter attribute. Such mothers refuse to give up when the welfare of their children is involved. Many special education classes for handicapped children exist because a Demeter mother fought to get what her child needed. And the Argentine mothers of missing sons and daughters who were abducted by the state police were also like Demeter in their persistence. Called the *Madres de la Plaza de Mayo* (The Mothers of the May Plaza), they refused to resign themselves to the loss of their children and continued to protest against the dictatorship, even though it was dangerous to do so. Stubborness, patience, and perseverance are Demeter qualities that—as Zeus ruefully discovered—may eventually influence a powerful man or an institution.

GENEROUS MOTHER

In her mythology, Demeter was the most generous goddess. She gave humanity agriculture and harvests, helped raise Demophoön (and would have made him immortal), and provided the Eleusinian Mysteries. These expressions of bountifulness are all found in Demeter women. Some naturally provide tangible food and physical care, some provide emotional and psychological support, while others give spiritual nourishment. Many famous women religious leaders have had Demeter qualities and been seen by their followers as maternal figures: the saintly recipient of the Nobel Peace Prize, Mother Teresa of Calcutta; Mary Baker Eddy, who founded the Christian Science religion; the woman referred to simply as "The Mother," spiritual leader of the Aurobindo Ashram in India.

These three levels of giving also parallel what Demeter women give their own children. First their children depend on their mothers to take care of their physical needs. Then they turn to their mothers for emotional support and understanding. And, finally, they may look to their mothers for spiritual wisdom as they cope with disappointments and grief or seek to find some meaning in life.

THE GRIEVING MOTHER:
SUSCEPTIBILITY TO DEPRESSION

When the Demeter archetype is a strong force and a woman cannot fulfill it, she may suffer from a characteristic "empty nest and emptiness" depression. A woman who yearns to have a child may be barren, or a child may die or leave home. Or her job as surrogate mother may end, and she may miss her clients or students. Then, rather than rage or actively strike out at those she holds responsible (Hera's way of reacting), the Demeter woman tends to sink into depression. She grieves, her life feels devoid of meaning and empty.

Dr. Pauline Bart, a professor of sociology at the University of Illinois, wrote an article about depressed Demeter women entitled "Mother Portnoy's Complaint."[4] Bart studied the records of over 500 women who were hospitalized for the first time between the ages of forty and fifty-nine. She found that extremely nurturant, overly involved mothers who lost their maternal role were the most depressed.

Prior to their illnesses, these women were "super-mother" types with a history of making sacrifices. Quotes from these depressed women revealed their emotional investment in providing for others and the emptiness they felt when their children left. One woman said, "Naturally as a mother you hate to have your daughter leave home. I mean it was a void there." Another commented, "I was such an energetic woman. I had a big house, and I had my family. My daughter said, 'Mother didn't serve eight courses, she served ten.' " Asked what they were most proud of, all these women replied, "My children." None mentioned any other accomplishment of their own. When they lost their maternal roles, life lost its meaning.

When a woman of late middle age becomes depressed, angry, and disappointed because her adult children are emotionally or physically distant, she becomes a grieving Demeter. She is obsessed by her sense of loss and constricts her interests. Her psychological growth stops. "Possessed" by the grieving aspect of the Demeter archetype, she is practically indistinguishable from other similarly suffering women. Such depressed patients show symptoms that are very much alike: their depressed facial expressions; the way they sit, stand, walk, and sigh; the way they express pain and make others feel defensive, guilty, angry, and helpless.

THE DESTRUCTIVE MOTHER

When grieving Demeter stopped functioning, nothing would grow, and famine threatened to destroy humankind.

Similarly, the destructive aspect of Demeter is expressed by withholding what another person needs (in contrast to Hera and Artemis who are actively destructive in their rage). A gravely depressed, nonfunctioning new mother can be life endangering to her infant: emergency room staff or a pediatrician may diagnose "failure to thrive." The baby has not gained weight, is listless, and may be emaciated in appearance. Failure to thrive results when a mother withholds emotional and physical contact from her infant, as well as needed nutrition.

Mothers who refuse to speak to their young children for days, or even longer periods, or who isolate their small children inflict psychological damage through this form of withholding. Such mothers are themselves usually seriously depressed and hostile.

Much more common than these extreme forms of withholding are Demeter mothers who withhold approval as their children grow more independent of them. While the mother's depression is less evident in these circumstances, withholding approval (which a child needs for self-esteem) is also connected with depression. She experiences her child's growing autonomy as an emotional loss for herself. She feels less needed and rejected, and as a result may be depressed and angry.

CULTIVATING DEMETER

Without realizing it, women are cultivating Demeter and inviting the archetype to become more active when they seriously consider whether to have a child. As they consider the choice, they notice pregnant women (who were seemingly invisible before, and now seem ever present), they notice babies, they seek out people with children, and they pay attention to children themselves. (All of these activities are what Demeter women naturally do.) Women cultivate Demeter by imagining themselves pregnant and having children. As they notice pregnant women, hold babies, and give children their full attention, the archetype may be evoked in them. Efforts to test the strength of the maternal instinct can bring it forth if the archetype is easily evocable, not otherwise.

A woman may seek to shift gears and be more maternal toward a particular child, or she may want to be loved by a particular child. The child pulls for (or constellates) the archetype in the woman. Motivated by her feelings for the child, she will work at being more patient, or be persistent on the child's behalf. As she seems to be more maternal, and works at being so, the archetype of Demeter grows within her.

DEMETER THE WOMAN

A Demeter woman is first and foremost maternal. In her relationships, she is nurturing and supportive, helpful and giving. She is often a Lady Bountiful, providing whatever she sees is needed—chicken soup, a supportive hug, money to tide a friend over, a standing invitation to "come home to Mother."

A Demeter woman often has an aura of the Earth Mother about her. She is solid and dependable. Others describe her as having her "feet on the ground," as she goes about doing what needs to be done with a mixture of practicality and warmth. She is usually generous, outer-directed, altruistic, and loyal to individuals and principles, to the point that others may see her as stubborn. She has strong convictions and is difficult to budge when something or someone important to her is involved.

YOUNG DEMETER

Some little girls are clearly budding Demeters—"little mothers" who cradle baby dolls in their arms. (Little Hera prefers Barbie and Ken dolls, and little Athena may have a collection of historical dolls in a glass case.) Young Demeter also likes to hold real babies; at nine or ten she's eager to babysit for her neighbors.

PARENTS

The relationship that Demeter women have with their parents can be better understood if we first look at the goddess Demeter's relationship with her parents. Demeter the goddess was the daughter of Rhea and the granddaughter of Gaea. Gaea was the primal Earth Mother from whom all life came, including the Sky God, Uranus, who became her husband. Rhea was also known as an Earth goddess, although she is most famous for being the mother of the first-generation Olympians.

As goddess of Grain, Demeter continues the lineage of female goddesses concerned with fertility. She shares other similarities with her mother and grandmother as well. For example, all three suffered when their husbands hurt their children. Gaea's husband buried her children in her body when they were born. Rhea's husband swallowed her newborn children. And Demeter's husband allowed their daughter to be abducted into the underworld. All three biological fathers displayed a lack of paternal feelings.

For three generations, these mother goddesses suffered. Less powerful than their husbands, they were unable to stop their husbands from harming their children. However, they refused to accept the abuse, and they persisted until their children were freed. Unlike Hera, whose primary bond was the wife-husband relationship, the strongest bond of these Earth-Mother goddesses was mother-child.

Real life parallels the Demeter myth when maternal women are married to unpaternal men. In this situation, a Demeter daughter grows up closely identified with her mother and unconnected to her father. The father's attitude toward his children may range from disinterest to competitiveness and resentment or even abusiveness—if he sees them as successful rivals for the affection of his wife. In such a household, a young Demeter's self-esteem suffers, and she develops a victim attitude. Or, a Demeter daughter's maternal qualities may result in her reversing roles with immature or incompetent parents. As soon as she's old enough, she may look after her parents or become a surrogate parent for younger siblings.

In contrast, if a young Demeter has a father who is affectionate and approving of her, she will grow up feeling his support for her wish to be a good parent herself. She will view men positively and will have positive expectations of a husband. An archetypal susceptibility to become victimized will not be enhanced by her childhood experience.

ADOLESCENCE AND EARLY ADULTHOOD

At puberty, a baby of her own becomes a biological possibility as the archetypal maternal drive gets a boost from hormones. Then some Demeter girls start yearning to become pregnant. If other aspects of her life are empty and she is herself little more than a neglected child, a young Demeter who has been coerced into sex and becomes pregnant may welcome the child. One pregnant fourteen-year-old girl at a shelter for unwed mothers said, "When other girls my age wanted bicycles or other things, I always wanted a baby of my own. I'm happy I'm pregnant."

However, most Demeter adolescents do not become pregnant. Lacking Hera's deep wish to be part of a couple or Aphrodite's erotic drives, Demeter is not motivated to have early sexual experience.

Many Demeters marry young. In working-class families, a girl may be encouraged to get married right after high school. This push may fit with a girl's own Demeter proclivities to have a family rather than an education or a job.

If a young Demeter woman does not marry and begin a family, she will go to work or college. In college, she will probably take courses geared toward preparing her to enter a helping profession. A Demeter woman is not typically ambitious, intellectual, or competitive for grades, though she may do well is she's bright and interested in her classes. Status, which Hera women find important, is inconsequential to a Demeter. Her friends are often chosen across a wide social and racial range. She will go out of her way to make an ill-at-ease foreign student feel comfortable, to aid a physically handicapped student, and to help a social misfit.

WORK

The maternal nature of the Demeter woman predisposes her to enter the nurturing or helping professions. She is drawn toward "traditionally feminine" jobs such as teaching, social work, or nursing. Helping people to get well or grow is a satisfaction and an underlying motivation when Demeter is present. Women who become psychotherapists, physical therapists, rehabilitation therapists, or pediatricians are often expressing some Demeter inclinations in their occupational choice. Many women volunteers at nursery schools and elementary schools, at hospitals and nursing homes, also are putting their Demeter tendencies to work.

Some Demeter women become key figures in organizations, which receive their maternal energy. Typically, the Demeter woman in such a situation is personally impressive. She may have envisioned and founded the organization, thrown her considerable energy into it, and been personally responsible for its early success.

Demeter women in leadership and founding mother positions may seek counseling for several reasons: The organization can take so much effort that it leaves her virtually no time or energy for anything else. Personal yearnings for a mate (if Hera is also present) and for a child of her own go unmet. Conflicts arise within her and between her and those she supervises because she is a person with authority who sees herself and is seen by others as a nurturing figure. It is difficult for her to fire or confront an incompetent employee, for example, because she feels sorry for the person and guilty for causing pain. Moreover, employees expect her to look after them personally (an expectation they usually do not have of male supervisors) and are resentful and angry whenever she doesn't.

RELATIONSHIPS WITH WOMEN

Demeter women are not competitive with other women for either men or achievements. Any envy or jealousy of other women will concern children. A Demeter woman without children compares herself unfavorably to women her age who are mothers. If she is infertile, she may feel bitter at the ease with which others get pregnant—especially if they have abortions. Later in life, if her grown children live far away or are emotionally distant, she will envy the mother who has frequent contact with her children. At that stage of life, envy may resurface after twenty-five years, this time over grandchildren.

Demeter women have mixed feelings about feminism and the women's movement. Many Demeter women resent feminists for devaluing the role of motherhood; they want to be full-time mothers and now feel pressured to work outside the home. On the other hand, Demeter women strongly support many women's issues; for example, protecting children against abuse, and providing shelters for battered women.

Usually Demeter women have solid friendships with other Demeter women. Many such friendships date back to when they were new mothers together. Many rely more on their women friends than on their husbands for emotional support, as well as for tangible help. For example, one woman said, "When I was in the hospital, my friend Ruth took the kids in, and had my husband Joe over every night for dinner . . . for two weeks, she fed nine kids, her four and my five, and three adults. . . . I'd have done the same for her." Typically, this woman made arrangements for help rather than expect her husband to take care of the home and children in her absence.

Within families, mothers and daughters who are all Demeter women may remain close for generations. These families have a decided matriarchal cast. And the women in the family know what is going on in the extended family, much more than the husbands do.

This mother-daughter pattern may also be duplicated with peers. She may take the Demeter maternal role with a Persephone-like friend who is inexperienced and indecisive. Or, if both are Demeter women who also share Persephone qualities, they may take turns mothering each other, and at other times can both be Demeters, sharing details of their lives and talking about their joys and difficulties. Or, yet again, they may both be playful, giggling Persephones.

Lesbian couples sometimes fit a Demeter-Persephone pattern, in which a Demeter woman's well-being depends on the intactness of a relationship with a younger or less mature lover. As long as they are together, the Demeter woman feels productive and fertile. Her work and her creativity thrive as a result of being with a woman who is like a goddess to her. She may be possessive of her Persephone if she fears that she may lose her. And she may foster dependence and exclusiveness, which eventually harms the relationship.

However, a Persephone woman is a young, undifferentiated personality. Everything about her is unformed and indistinct. She is a receptive, feminine woman whose sexual preference may be as malleable as the rest of her. Even though she may be in a lesbian relationship, for example, she may also be attracted to a man. If a Persephone woman leaves her Demeter lover when her heterosexuality emerges in response to a man's attentions, the Demeter woman feels as if the myth itself has been reenacted. Unexpectedly, her Persephone has been "abducted by Hades," which is a devastating loss.

RELATIONSHIPS WITH MEN

A Demeter woman attracts men who feel an affinity for maternal women. A true-to-type Demeter woman does not do the choosing. She responds to a man's need for her and may even be with a man because she feels sorry for him. Demeter women don't have high expectations of men. More often they feel that "men are just little boys."

A common type of couple where the woman is Demeter fits the pattern of Great Mother mated to a son-lover. This archetypal mother-son relationship does not refer to a difference in chronological years, although the man may be younger. Usually he is a talented, sensitive man who feels unappreciated or misunderstood by others who do not value his specialness (as she does) and who won't overlook his irresponsibility (as she does). He is an immature, self-absorbed boy with a sense of specialness, more than he is a man. She agrees with his self-assessment and repeatedly overlooks behavior toward her that others consider selfish and thoughtless.

As far as she is concerned, the world is unkind to him. It should make exceptions for him, as she does. His thoughtlessness often hurts and angers her—but if he then tells her how much he appreciates her, or how she's the only person in his life that really cares about him, all is again forgiven.

Like a mother of a handsome son, who wonders how she could have given birth to such a young god, the Demeter woman playing Great Mother to his son-lover role may also be in awe of his appearance (or his talent). She may say, as one Demeter woman said to me, "He looked to me like Michelangelo's statue of David. I was happy taking care of him. I spoiled him rotten." She said this with pride rather than bitterness.

A Demeter woman's maternal qualities and her difficulties in saying no make her vulnerable to being used by a sociopath, another type of man often found in relationships with Demeter women. The Demeter-sociopath relationship may superficially resemble a Great Mother–son-lover relationship—

and there is some overlap—but the son-lover has the ability to love, be loyal, or be remorseful. The sociopath lacks these capacities, which makes a crucial difference. The sociopath acts on the assumption that his needs entitle him to receive. He is incapable of emotional intimacy or appreciation. His attitude suggests the question "What have you done for me lately?" He forgets past generosity or sacrifices on the part of the Demeter woman, as well as his past exploitative behavior. He magnifies his needs—and that neediness invites a generous Demeter response. A relationship with a sociopath may tie up a Demeter woman's emotional life for years and may drain her financially.

Another typical Demeter mate is the man who wants "a girl just like the girl who married dear old Dad." As Little Oedipus, he may have just been biding his time—he was the little boy of four or five who wanted to marry his Mommy. Now he is a grown man who seeks a maternal woman who will be a good mother to him. He wants her to be nurturing, warm, responsive, and caretaking; to look after his meals, buy and take care of his clothes, make sure he goes to the doctor and dentist when he needs to, and arrange his social life.

Of all the men who are attracted to Demeter qualities, the "family man" is the only one who is himself mature and generous. This man is strongly motivated by his wish to have a family, and he sees in the Demeter woman a partner who shares the dream. Besides being "a good daddy" for their children, this type of man also looks out for her. If she has trouble saying no to people who would take advantage of her Demeter good nature, he can help her look out for herself.

The family man also helps her fulfill herself through bearing children. The other three types are threatened by the idea of children and may insist on an abortion if she gets pregnant. This insistence will put her into a maternal crisis: either reject the man she mothers, or reject motherhood. The choice makes her feel like a mother given the impossible choice of sacrificing one of two children.

SEXUALITY

When Demeter is the strongest goddess element in a woman's personality, her sexuality is usually not very important. Demeter does not usually have a strong sexual drive. She is often a warm, affectionate, feminine person who would just as soon cuddle as make love—a "huggy" woman rather than a sexy woman. Many Demeter women have a puritanical attitude toward sex. For them, sex is for procreation, not for pleasure. Some Demeter women think of sex as what a wife provides in the context of giving or nurturing—she is providing what her husband needs. And many Demeter women keep a "guilty" secret to themselves—for them, the most sensual physical act is breastfeeding their infants, not making love to their husbands.

MARRIAGE

For a Demeter woman, marriage in itself is not an overriding priority, as it is for a Hera woman. Most Demeter women want to get married mainly in order to have children. Unless she has Aphrodite or Hera as active archetypes, the Demeter woman views marriage as a simply necessary step that paves the way for children and the best situation in which to have children.

CHILDREN

A Demeter woman feels a deep need to be a biological mother. She wants to give birth and nurse her own child. She also may be a loving foster mother, adoptive mother, or stepmother, but if she cannot also have child of her own, a deep longing will go unmet and she will feel barren. (In contrast, many Artemis or Athena women would just as soon inherit a ready-made family, by marrying a man with children.)

Demeter women uniformly perceive themselves as good mothers who have the best interests of their children in mind. From the standpoint of their impact on their children, however, Demeter women seem to be either superbly able mothers or terrible, all-consuming mothers.

When her adult children resent her, a Demeter woman is deeply wounded and confused. She cannot understand why her children treat her so badly, while other mothers have children who love and appreciate them. She also cannot see that she may have contributed to her children's difficulties. She is conscious only of her positive intentions, not of the negative elements that poisoned the relationship with her children.

Whether or not a Demeter mother has had a positive effect on her children and is positively regarded by them depends on whether she was like the goddess Demeter "before the abduction" or "after the abduction." Before the abduction of Persephone, Demeter trusted that all was well (as Persephone played in the meadow) and went about her activities. After the abduction, Demeter was depressed and angry; she left Mt. Olympus and ceased to function.

The "before" phase takes many forms in real life. For the woman who faces an empty nest when her last child leaves home and then feels as if her sense of meaning has been "abducted," the before phase was the close and caring family life that lasted for some twenty-five years. For the woman whose daughter defies her to live with a man the mother considers an abducting Hades, the before phase was when her daughter seemed an extension of herself who shared the same values and hopes for the future.

Some Demeter mothers always fear that something bad may happen to their child. These mothers may act as if they anticipate the possibility of "an abduction" from the time a child is born. They consequently limit the child's independence and discourage the formation of relationships with others. At the heart of the anxiety that motivates them to act this way is a feared loss of the child's affection.

Circumstances may also be responsible for activating the negative side of Demeter. One woman recalled that for six years after her daughter was born she existed as though in a state of grace. The world was safe, motherhood was fulfilling and fun. Then an event occurred that was as distressing and sudden as Hades emerging from a vent in the earth. One afternoon the mother left her daughter in the care of a sitter. The daughter wandered off to a neighbor's house and was sexually molested. Afterward, the child became fearful and anxious, had nightmares, and was apprehensive around men—even her father.

The mother raged, grieved, and felt guilty because she had not been there to prevent the incident. Before, she had been generous, trusting, and somewhat casual in her mothering style. Afterward, she felt guilty and responsible, unsure of herself, and anxious that something bad could happen again. She became overcontrolling and overprotective. Gone was her fun and spontaneity, her sense of living in a safe world, her feeling of self-confidence.

A Demeter mother may feel guilty for any event that has an adverse effect on her child. Until she has some insight into her unrealistic expectations that she should be the perfect mother, she expects herself to be all-knowing and all-powerful, capable of foreseeing events and protecting her child from all pain.

With the intention of protecting her child, a Demeter woman may become overcontrolling. She hovers over every move, intercedes on the child's behalf, and takes over when there is any possibility of harm. Consequently, the child stays dependent on her to deal with people and problems.

The children of a controlling Demeter mother sometimes stay forever close to her, the psychological umbilical cord still quite intact. Dominated by her personality, they remain Mother's little girls or Mama's boys well into adulthood. Some such children may never marry. When they do, they often maintain stronger filial bonds than conjugal ones. For example, a Demeter's son may be at his mother's beck and call, to the dismay of his wife, whose wishes always take a backseat. Or a Demeter's daughter may never agree to go on a long vacation with her husband, because she cannot leave her mother for that length of time.

In an effort to lead their own lives, some children of an overcontrolling Demeter mother may break away and stay away, creating both a geographical and an emotional distance between them. Often they do so when a mother has unconsciously tried to make them feel beholden, guilty, or dependent.

Another negative mother model for Demeter women is the mother who can't say no to her children. She sees herself as the selfless, bountiful, providing mother, who gives and gives. Beginning when they are young, this Demeter mother wants her children to have whatever they want. If it's much more expensive than she can afford, she either will make sacrifices to get it or will feel guilty. Moreover, she fails to set limits on behavior. From toddlerhood on, she gives in to her children's demands, nourishing their selfishness. As a consequence, her children grow up feeling entitled to special consideration and ill-prepared to conform. Their behavior problems arise in school; their conflicts with authority disrupt employment. In her attempts to be an all-providing "good mother," such a mother can become the opposite.

MIDDLE YEARS

The midlife period is an important time for Demeter women. If a woman has not had a child, she is preoccupied with the awareness that the biological clock is running out on the possibility of becoming pregnant. Married Demeter women raise the baby issue with reluctant spouses, and they visit fertility specialists if there are problems with conception or miscarriages. Adoption may be considered. And unmarried women contemplate becoming single mothers.

Even if a Demeter woman has children, her midlife years are no less crucial, though she may be unaware of their importance in shaping the rest of her life. Her children are growing, and each step they take toward independence tests her ability to let go of their dependence on her. She, too, may now feel the pull to have a late-life baby. One woman came to see me in the middle of a midlife crisis: Her children were in school and now, at age forty, it was time for her to go back to school herself if she were to grow beyond Demeter. She discovered that she was afraid that she would fail at graduate school, and that another child was the only excuse she herself would accept for not enrolling. She could then separate the desire to have another baby from the fear that she would fail as a student and could focus on exploring this concern. As it turned out, she did go to graduate school, studied a subject she loved, and now is an inspired teacher.

In her middle years, a founding mother of an organization may face a crisis when it gets large enough for others to covet her position and power. Unless she also has Athena's strategist mind and can play politics well, ambitious managers may "abduct" the organization she gave birth to and reared through its early years. The loss will plunge her into being an angry, grieving Demeter.

Even if there are no power struggles or she survives this crisis, personal issues now arise for her—and for all Demeter women who have put their maternal energy into their work. Now it is time to consider what is missing in her life, and what she might do to fulfill herself.

LATER YEARS

In their later years, Demeter women often fall into two categories. Many find this phase of life very rewarding. They are active, busy women—as they always were—who have learned from life and who are appreciated by others for their down-to-earth wisdom and generosity. They are Demeter women who have learned not to tie people to them or to allow them to take advantage. Instead, these woman have fostered independence and mutual respect. Children, grandchildren, clients, students, or patients who span generations may love and respect her. She is like the goddess Demeter at the end of her myth, who gave humankind her gifts and was greatly honored.

The opposite fate befalls a Demeter woman who considers herself a victim. The source of her unhappiness usually stems from the disappointments and unfulfilled expectations of midlife. Now, identified with the mourning, betrayed, angry Demeter who sat in her temple and allowed nothing to grow, such a woman does nothing with her later years but grow older and more bitter.

PSYCHOLOGICAL DIFFICULTIES

The goddess Demeter was a major presence. When she stopped functioning, life ceased to grow and all the Olympians trooped down to plead with her to restore fertility. Yet she could not prevent the abduction of Persephone or force her immediate return, she was victimized, her pleas were ignored, and she suffered depression. The difficulties faced by Demeter women have similar themes: victimization, power and control, expression of anger, and depression.

IDENTIFYING WITH DEMETER

A woman who identifies with Demeter acts like a bountiful, maternal goddess with an unlimited capacity to provide. She can't say no if someone needs her attention or help. This Demeter trait makes a woman stay on the phone longer than she wants to with a depressed friend, or agree to be the homeroom mother when she'd rather not, or give up her one free afternoon to help someone instead of reserving this time for herself. And Demeter is present in the therapist who gives her anxious client the extra hour that was her only break in the day's heavy schedule, whose evenings are invariably interrupted by lengthy phone calls, and whose sliding-scale fees are always at the lower end of the scale. This instinct to nurture can eventually deplete a woman in a helping profession and can lead to "burnout" symptoms of fatigue and apathy.

When a woman instinctively says yes to everyone who needs something from her, she will rapidly find herself overcommitted. She is not an unlimited natural resource, even if other people and the Demeter within her expect her to be so. A Demeter woman must confront the goddess time and time again, if she is to take charge of her own life. Instead of an instinctive yes, which is Demeter's response, she must be able to choose when and how and to whom she will give. To do so, she must learn to say no—both to a person who needs something from her and to the goddess within.

MATERNAL INSTINCT

If this archetype has its way, a Demeter woman may also not be able to say no to getting pregnant. Because maternity is an inner imperative for her, a Demeter woman may unconsciously collude with the Demeter archetype, may "forget" when she is fertile, or may "be careless" about birth control. Thus she may find herself pregnant when circumstances are far from ideal.

A Demeter woman must be able to choose when and with whom she will have a baby. She needs to recognize that the Demeter within her has no interest in the realities of her life and no concern for timing. If pregnancy is to happen at the right time in her life, she must resist Demeter by being vigilant about birth control.

Fatigue, headaches, menstrual cramps, ulcer symptoms, high blood pressure, and back pains are common in Demeter women who have trouble saying no or expressing anger when they are overworked and overloaded with too many responsibilities or children. The message indirectly conveyed through these symptoms is "I am worn out, pressured, and in pain—don't ask me to do any more!" They are also expressions of low-grade, chronic depression, which results when a woman cannot protest effectively, represses her anger, and resents a situation of Demeter's making.

FOSTERING DEPENDENCY

A Demeter woman's superabundant capacity for mothering can be flawed by her need for her child to need her and by her anxiety when her child is "out of her sight." She will foster dependency and keep her child "tied to her apron strings." She may also do so in other relationships. For example, she may mother "the dependent child" as she mothers "the poor little boy" in her lover and takes care of "the anxious child" in her friend.

Such a woman infantilizes others by her attempts to be indispensable ("Mother knows best") or overcontrolling ("Let me do it for you"). This tendency fosters feelings of insecurity and inadequacy in the other person. In the kitchen, for example, she may encourage her young daughter to learn to cook. But she supervises closely and then always adds the final touches at the end. Whatever the daughter does, the mother gives her message that "It's not good enough" and "You need me to do it right." In a work situation, it is the same. She is the supervisor, editor, or mentor that "knows best" how the work should be done and thus may take it over, which stifles originality and self-confidence in her "child" and increases her own workload.

If people in her life need her, an anxious Demeter woman feels secure. If they grow in independence and competence, she may be threatened. To stay in her good graces, and to be the recipient of her care and concern, often requires staying in a dependent role.

Whether a Demeter woman fosters dependency or, on the contrary, creates a sense of security in which the other person can grow and thrive, depends on whether she herself has a sense of bountifulness or scarcity. If she is afraid that she will lose the other person or that her "child" is "not good enough," she may become possessive, controlling, and constricting. This insecurity makes her into a hovering or a smothering mother.

One young mother in my practice realized, while her child was still an infant, that she was the type who was going to find it hard to let her daughter grow up. The first struggle came when it was time to introduce baby food. She had been breastfeeding, enjoying the exclusiveness of the relationship and the dependency of her infant. As the time came to introduce solids, her husband looked forward to spoonfeeding their daughter, which would be a major new step in the father-daughter bonding. Luckily, the altruistic mother in her knew it was time to start solids and share the child more with her husband, although the possessive mother in her wanted to resist as long as possible. Her wish to do what was best for the child won out. Even so, she did transiently feel like mourning Demeter, grieving over the loss.

Possessive Demeter women grow as they let go of their need to keep other people dependent and tied to their apron strings. In doing this, mutual dependency can get transmuted into mutual appreciation and love.

PASSIVE-AGGRESSIVE BEHAVIOR

A Demeter woman who can't say no will get overburdened. She may then become depleted and apathetic, or resentful and angry. If she feels exploited, she typically doesn't express it directly, showing the same lack of assertiveness on her own behalf that had her say yes when she should have said no. Instead of expressing her anger or insisting that something change, a Demeter woman is likely to discount her feelings as ungenerous and to work harder at getting everything done.

When she tries to suppress her true feelings and they leak out anyway, she begins to show passive-aggressive behavior. She then forgets to "go a little out of her way" and doesn't shop for the item her next-door neighbor asked her to pick up; she misses the deadline or is late for an important meeting. In this way she drops the burdens she was expected to carry, unconsciously acts out her hostility with noncompliant behavior, and indirectly expresses her resentment and asserts her independence. It would be far better if she could learn to say no in the first place, because passive-aggressive behavior makes her appear incompetent and feel guilty.

Purposefulness makes the same action significantly different. To straightforwardly refuse to do what someone else expects you to do, and state why, is a clear message; a passive-aggressive action is a muddled message encoded in a hostile act. If the other person cares about your needs, the clear statement is enough. Backing up the statement with action is often required when the other person is exploitive and expects to get his or her way at your expense. Zeus did not heed Demeter until she "went on strike."

Until Demeter refused to function as Goddess of Grain, Zeus did not pay any attention to her suffering. When her refusal to let anything grow threatened the earth with famine, he became concerned because there would be no mortals to honor the gods if she persisted. Only then did he heed her, and send Hermes to bring Persephone back from the underworld. Once a Demeter woman becomes aware of her needs (which she herself suppresses) and of her anger at having those needs discounted by others, she can consider following Demeter's example. An underpaid and overworked essential employee can state her case for a deserved raise and additional help, for example, and not be heard until she makes it clear to her boss that she will not continue as she has been doing.

DEPRESSION: EMPTY NEST AND EMPTINESS

When a Demeter woman loses a relationship in which she has been the maternal figure, she not only loses that relationship and misses the person, but she also loses her mother role, which gave her a sense of power, importance, and meaning. She is left with an empty nest and a feeling of emptiness.

The term "empty-nest depression" describes the reaction of women who have devoted their lives to their children only to have them move away. Demeter women in love relationships that end may also react thus, as well as a Demeter woman who has "mothered" a project for years, only to have it fail or be taken over by others. Such organizational difficulties leave her feeling "ripped off" and barren.

When the archetype is at its most extreme, a depressed Demeter woman becomes unable to function and needs psychiatric hospitalization. She may become a personification of the grieving goddess who searched fruitlessly over the earth for Persephone. Like Demeter, she may not eat, sleep, or bathe. She may pace back and forth, restlessly moving all the time, wringing her hands and grieving, deep in a severe agitated depression. Or she may sit, like Demeter at Eleusis, withdrawn, unmoving, and unresponsive. Everything looks bleak and barren to her, the world is devoid of meaning. She feels no green and growing quality in her arid life. This reaction is a severe apathetic depression. In both reactions, agitated and apathetic, hostility underlies her depression: she is angry that a source of meaning has been taken away.

When a grieving Demeter is hospitalized, of course, she needs professional help. But had she known that she was so susceptible to an empty-nest depression, and had she taken four preventive mental health measures, her reaction would have been much less severe. Learning how to express anger instead of bottling it up inside reduces depression. Learning to say no helps avoid getting depleted and depressed from being overextended and feeling unappreciated and martyred. Learning to "let go and let grow," spares her the wrenching pain of having children (or her supervisees, staff, or clients) resent her and need to break away. Developing other goddesses within herself provides her with additional interests besides mothering.

WAYS TO GROW

Demeter women find it easy to recognize the maternal pattern they embody, including the difficulty of saying no. However, there's too often a blind spot when it comes to looking at their negative feelings and negative behavior toward others. Since these feelings and actions are what most need to be changed, a Demeter woman's growth is thwarted until she can see the whole picture. Demeter women have good intentions—which, coupled with the need to see themselves as good mothers, block their receptiveness to these insights. Such women are often very defensive. They counter criticism with statements about their good intent ("I was only trying to help") or with a list of the many positive and generous actions that they, in fact, do.

Just as the Demeter woman has difficulty saying no because she identifies with the good and giving mother, so she also resists acknowledging her anger at those she loves. For the same reasons, she denies the possibility that she may be engaging in passive-aggressive behavior and that she may be overcontrolling or fostering dependency. However, she does know that she is disappointed at not being appreciated, and she can admit to feeling depressed. If she is willing to explore these avenues, then she may gradually allow knowledge of her negative Demeter traits to become conscious. Acknowledging them is the biggest obstacle. Changing her behavior is the easier task.

BECOMING HER OWN GOOD MOTHER

A Demeter woman needs to "employ" Demeter on her own behalf instead of instinctively responding to others as if she herself were Demeter. When she's asked to take on another responsibility, she needs to learn to focus on herself the caretaking concern she so readily feels for others. She can ask herself, "Is this something you really want to do now?" and "Do you have enough time and energy?" When she has been treated badly, she needs to reassure herself that "You deserve better treatment" and encourage herself to "Go tell them" of her needs.

EXPANDING BEYOND DEMETER

Unless a Demeter woman consciously makes room in her life for other-than-Demeter relationships, she may stay locked in one pattern, being "just Demeter." If she is a married woman with children, will she make the effort to get away with her husband without the children? Will she put time aside for a solitary activity and take the time to jog, meditate, paint, or play a musical instrument? Or, as is typical of Demeter, will she never find any time? If she is a professional Demeter woman, all her energy may go into her work. She may head a nursery school or a professional program and devote all her time and energy to it, coming home depleted at the end of every day. A professional Demeter needs to resist being "just Demeter" every bit as much as does the Demeter woman with five children. If she does not expand beyond Demeter, she increases the likelihood of an empty-nest depression when she is no longer needed and finds that she is dispensable after all.

RECOVERING FROM DEPRESSION

A Demeter woman who becomes a grieving, depressed Demeter has suffered a significant loss. The loss can be anything of great emotional value to her—a relationship, a role, a job, an ideal—whatever gave her life meaning that is now gone. And, as with each of the goddess mythologies, it is possible for a woman to get "stuck" in any phase or to move through a myth pattern and grow. Some depressed Demeter women never recover; their existence remains empty, bitter, and barren.

But recovery and growth are possible. The myth itself presents two solutions. First, after she knew that Persephone had been abducted, Demeter left Mt. Olympus to wander on earth. At Eleusis, the depressed and grieving goddess was welcomed into a household, where she became the nursemaid of Demophoön. She fed him nectar and ambrosia, and would have made him into an immortal had his mother Metanira not interrupted. Thus she coped with her loss by loving and caring for someone else. Risking another relationship is one way for a grieving Demeter woman to recover and function again.

Second, reunion with Persephone led to Demeter's recovery. The grieving mother was reunited with her eternally maiden daughter and ceased being depressed, functioned again as grain and fruit goddess, and restored fertility and growth to the earth.

Metaphorically, this is what ends a depression: the archetype of youth returns. How it happens often seems mysterious. It follows weeping and rage. Time passes. Then a budding feeling stirs. Perhaps the woman notices what a beautiful blue the sky is. Or she is touched by someone's compassion. Or she has an urge to complete a long-abandoned task. Emotionally, these are small signs of spring. Shortly after the first signs of returning life, the woman is herself again, once more full of vitality and generosity, reunited with that part of herself that has been missing.

More than simple recovery is possible. The Demeter woman can also emerge from a period of suffering with greater wisdom and spiritual understanding. As an inner experience, the myth of Demeter and Persephone speaks of a capacity to grow through suffering. A Demeter woman may then, like Demeter herself, come to accept the existence of human seasonal changes. She may acquire an earth wisdom that mirrors nature. Such a woman learns that she can live through whatever happens, knowing that just as spring follows winter, so changing human experience follows certain patterns.

10.

Persephone:
The Maiden and
Queen of the Underworld,
Receptive Woman and
Mother's Daughter

PERSEPHONE THE GODDESS

The goddess Persephone, whom the Romans called Proserpina or Cora, is best known through the Homeric "Hymn
to Demeter," which describes her abduction by Hades. She
was worshipped in two ways, as the Maiden or the Kore (which
means "young girl"), and as Queen of the Underworld. The
Kore was a slender, beautiful young goddess, associated with
symbols of fertility—the pomegranate, grain, and corn, as
well as the narcissus, the flower that lured her. As Queen of
the Underworld, Persephone is a mature goddess, who reigns
over the dead souls, guides the living who visit the underworld, and claims for herself what she wants.

Although Persephone was not one of the twelve Olympians, she was the central figure in the Eleusinian Mysteries,
which for two thousands years prior to Christianity was the
major religion of the Greeks. In the Eleusinian Mysteries, the
Greeks experienced the return or renewal of life after death
through Persephone's annual return from the underworld.

GENEALOGY AND MYTHOLOGY

Persephone was the only daughter of Demeter and Zeus.
Greek mythology is unusually silent about the circumstances
of her conception.

In the beginning of the Demeter-Persephone myth (told in detail in the previous chapter), Persephone was a carefree girl who gathered flowers and played with her friends. Then Hades in his chariot suddenly appeared out of a vent in the earth, took the screaming maiden by force and carried her back to the underworld to be his unwilling bride. Demeter did not accept the situation, left Mt. Olympus, persisted in seeking Persephone's return, and finally forced Zeus to heed her wishes.

Zeus then dispatched Hermes, the Messenger God, to fetch Persephone. Hermes arrived in the underworld and found a disconsolate Persephone. But her despair turned to joy when she found that Hermes had come for her and Hades would let her go. Before she left him, however, Hades gave her some pomegranate seeds, which she ate. Then she got into the chariot with Hermes, who took her swiftly to Demeter.

After the reunited mother and daughter had joyfully embraced, Demeter anxiously inquired if she had eaten anything in the underworld. Persephone replied that she had eaten pomegranate seeds—because Hades had forced her "unwillingly, violently" to eat them (which was not true). Demeter accepted the story and the cyclic pattern that followed. Had Persephone not eaten anything, she would have been fully restored to Demeter. Having eaten the pomegranate seeds, however, she would now spend one-third of the year in the underworld with Hades, and two-thirds of the year in the upper world, with Demeter.

Later, Persephone became Queen of the Underworld. Whenever the heroes or heroines of Greek mythology descended to the lower realm, Persephone was there to receive them and be their guide. (None found her absent. There was never a sign on the door saying, "Gone Home to Mother," although the Persephone-Demeter myth says she did so two-thirds of the year.)

In the *Odyssey*, the hero Odysseus (Ulysses) journeyed to the underworld, where Persephone showed him the souls of women of legendary fame. In the myth of Psyche and Eros, Psyche's last task was to descend into the underworld with a box for Persephone to fill with beauty ointment for Aphrodite. The last of the Twelve Tasks of Heracles (Hercules) also brought him to Persephone: Heracles had to get her permission to borrow Cerberus, the ferocious three-headed guard dog, which he subdued and put on a leash.

Persephone contended against Aphrodite for the possession of Adonis, the beautiful youth who was loved by both goddesses. Aphrodite had concealed Adonis in a chest and sent him to Persephone for safekeeping. But on opening the chest, the Queen of the Underworld was herself charmed by his beauty, and refused to give him back. Persephone now struggled with another powerful deity for possession of Adonis, as Demeter and Hades once did over her. The dispute was brought before Zeus, who decided that Adonis should spend one-third of the year with Persephone and one-third of the year with Aphrodite, and should be left to himself for the remaining time.

PERSEPHONE THE ARCHETYPE

Unlike Hera and Demeter, who represent archetypal patterns that are linked to strong instinctual feelings, Persephone as a personality pattern does not feel that compelling. If Persephone provides the structure of the personality, it predisposes a woman not to act but to be acted on by others—to be compliant in action and passive in attitude. Persephone the Maiden also allows a woman to seem eternally youthful.

The goddess Persephone had two aspects, as the Kore and as Queen of the Underworld. This duality is also present as two archetypal patterns. Women can be influenced by one of the two aspects, can grow through one to the other, or can have both Kore and Queen present in their psyches.

THE KORE—THE ARCHETYPAL MAIDEN

The Kore was the "nameless maiden"; she represents the young girl who does not know "who she is" and is as yet unaware of her desires or strengths. Most young women go through a phase of being "the Kore" before they marry or decide on a career. Other women remain the maiden for most of their lives. They are uncommitted to a relationship, to work, or to an educational goal—even though they may, in fact, be in a relationship, have a job, or be in college or even graduate school. Whatever they are doing, it doesn't seem "for real." Their attitude is that of the eternal adolescent, indecisive about who or what they want to be when they "grow up," waiting for something or someone to transform their lives.

MOTHER'S DAUGHTER

Persephone and Demeter represent a common mother-daughter pattern, in which a daughter is too close to a mother to develop an independent sense of herself. The motto for this relationship is "Mother knows best."

The Persephone daughter wants to please her mother. This desire motivates her to be "a good girl"—obedient, compliant, cautious, and often sheltered or "protected" from experience that carries even the hint of risk. This pattern is echoed in the Mother Goose rhyme:

"Mother, may I go out to swim?"
"Yes, my darling daughter.
"Hang your clothes on a hickory limb,
"but don't go near the water."

Although the mother appears to be strong and independent, this appearance is often deceptive. She may foster her daughter's dependence in order to keep her close. Or she may need her daughter to be an extension of herself, through whom she can live vicariously. A classic example of this relationship is the stage-manager mother and actress daughter.

Sometimes the father is the dominating and intrusive parent who fosters the dependent daughter. His overcontrolling attitude may also be deceptive, covering a too-close emotional attachment to his daughter.

In addition to family dynamics, the culture we live in also conditions girls to equate femininity with passive, dependent behavior. They are encouraged to act like Cinderellas waiting for a prince to come, Sleeping Beauties waiting to be awakened. Passivity and dependency are the core ("Kore") problems for many women because the environment reinforces the archetype and thus other aspects of the personality do not develop.

"ANIMA WOMAN"

M. Esther Harding, a distinguished Jungian analyst, began her book *The Way of All Women* by describing the type of woman who is "all things to all men." This type is the "anima woman" who "adapts herself to his wishes, makes herself beautiful in his eyes, charms him, pleases him." She is "not sufficiently aware of herself to be able to give a picture of what her subjective life is like." She is "generally unself-conscious; she doesn't analyze herself or her motives; she just is; and for the most part she is inarticulate."[1]

Harding described the ease with which an "anima woman" receives the projection of a man's unconscious image of woman (this anima) and unconsciously conforms to the image. Harding describes her thus: "She is like a many-sided crystal which turns automatically without any volition on her part . . . by this adaptation, first one facet and then another is presented to view and always that facet which best reflects his anima is presented to the gazer."[2]

A Persephone woman's innate receptivity makes her very malleable. If significant people project an image or expectation onto her, she initially does not resist. It is her pattern to be chameleonlike, to "try on" whatever others expect of her. It is this quality that predisposes her to be an "anima woman"; she unconsciously conforms to what a man wants her to be. With one man, she's a tennis buff who fits into the country club set; in the next relationship, she's on the back of his motorcycle as they roar down the highway; she's a model for the third, who paints her as an innocent ingenue—which she is, to him.

CHILD-WOMAN

Prior to her abduction, Persephone was a child-woman, unaware of her sexual attractiveness and her beauty. This archetypal combination of sexuality and innocence permeates the United States' culture, where the woman who is considered desirable is a sex kitten, a woman with a girl-next-door look posing nude for *Playboy* Magazine. In the film *Pretty Baby*, for example, Brooke Shields played the archetypal child-woman—a virginal, desirable, twelve-year-old girl in a brothel, whose virginity was sold to the highest bidder. This image was continued in her next films, *Blue Lagoon* and *Endless Love,* and in her advertisements for Calvin Klein jeans. At the same time, the media described her as a sheltered and obedient Persephone-type daughter of a mother who firmly managed her career and her life.

A Persephone woman does not need to be young in age or to be sexually inexperienced to lack a sense of herself as a sensual or sexual woman. As long as she is psychologically the Kore, her sexuality is unawakened. Although she likes men to like her, she lacks passion and is probably nonorgasmic.

In Japan, even more than the United States, the ideal woman resembles Persephone. She is quiet, demure, compliant—she learns that she must never say no directly: she is brought up to avoid disturbing the harmony by disagreeing or being disagreeable. The ideal Japanese woman graciously remains present but in the background, anticipates the needs of men, and outwardly accepts her fate.

GUIDE TO THE UNDERWORLD

Although Persephone's first experience with the underworld was as a kidnap victim, she later became Queen of the Underworld, the guide for others who visited there. This aspect of the Persephone archetype develops, as in the myth, as a result of experience and growth.

Symbolically, the underworld can represent deeper layers of the psyche, a place where memories and feelings have been "buried" (the personal unconscious) and where images, patterns, instincts, and feelings that are archetypal and shared by humanity are found (the collective unconscious). When these areas are explored in analysis, underground images are produced in dreams. The dreamer may be in a basement, often with many corridors and rooms that are sometimes like labyrinths. Or she may find herself in an underground world or a deep cave, where she encounters people, objects, or animals and is awed, afraid, or interested—depending on whether or not she fears this realm in herself.

Persephone the Queen and Guide of the Underworld represents the ability to move back and forth between the ego-based reality of the "real" world and the unconscious or archetypal reality of the psyche. When the Persephone archetype is active, it is possible for a woman to mediate between the two levels and to integrate both into her personality. She may also serve as guide for others who "visit" the underworld in their dreams and fantasies, or may help those who are "abducted" and who lose touch with reality.

In *I Never Promised You a Rose Garden*, Hannah Green wrote her autobiographical story of the illness, hospitalization, and recovery of a sixteen-year-old schizophrenic girl who retreated from reality into the bondage of an imaginary kingdom. Green had to vividly recall her experience in order to write of it. Initially, "the Kingdom of Yr" was her refuge, a fantasy world that had its own "secret calendar," its own language and characters. But eventually this "underground" world took on a terrifying reality. She became a prisoner in it and could not leave; "she could not see except in outlines, gray against gray, and with no depth, flatly, like a picture."[5] This girl was an abducted Persephone.

Ex-psychiatric patients, like Persephone, can help guide others through the underworld. Hannah Green's *I Never Promised You a Rose Garden*, Sylvia Plath's novel *The Bell Jar* and her poetry, and Doree Previn's songs have served as guides for others who were pulled into their depths and needed help making sense of the experience. These women were hospitalized psychiatric patients who recovered and wrote of their "abductions" into the world of depression and madness. I also know several superb therapists who as young women were hospitalized for psychiatric illnesses. They were, for a time, "held captive" by elements in the unconscious, and were out of touch with ordinary reality. Because of their firsthand experience of the depths, and their recovery, they now are especially helpful to others. Such people know their way around in the underworld.

Finally, some people know Persephone the Guide without the experience of being captive Kore. This is true for many therapists who work with dreams and images that arise in the imagination of their patients. They have a receptivity to the unconscious without having been held captive there. They intuitively know and are familiar with the underworld realm.

Persephone the Guide is part of that person's psyche, the archetype responsible for the sense of familiarity the person feels when she encounters symbolic language, ritual, madness, visions, or ecstatic mystical experience.

SYMBOL OF SPRING

Persephone the Kore or "nameless maiden" is familiar to many a woman as the stage of life when she was young, uncertain, and full of possibilities. It was the time when she waited for someone or something to come along to shape her life, before another (any other) archetype became activated and ushered in a different phase. In the seasons of a woman's life, Persephone represents spring.

Just as spring cyclically follows the fallow period after harvest and the barren months of winter, bringing warmth, more light, and new green growth, so can Persephone become reactivated in women after times of loss and depression. Each time Persephone resurfaces in a woman's psyche, it is once again possible for her to be receptive to new influences and change.

Persephone is youthfulness, vitality, and the potential for new growth. Women who have Persephone as a part of them may stay receptive to change and young in spirit all their lives.

CULTIVATING PERSEPHONE

The receptivity of the Persephone archetype is the quality many women need to cultivate. This is especially so of focused Athena and Artemis women, who are in the habit of knowing what they want and acting decisively. They do not do well when they encounter a lack of clarity about how and when to act, or an uncertainty about what has the highest priority. For this, they need to cultivate Persephone's ability to wait for the situation to change, or for their feelings to become clear.

The ability to be open and flexible (or malleable) that typifies Persephone (at times to a fault) are attributes that Demeter and Hera women often also need to develop, if they are locked into their expectations (Hera) or their conviction that they know best (Demeter).

Placing a positive value on receptivity is the first step in its cultivation. A receptive attitude toward other people can be consciously developed by listening to what others have to say, attempting to see matters from their perspective, and refraining from critical judgments (or prejudices).

A receptive attitude toward one's own psyche also can be developed. A necessary first step is kindness toward oneself (rather than impatience and self-criticism), especially during periods when a woman feels that she is "lying fallow." Many women learn that fallow periods can be healing respites that precede a surge of activity or creativity, only after they have learned to accept them as a phase and not a sin.

Cultivating dreams often turns out to be rewarding. An effort to recall and write them down each morning keeps images alive. Insights into their meaning often develop when this is done, as one now remembers dreams and thinks about them. Extrasensory perception can also be developed by many people when they attempt to pick up ESP impressions, and learn to be receptive to images that arise spontaneously in their minds.

PERSEPHONE THE WOMAN

The Persephone woman has a youthful quality. She may actually look younger than her age or may have something "girlish" in her personality, a "Take care of Little Me" element that may endure through middle age and beyond. I think of the Persephone woman as having something willowy about her that bends to conform with circumstances or with stronger personalities. Going first in one direction and then another, depending on how "the wind blows," she springs back when the force lets up, remaining unaffected in some significant way by experience unless she makes a commitment that will change her.

YOUNG PERSEPHONE

The typical little Persephone is a quiet, unassuming, "good little girl," the kind who is often "dolled up" in pink, frilly dresses. She's usually a well-behaved child, who wants to please, does what she is told, and wears what is chosen for her.

An oversolicitous mother compounds little Persephone's own tendency to be cautious and compliant, if from infancy she treats her daughter like a fragile doll in need of protection and supervision. When she is more concerned that her little girl may fall and hurt herself than delighted when her daughter takes her first wobbly steps, she is sending the first of many similar messages that equates trying something new and thus difficult with risk and worry. When she chides her daughter for trying something on her own, saying, "You should have asked me first," her message really is "Wait for me to help." Stay dependent is the unspoken admonition.

Chances are that a young Persephone is an introverted child, who appears cautious by nature because she prefers to observe first and join in later. She'd rather watch from the sidelines until she knows what is going on and what the rules are, instead of plunging in and learning firsthand, as a more extraverted child would do. She needs to imagine herself doing something before she decides whether she wants to participate. But her mother often misinterprets her natural introversion as timidity. By pushing her to do something before she is ready, a well-intentioned, extraverted mother often does not allow her Persephone daughter time to discover what her own preferences are. Pressured to "Make up your mind!" a young Persephone is likely to do what will please the other person, rather than resist; thus she learns to be passive.

In contrast, with support to do so, a young Persephone can also learn to trust her inward way of knowing what she wants to do. She gradually learns to trust her innately receptive style and becomes confident of her ability to make decisions in her own way and in her own time. Her preferences are subjectively arrived at, and they are right for her; yet she cannot state her reasons because she senses what to do inwardly and cannot explain herself logically.

PARENTS

A Persephone daughter is often "a Mommy's little girl," fixed in a Demeter-Persephone pattern with her mother. This type of mother often treats her daughter like an extension of herself who contributes or detracts from her own self-esteem. This pattern can result in a relationship in which mother's and daughter's psyches overlap. The mother chooses her child's parties, dancing or piano lessons, even friends, as if she were mothering herself. She provides for her daughter what she herself wanted or missed when she was a child, without considering that the daughter might have different needs.

A Persephone daughter doesn't do much to contradict the impression that she wants the same things for herself that her mother wants for her. By nature, she is receptive and compliant and wants to please. (In contrast, little Artemis and Athena at age two distinctly say "No!" to the dress they don't want to wear, or "No!" at efforts to divert them from something they are intent on doing.)

A career-minded Athena mother with a Persephone daughter may wonder, "How did I get such a little princess?" She may take pleasure in being this child's mother one moment, and be frustrated at her daughter's apparent indecisiveness and inability to say what's on her mind, the next. An Artemis mother's frustration is different. She's much better at accepting her daughter's subjective feelings; her irritation is directed toward her daughter's lack of will. She exhorts her daughter to "Stand up for yourself!" Both Artemis and Athena mothers may help their Persephone daughters to develop these qualities that they value, or they will instill a sense of inadequacy.

Many young Persephones do not have close relationships with their fathers. The father may have been discouraged by the possessiveness of a Demeter mother who wanted a very exclusive relationship with her daughter. Or if he was a traditional husband who prided himself on never changing a diaper, he may have chosen to remain uninvolved, as do certain men who leave a daughter to be raised by her mother, yet take an active interest in a son.

Ideally, a young Persephone would have parents who respected her inward way of knowing what was important to her, and trusted her conclusions. They would provide her with a variety of experiences, but not push her into them. These are parents who have learned to value the introversion in themselves.

ADOLESCENCE AND EARLY ADULTHOOD

Young Persephone's high school experience is usually a continuation of her early life. If she has grown up in a "Mother knows best" relationship, her mother shops with her, chooses her clothes, and influences her choice of friends, interests, and now dates. Living vicariously through her daughter's experience, she may devour details of her daughter's dates and activities, and may expect her daughter to confide in her and share secrets.

However, adolescents need to keep some secrets and have some privacy. At this stage of growth, an overly intrusive parent handicaps the development of a separate identity. By sharing everything, an adolescent daughter allows her mother to color what should be her own experience. Her mother's anxieties, opinions, and values influence her perceptions.

Typically, a middle- or upper-class Persephone woman attends college because that is where young women of her social class and background are expected to be—the contemporary equivalent of the meadows where Persephone and her friends played. Education is usually a pastime for such a girl, not an occupational prerequisite. She struggles to get assignments done and papers written, because she is easily diverted and/or lacks confidence. Characteristically, she tries several possible academic majors. If she manages to settle on one, she does so often by default or by following the path of least resistance rather than by active choice.

WORK

The Persephone woman may stay a "professional student," or she may go to work. Whether after high school or after college, she tends to have a series of jobs, rather than a profession or a career, and gravitates to where her friends or family are. She moves from job to job in the hope that one will really interest her. Or she may be fired when she doesn't meet deadlines or takes too much time off.

Persephone women do best at jobs that do not require initiative, persistence, or supervisory skills. She does very well when she has a boss she wants to please, who gives her specific assignments that must be done right away. On long assignments, Persephone procrastinates. She acts as if she expected to be rescued from the task or as if she had all the time in the world. When neither turns out to be true, and it is time to deliver, she is ill prepared. At best, she manages to get the work done in a last-minute, stay-up-all-night effort.

Although work is never important to a woman who resembles the Kore, the situation is quite different if she matures into Queen of the Underworld. Then she is likely to enter a creative, psychological, or spiritual field; for example, working as an artist, poet, therapist, or psychic. Whatever she does is usually deeply personal and often unorthodox; she works in a highly individual way, commonly without the "proper" academic degrees.

RELATIONSHIPS WITH WOMEN

A young Persephone woman is comfortable with other young women who are like herself. She is often a sorority sister in high school or college and habitually tries out new situations in the company of other girls rather than on her own.

If she is pretty, she may attract women friends who do not think of themselves as very feminine, who project their own undeveloped femininity onto her and then treat her as special. If she has been treated as fragile and precious all her life, she'll take such treatment for granted. Her closest friend often is a girl with a stronger personality. The Persephone evokes maternal responses in peers and older women, who do favors for her and look out for her.

RELATIONSHIPS WITH MEN
(WHO PREFER GIRLS)

With men a Persephone woman is a child-woman, unassertive and youthful in attitude. She fits the pattern of Persephone the Kore as the most indistinct and unthreatening of all the goddesses. She means it when she says, "Let's do whatever you want to do."

Three categories of men are drawn toward Persephone women: men who are as young and inexperienced as she is;

"tough men" drawn to her innocence and fragility; and men who are uncomfortable with "grownup" women.

The label "young love" fits the first category. In these high school and college relationships, the young man and woman are exploring, as equals, being with the opposite sex.

The second category pairs Persephone—the archetypal "nice girl from a good family"—with a tough, streetwise man. He is fascinated by this protected and privileged girl who is so much his opposite. She, in turn, is captivated by his personal magnetism, sexual aura, and dominating personality.

The third stereotypical category involves men who for various reasons are uncomfortable with "grownup women." The May-December relationship between an older man and a much younger woman, for example, is an exaggeration of this archetypal patriachal model. The man is supposed to be older, more experienced, taller, stronger, and smarter than his spouse. The woman is supposed to be younger, less experienced, smaller, weaker, less educated, and less intelligent. The type who most closely fits this ideal is a young Persephone. Moreover, Persephone is quite unlike the image many men have of "mother"—as a powerful or difficult to please woman—which is another reason why some men like younger girls. With a Persephone, a man feels he can be perceived as a powerful, dominant man and not have his authority or ideas challenged. He also feels that he can be innocent, inexperienced, or incompetent and not be criticized.

A relationship with a man can be the means through which a Persephone woman separates from a dominating mother. She then goes through a stage of being Persephone "the pawn," in which she is the object to be possessed in a power struggle between a man and her mother. She falls in love with a man her mother doesn't like, someone different from "the nice young man" her mother had in mind. Sometimes, Persephone chooses a man of a different social class or even a different race. The mother may object to his personality: "He's standoffish and rude!" or "He's disagreeable . . . always has to take the other point of view!" He may be the first person who hasn't treated the daughter like a pampered princess, and won't put up with it when she acts the part. Her mother is appalled. Confident that she can influence her usually compliant daughter, the mother attacks her choice. She deplores the man's personality, character, or background, sometimes also calling into question her daughter's judgment, competence, and morals. Often the mother recognizes that he is a potential adversary—in fact, this ability to resist her mother was one reason why the Persephone daughter was attracted to him.

Now, for the first time in her life, the Persephone daughter may be at odds with her mother and her standards of good-girl behavior. Her mother or her family may forbid her to see the man she's chosen. She may agree (rather than defy them openly) and then sneak off to see him. Or she may try to convince her mother of his good qualities.

After a certain amount of this struggle, the man usually demands that she confront her mother or else give up trying to get her mother's approval. He may demand that she live with him, marry him, leave the area with him, or break off contact with her mother. Caught between the two, she either goes back to the mother and acts the part of the restored, compliant daughter, or she casts in her lot with him and makes the break.

If she literally or figuratively does move away from her mother, she may have begun her journey toward becoming a separate, self-determining human being. (She does so at the risk of trading a dominating mother for a dominating man; but usually, having defied her mother, she has changed and is no longer the compliant person she once was.) Reconciliation with her mother can come later, after she herself has gained emotional independence.

SEXUALITY

A woman who is in the phase of Persephone the Maiden is like Sleeping Beauty or Snow White—asleep or unconscious of her sexuality, waiting for the prince to come along to awaken her. Many Persephones eventually are awakened sexually. They discover that they are passionate, orgasmic women, a discovery that has a positive effect on their self-esteem. Before, they felt like girls masquerading as women. (This aspect of Persephone is further discussed later in this chapter.)

MARRIAGE

Marriage is something that often "happens to" a Persephone woman. She gets "abducted" into marriage when a man wants to get married and persuades her to say yes. If she is a typical Persephone, she may not be sure that she wants to marry. She is swept away by the man's insistence and certainty and is influenced by the cultural assumption that marriage is what she is supposed to do. By nature, Persephone women have "traditionally feminine" personalities. They defer to the stronger person, are receptive rather than active, are not competitive or pushy. Men choose them, not vice versa.

Once married, the Persephone woman may go through stages paralleling the Persephone myth and may become the unwillingly bride or pawn caught between her husband and mother. Marriage may also turn out to be an unsought transformative event through which the eternal girl or maiden becomes the married matron, mother, or sexual woman as the Hera and/or Demeter and/or Aphrodite archetypes become activated by marriage.

A newlywed husband described the painful dramas between him and his Persephone wife: "She treats me as if I were responsible for ruining her life, when all I did was fall in love with her and want to get married right away. Last week I needed to get a form to the bank that day and my day was back-to-back appointments, so I asked her—and she accused me of treating her like a servant. Lovemaking happens only when I initiate it; and then she acts as if I were a rapist." He was confused, angry, and depressed by what went on between them. He felt she treated him as if he were an insensitive, oppressive beast; he felt wounded and powerless because his wife reacted as if she were a captive Persephone and he were Hades the abductor, who held her prisoner.

Persephone women who are unwilling brides only make a partial commitment. They get married with mental reservations. One said, "I was living with some roommates and had a boring job. He wasn't the Prince Charming I had dreamed of, but he wanted the same things I thought I did—a home and a family—and was dependable, so I said yes. This Persephone was only partially committed to her husband. Emotionally, she spent only part of the time married, and the rest fantasizing about other men.

CHILDREN

Although a Persephone woman may have children, she won't feel authentic as a mother unless some Demeter is activated in her. She may stay a daughter who thinks of her own mother as a "real mother" and of herself as merely playing at the role. An intrusive mother who, as grandmother, takes over her grandchild makes her Persephone daughter feel incompetent and accentuates the difficulty. She may say, "You don't know how to hold a fussy baby, let me do it!" Or "I'll take care of that, you rest." Or "You aren't making enough milk for the baby—maybe you should switch to a bottle." These typical comments undermine her daughter's self-confidence.

The children of a Persephone woman react to her in various ways. A daughter who has a stronger will and more definite ideas than her Persephone mother may end up telling her mother what her mother ought to do rather than vice versa. As she grows older—sometimes as early as age twelve—a daughter may reverse roles with a dependent Persephone mother. As adults looking back on their childhood and adolescence, many such daughters say, "I didn't have a mother—I *was* the mother." If both mother and daughter are Persephones, they may become too much alike, especially if they live together and become mutually dependent on one another. As the years go by, they may resemble inseparable sisters.

Persephone mothers of assertive sons may feel "run over" by them. Even as toddlers, little boys can intimidate their Persephone mothers because when the boys are insistent and angry they appear to be smaller versions of powerful men. Since it's foreign to a Persephone woman to use power in any relationship, it's unlikely that she will show such a child "who's boss." She may give in to the demand, fail to set limits, and feel impotent and victimized. Or she may find an indirect way to shift the focus: charm him into a better mood, cajole him to change his mind, divert his attention, or get upset and make him feel guilty or ashamed.

Some sons and daughters of Persephone mothers thrive

on having nonintrusive mothers who love them and admire their independent spirit, which is so different from their own. A Persephone mother may also nurture her children's imagination and capacity to play by sharing these aspects of herself with them. If she herself has grown beyond Persephone the Kore, she can guide them toward valuing the inner life as a source of creativity.

MIDDLE YEARS

Although the archetype of Persephone the Kore remains eternally young, the woman herself grows older. As she loses her youthful bloom, she may become distressed by every facial wrinkle and line. Realistic barriers now arise that make her aware that dreams she once entertained as possibilities are now beyond reach. A midlife depression results when these realities become obvious to her.

If she stays identified with "the Maiden" she may work at denying reality. She may have a facelift as she concentrates on trying to maintain an illusion of youthfulness. Her hairstyle and clothes may be more suitable for a woman many years her junior; she may act helpless and try to be cute. And with each passing year her behavior will be less appropriate. For such a woman, depression is never far from the surface.

If she is no longer identified with Persephone the Kore at midlife—because she made commitments or had experiences that changed her—she will be spared a depression. Otherwise, a depression will be the turning point in her life; a turning point that may have positive or negative consequences. This may mark the beginning of a lasting depression, after which she remains defeated by life. Or the depression will mark the end of a prolonged adolescence and the beginning of maturity.

LATER YEARS

If in the course of her life a Persephone woman has evolved from Kore to Queen, at sixty-five years of age and older she may have the regal presence of a wise elder who knows the mysteries that make life and death meaningful. She has had mystical or psychic experiences and has tapped a source of spirituality deep within herself that dispels her fears about growing old and dying. If she matured, made commitments, developed other aspects of herself, and yet retained a connection to Persephone the Kore, a part of her stays eternally young in spirit.

In her later years, it's also possible that there may be hardly a trace of Persephone left in a woman who started out in life following a Persephone pattern and then in early or middle adulthood had Hera, Demeter, or Aphrodite activated. Or, if the worst possible scenario for Persephone is followed, she may have never recovered from a depression, and remained from that point on, defeated by life or withdrawn from reality, captive in her own underworld.

PSYCHOLOGICAL DIFFICULTIES

The goddess Persephone was a carefree daughter until she was abducted and raped by Hades and was for a time, a powerless, captive, unwilling bride. Although freed through her mother's efforts, she ate some pomegranate seeds, which meant that she would spend part of the year above ground with Demeter and part of the time in the underworld with Hades. Only later would she come into her own as Queen and Guide of the Underworld. Each distinctly different phase of the myth has a corresponding real-life parallel. Like the goddess, Persephone women can evolve through these phases and mature in response to what happens to them. But they can also become stuck in one phase.

Unlike Hera and Demeter, who represent strong instincts that often must be resisted in order for a woman to grow, Persephone influences a woman to be passive and compliant. Thus she is easily dominated by others. The most formless and indistinct of the seven goddesses, she is characterized by a lack of direction and lack of drive. Of them all, however, she also has the most possible routes for growth.

IDENTIFYING WITH PERSEPHONE THE KORE

To live as the Kore means being the eternal girl who doesn't commit herself to anything or anyone, because making a definite choice eliminates other possibilities. Besides, such a woman feels as if she had all the time in the world to make up her mind and thus can wait until something moves her. She lives in a Never-Never Land, like Wendy with Peter Pan and the lost boys, drifting and playing at life. If she is to grow, she must return to real life. Wendy, of course, made this choice. She said goodbye to Peter and returned through the window into the children's room she had left long ago, knowing that she now would grow older. The threshhold a Persephone woman must cross is a psychological one.

To grow, a Persephone woman must learn to both make commitments and live up to them. She has difficulty saying yes and following through with whatever she has agreed to do. Meeting deadlines, finishing school, entering marriage, raising a child, or staying with a job are all hard tasks for someone who wants to play at life. Growth requires that she struggle against indecisiveness, passivity, and inertia; she must make up her mind and stay committed when the choice stops being fun.

Between age thirty and forty, reality intrudes on a Persephone woman's illusion that she is eternally young. She may begin to sense that something is wrong. By the biological clock, she is running out of time to have a child. She may realize that her job has no future, or she may look at herself in a mirror and see that she is growing older. Looking around at her friends, she realizes that they have grown up and left her behind. They have husbands and families or are established in careers. What they do really matters to someone else, and in some definite but intangible way they are different from her, because life has affected them and left its mark.

As long as a woman's attitudes are those of Persephone the Kore, she will either never marry, or she will go through the motions but not make the commitment "for real." She will resist marriage because she sees it from the archetypal perspective of the maiden, for whom the model of marriage is death. From the standpoint of Persephone, marriage was an abduction by Hades, the death-bringer. This view of marriage and husband was quite different from Hera's contrasting model of marriage as fulfillment and from Hera's expectation of her husband Zeus as bringer to fulfillment. The Hera woman must know the man and resist entering into a bad marriage by the positive expectations held by the archetype. Otherwise, she will be disillusioned when marriage is not fulfilling. In marked contrast, the Persephone woman must resist an equally unsubstantiated assumption that marriage is always an abduction or death, to be fought or resented.

PITFALLS FOR PERSEPHONE: CHARACTER FLAWS

When Persephone was reunited with Demeter, the first question her mother asked was "Did you eat anything in the underworld?" Persephone replied that she had eaten some pomegranate seeds, and then lied by saying she had done so only because Hades had forced her to. Persephone did what she wanted without disturbing the image her mother had of her. While giving the impression that she had no control over her fate and therefore could not be held accountable, she actually determined her own fate. By swallowing the seeds, Persephone guaranteed that she would spend part of the time with Hades.

Deviousness, lying, and manipulation are potential character problems for Persephone women. Feeling powerless and dependent on others who are more powerful, they may learn to get what they want indirectly. They may wait for the opportune time to act, or they may use flattery. They may tell only part of the truth or may lie outright rather than directly confront the other person.

Usually Persephone women avoid anger. They do not want people to get mad at them. They feel dependent on the generosity and goodwill of others whom they correctly perceive as more powerful. Therefore, they often treat their mothers, fathers, husbands, employers, and teachers like patrons whose good graces need to be courted.

Narcissism is yet another pitfall for some Persephone women. They may become so anxiously fixed on themselves that they lose their capacity to relate to others. Their thoughts are dominated by self-questions: "How do I look? Am I witty enough? Do I sound intelligent?" And their energy goes into makeup and clothes. Such women spend hours in front of mirrors. People exist only to give them feedback, to provide them with reflecting surfaces in which to see themselves.

IN THE UNDERWORLD: PSYCHOLOGICAL ILLNESS

During part of her myth, as captive in the underworld, Persephone was a sad maiden who did not eat and did not smile. This phase is analogous to a period of psychological illness through which some Persephone women must go.

A Persephone woman is susceptible to depression when she is dominated and limited by people who keep her bound to them. An unassertive person, she bottles up her anger or differences rather than express them or actively change the situation. Instead, she holds in her negative feelings, and becomes depressed (anger turned inward—which is *re*pression—becomes *de*pression). Feelings of isolation, inadequacy, and self-criticism further contribute to her depression.

When a Persephone woman becomes depressed, it's an undramatic, fade-into-the-woodwork depression. Her retiring personality recedes even further, her passivity becomes even greater, and her emotions are inaccessible. She seems wispy and insubstantial. Like Persephone when she was first abducted to the underworld, she doesn't eat, and she doesn't have anything to say. Physically as well as psychologically, the insubstantiality becomes more marked over time. Watching a depressed Persephone is like watching a flower fade.

In contrast, a depressed Demeter woman looms large and has a big effect on everyone around her. Before she became depressed, she may have been an energetic, central figure, so there is a dramatic change in her behavior when she gets depressed—while a Persephone woman was unassuming to begin with, and merely fades away more when she's depressed.

Moreover, a depressed Demeter makes everyone around her feel guilty, powerless, or angry at the blame she implies. A depressed Persephone, in contrast, doesn't stir up these feelings in others. Instead, they feel cut off from her. She is the one who feels guilty, blameworthy, and powerless. And often she feels inappropriately guilty for something she said, thought, or did. Consequently, a depressed Demeter is an enormous presence in the center of the household, while a depressed Persephone seems to disappear into the back rooms.

Some Persephones withdraw into a shadowy world of inner images, musings, and imagined life—a world to which only they have access. A woman may have spent too much time by herself or may have retreated there to get away from an intrusive mother or an abusive father. One of my Persephone patients said, "I had my special places—behind the big brown chair in the corner of the living room, under my tree where the branches touched the ground and hid me from view—where I'd go hide. I spent hours there as a kid, mostly daydreaming, pretending I was anywhere else but in that house with those people."

Sometimes her preoccupation with her inner world cuts her off from people, and she retreats there whenever the real world seems too difficult or demanding. At some point, however, what was once a sanctuary may become a prison. Like Laura in the Tennessee Williams play *The Glass Menagerie,* a Persephone woman may become confined in her fantasy world and be unable to come back to ordinary reality.

Withdrawing gradually from reality, some Persephones seem to slip into psychosis. They live in a world full of symbolic imagery and esoteric meaning, and have distorted perceptions of themselves. And sometimes, psychotic illness can serve as a metamorphosis, a way for such women to break out of the limitations and prohibitions that were constricting their lives. By becoming temporarily psychotic, they may gain access to a wider range of feeling and a deeper awareness of themselves.

But psychotics risk being held captive in the underworld. Some Persephone women (like Ophelia in Shakespeare's play *Hamlet*) avoid what is really happening by staying psychotic when reality is too painful. Many others, however, go through the experience with the help of therapy, and learn to grow, assert themselves, and become independent.

After Persephone emerged from the underworld, Hecate was her constant companion. Hecate, Goddess of the Dark Moon and the Crossroads, ruled over the uncanny realms of ghosts and demons, sorcery and magic. The Persephone woman who emerges from a psychotic illness may gain a reflecting discernment that intuits the symbolic meaning of events. When she recovers and returns to the world from the hospital, she often has an awareness of another dimension, which can be symbolized as having Hecate as a companion.

WAYS TO GROW

To make a commitment, a Persephone woman must wrestle with the Kore in her. She must decide to marry and say yes without mentally crossing her fingers. If she does, marriage may gradually transform her from an eternal girl into a mature woman. If she embarks on a career, she also needs to make a commitment and stay with it, both for her personal growth and in order to succeed.

A Persephone woman may grow beyond Persephone the Kore if she must face life on her own and take care of herself. For many privileged daughters, the first time such independence is possible is after they become divorced. Until then, they have done exactly what was expected of them. They were protected daughters who married suitable young men. They divorce in part because they view marriage as captivity. They were not transformed by marriage; instead, they now find that divorce becomes their rite of passage. Only when they lack someone to do things for them or someone to blame can some Persephone women grow. Necessity becomes the teacher when they have to cope with leaky faucets, bank balances, and the need to work.

A Persephone woman can grow in several different directions that are inherent potentials of the archetype (these are discussed next), through the activation of other goddess archetypes (described throughout this book), or by developing her animus (described in the Aphrodite chapter).

BECOMING A PASSIONATE, SEXUAL WOMAN

The Persephone woman may be a sexually unresponsive woman who feels either raped or merely compliant when she has sex. Such a woman may say, "A week goes by, and I know he's annoyed with me about sex;" "I think about recipes when it's happening;" or "Sometimes, I really do have a headache;" or "I resent sex." But she may also transform into a sensual, sexy lady. I've heard about this transformation happening often in women I've seen in my office, or in the wives of men who have talked about it with me.

And in fact a sexual initiation that puts a woman in touch

with her own sexuality is a potential of the Persephone archetype consistent with mythology. Once Persephone was Queen of the Underworld, she had a connection or a bond with Aphrodite, Goddess of Love and Beauty. Persephone may represent the underworld aspect of Aphrodite; Persephone is a more introverted sexuality, or a dormant sexuality. In the mythology, Adonis was loved by both Aphrodite and Persephone. And both goddesses shared the pomegranate as a symbol.

Morever, Persephone's acceptance of the pomegranate seeds from Hades meant that she would be voluntarily returning to him. By this act, she ceased being the unwilling bride. She became his wife and Queen of the Underworld, instead of the captive. In real life, sometimes after years of marriage, a Persephone wife may cease feeling that she is a captive of an oppressive, selfish husband to whom she has resentfully stayed married. She feels differently only when she is able to see him as a vulnerable, decent, imperfect man and can appreciate that he loves her. When her perception changes, he may know for the first time in their marriage that she is with him to stay and that she loves him. In this new context of trust and appreciation, she may become orgasmic for the first time and view him as Dionysus the evoker of passion, rather than Hades the captor.

In ancient Greece, Dionysus's intoxicating spirit moved women to ecstatic sexual heights. He was worshipped in mountain revels by Greek women who would periodically leave their traditional respectable roles, their hearths and homes, to participate in religious orgies. Dionysus transformed them into passionate maenads. And tradition and myth link Hades and Dionysus together: Dionysus was said to sleep in the house of Persephone in the intervals and between his reappearances. The philosopher Heraclitus said, "Hades and Dionysus, for whom they [the women] go mad and rage, are one and the same."[4]

A contemporary Persephone woman can have a parallel "Dionysian" encounter. One woman said, "After I left my husband, I went out looking for what had been missing in the marriage. I figured a lot of it was me—uptight, well-brought-up, I saw myself as Miss Priss." In a coffeehouse she met a man who became her lover. He was very sensual, and helped her become aware of "nerve endings I never even knew about before."

UNCOVERING A CAPACITY FOR
ECSTATIC RELIGIOUS EXPERIENCE

The archetypal affinity of the goddess Persephone for Hecade and Dionysus may provide a clue to the ecstatic, numinous priestess qualities that some Persephone women develop. They become intoxicated by ritual and feel possessed by a god or goddess. Within Christianity, they may be "charismatics" who "speak in tongues" when the spirit moves them. And today, with the revival of goddess worship, where spiral dances evoke the goddess spirit, some women who seem ordinary Persephones by day become uncanny Hecates or Dionysian maenads by night.

DEVELOPING POTENTIAL AS MEDIUMS OR PSYCHICS

As the guide for mortals who visited the underworld to speak to the shades of the dead, Persephone had a function metaphorically similar to that of mediums who hold seances and allow the spirits of the dead to speak through them. The diffuseness of her personality, with its generalized receptivity and lack of focus, also facilitates receiving ESP. To develop psychic ability, a Persephone woman must transcend her identification with the Kore to find the Persephone-Hecate element that is unafraid of the uncanny, at home in the underworld, and wisely knows when she is at a dangerous crossroad and must seek the safer route.

BECOMING A GUIDE TO THE UNDERWORLD

Once a Persephone woman descends into her own depths, explores the deep realm of the archetypal world, and does not fear returning to reexamine the experience, she can mediate between ordinary and nonordinary reality. She has had awesome or terrible irrational experiences, visions or hallucinations, or a numinous spiritual encounter. If she can transmit what she has thus learned, she can become a guide for others. For example, when I was a psychiatric resident a book written by "Renee," *Autobiography of a Schizophrenic Girl*, gave me vivid insights into the subjective experience of being psychotic.[5] And a Persephone woman who has been to the underworld and back can also be a therapist-guide who can connect others with their own depths, guiding them to find symbolic meaning and understanding of what they find there.

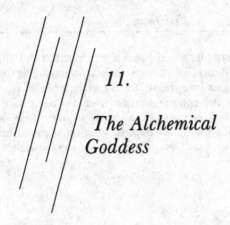

11.

The Alchemical Goddess

APHRODITE

Aphrodite, Goddess of Love and Beauty, I place in a category all her own as the alchemical goddess, a fitting designation for the magic process or power of transformation that she, alone, had. In Greek mythology, Aphrodite was an awesome presence who caused mortals and deities (with the exception of the three virgin goddesses) to fall in love and conceive new life. For Pygmalion, she turned a statue into a living woman (in contrast, Athena turned people into stone). She inspired poetry and persuasive speech, and symbolizes the transformative and creative power of love.

Although she has some characteristics in common with both virgin and vulnerable goddesses, she does not belong in either group. As the goddess who had the most sexual liaisons, Aphrodite was definitely not a virgin goddess—although she was like Artemis, Athena, and Hestia in doing what pleased her. Nor was she a vulnerable goddess—although she was like Hera, Demeter, and Persephone in being linked with male deities and/or in having children. Unlike them, however, Aphrodite was never victimized and did not suffer. In all her relationships, the feelings of desire were mutual; she was never a victim of a man's unwanted passion for her. She valued emotional experience with others more than either independence from others (which motivated the virgin goddesses), or permanent bonds to others (which characterized the vulnerable goddesses).

As the alchemical goddess, Aphrodite shares some similarities with the other two categories, yet is intrinsically different from both. For Aphrodite, relationships are important, but not as long-term commitments to other people (which characterized the vulnerable goddesses). Aphrodite seeks to consummate relationships and generate new life. This archetype may be expressed through physical intercourse or through a creative process. What she seeks differs from what the virgin goddesses seek, but she is like them in being able to focus on what is personally meaningful to her; others cannot divert her away from her goal. And in that what she values is solely subjective and cannot be measured in terms of achievement or recognition, Aphrodite is (paradoxically) most similar to anonymous, introverted Hestia—who on the surface is the goddess most unlike Aphrodite.

Whomever or whatever Aphrodite imbues with beauty is irresistible. A magnetic attraction results, "chemistry" happens between the two, and they desire union above all else. They feel a powerful urge to get closer, to have intercourse, to consummate—or "know" the other, which was the biblical term. While this drive may be purely sexual, the impulse is often deeper, representing an urge that is both psychological and spiritual. Intercourse is synonymous with communication or communion, consummation may speak of an urge toward completion or perfection, union is to join together as one, and to know is to really understand one another. The desire to know and be known is what Aphrodite generates. If this desire leads to physical intimacy, impregnation and new life may follow. If the union is also or either of mind, heart, or spirit, new growth occurs in the psychological, emotional, or spiritual spheres.

When Aphrodite influences a relationship, her effect is not limited to the romantic or sexual. Platonic love, soul connection, deep friendship, rapport, and empathic understanding all are expressions of love. Whenever growth is generated, a vision supported, potential developed, a spark of creativity encouraged—as can happen in mentoring, counseling, parenting, directing, teaching, editing, and doing psychotherapy and analysis—then Aphrodite is there, affecting both people involved.

QUALITY OF CONSCIOUSNESS: LIKE "LIMELIGHT"

The quality of consciousness associated with Aphrodite is unique. The virgin goddesses are associated with focused consciousness and are the archetypes that enable women to concentrate on what matters to them. The receptiveness of the vulnerable goddesses is equated with diffuse awareness. But Aphrodite has a quality of consciousness all her own, which I call Aphrodite consciousness. Aphrodite consciousness is focused, yet receptive; such consciousness both takes in what is attended to, and is affected by it.

Aphrodite consciousness is more focused and intense than the diffuse awareness of vulnerable goddesses. But it is more receptive and attentive to what it focuses on than the focused consciousness of the virgin goddesses. Thus it is neither like a living room lamp that illuminates everything within the radius of its glow with a warm, soft light, nor like a spotlight or a laser beam. I think of Aphrodite consciousness as analogous to theater lighting that illuminates the stage. What we behold in this limelight enhances, dramatizes, or magnifies the impact of the experience on us. We take in and react to what we see and hear. This special lighting helps us to be emotionally transported at a symphony, or to be moved by a play or by the words of a speaker; feelings, sense impressions, and memories are drawn out of us in response to what we see and hear. In turn, those onstage can become inspired by an audience, energized by the rapport they sense being directed toward them.

What is in the "limelight" absorbs our attention. We are drawn effortlessly toward what we see, and are relaxed in our concentration. Whatever we see in the golden light of Aphrodite consciousness becomes fascinating: a person's face or character, an idea about the nature of the universe, or the translucency and shape of a porcelain bowl.

Anyone who has ever fallen in love with a person, a place, an idea, or an object focuses on and takes it in with Aphrodite consciousness. But not everyone who uses Aphrodite consciousness is in love. Aphrodite's "in love" way of attending to another person as if he or she were fascinating and beautiful is characteristic of women who personify the archetype, and is a natural way of relating and gathering information for many women (and men) who like people and focus their total attention on them intently.

Such a woman takes in people in the same way that a wine connoisseur attends to and notices the characteristics of an interesting new wine. To appreciate the metaphor fully, imagine a wine buff enjoying the pleasure of getting acquainted with an unknown wine. She (or he) holds the goblet up to the light to note the color and clarity of the wine. She inhales the bouquet, and takes a lingering sip to capture the character and smoothness of the wine; she even savors the aftertaste. But it would be a mistake to assume that the "loving attention" and interest she pays the wine means that the particular wine is special, valued, or even enjoyed.

This is the mistake people often make when they respond to a woman who uses Aphrodite consciousness. Basking in the glow of her focus, they feel attractive and interesting as she actively draws them out and reacts in a loving or affirming way (rather than assessing or critical). It is her style to be genuinely and momentarily involved in whatever interests her. The effect on the other person can be seductive—and misleading if her way of interacting creates the impression that she is fascinated or enamored, when she is not.

APHRODITE CONSCIOUSNESS, CREATIVITY, AND COMMUNICATION

My own discovery of Aphrodite consciousness began with the observation that neither "focused consciousness" nor "diffuse awareness" described what I was doing in my psychotherapy work. Comparing notes with artists and writers, I found that in creative work a third mode was in operation, which I came to call "Aphrodite consciousness."

In a therapy session, I noticed that several processes go on simultaneously. I am absorbed in listening to my patient, who has my rapt attention and compassion. At the same time, my mind is active, mentally associating to what I am hearing. Things I already know about the person come to mind—perhaps a past dream, or knowledge about the family, a prior incident, or current events in his or her life that might have a bearing. Sometimes an image comes up, or a metaphor suggests itself. Or I may have an emotional response of my own, either to the material or to the way it's expressed, which I note. My mind is actively working, but in a receptive way, stimulated by my absorption in the other person.

What I respond to during an analytic session is like one part of a large mosaic, an important detail in a much larger, only partially completed picture of this person in therapy with me, who is also someone with whom I am involved in a reciprocal process. If we are engaged in transformative work, an emotional field is generated between us powerful enough to touch us both. As Jung noted, analysis involves the totality of both personalities. Both conscious attitudes and unconscious elements in doctor and patient are involved in a process in which both are deeply affected: "For two personalities to meet is like mixing two different chemical substances: if there is any combination at all, both are transformed."[1]

In doing therapy, I gradually became aware that—in addition to the interactive, receptive, Aphrodite consciousness that facilitates change and growth—I also had to keep an optimal emotional distance. If I feel too much or am too closely identified with my patient, I lack some essential objectivity. If I am too distant and lack love for my patient, I lose a crucial empathetic connection, without which there isn't enough transformative energy to bring about deeper change. Befitting Aphrodite, who had the invulnerability of a virgin goddess and the involvement of a vulnerable goddess, Aphrodite consciousness has both qualities.

Aphrodite consciousness is present in all creative work, including that done in solitude. The "relationship" dialogue is then between the person and the work, from which something new emerges. For example, observe the process when a painter is engaged with paint and canvas. An absorbed interchange occurs: the artist reacts or is receptive to the creative accidents of paint and brush; she initiates actively with bold stroke, nuance, and color; and then, seeing what happens, she responds. It is an interaction; spontaneity combines with skill. It is an interplay between artist and canvas, and as a result something is created that never before existed.

Moreover, while the painter focuses on the detail in front of her, she also holds an awareness of the whole canvas in her consciousness. At times, she steps back and objectively sees what she has been so subjectively involved in creating. She is absorbed, involved—and also somewhat detached and objective.

In both good communication and creative process, there is an interaction. Conversation, for example, can be banal, meaningless, wounding—or it can be an art form, as spontaneous, moving, and wonderful as musical improvisation or jam sessions, when the soul takes flight with the music and soars to rhapsodic heights one moment, and touches a deep chord the next. The interaction is spontaneous in form, yet its substance may be deep and moving. The conversants feel excitement and discovery as each in turn sparks a response in the other. They mutually experience Aphrodite consciousness, which provides the energy field or backdrop for communication or creativity to happen. Where the music will go, or how the conversation will evolve, is not known at the start, or planned for. Discovery—the birth of something new—is a key element in creativity and communication.

Whenever Aphrodite consciousness is present, energy is generated: lovers glow with well-being and heightened energy; conversation sparkles, stimulating thoughts and feelings. When two people truly meet each other, both receive energy from the encounter and feel more vitality than before, regardless of the content—which, in therapy, can be very painful material. Work becomes invigorating rather than draining. Absorbed by whom we are with, or by what we are doing, we lose track of time—a characteristic that Aphrodite shares with Hestia.

VISION CARRIERS

To make a dream come true, one must have a dream, believe in it, and work toward it. Often it is essential that another significant person believe that the dream is possible: that person is a vision carrier, whose faith is often crucial. Daniel Levinson, in *Seasons of a Man's Life*, describes the function of a "special woman" in the transition phase of a young man's entry into the adult world. Levinson claims that such a woman has a special connection to the realization of his Dream. She helps him to shape and live out the Dream. She shares it, believes in him as its hero, gives it her blessing, joins him on the journey, and provides a sanctuary where his aspirations can be imagined and his hopes nourished.[2]

This special woman is similar to Toni Wolf's description of the "hetaira woman"[3] (from the ancient Greek word for *courtesan*, who was educated, cultured, and unusually free for a woman of those days; she was like a Japanese geisha in some respects)—a type of woman whose relationships with men have both erotic and companionship qualities. She may be his *la femme inspiratrice* or muse. According to Wolf, the hetaira fertilizes the creative side of a man and helps him in it. Toni Wolf, a Jungian analyst and former patient of Jung's, was his colleague and, according to some people, also his mistress. She herself may have been Jung's "special woman," a hetaira woman who inspired Jungian theory.

Sometimes a woman has a gift for attracting several or many men to her who see her as the special woman; she has the ability to see their potential, believe in their dreams, and inspire them to achieve. Lou Salome Andreas, for example, was the special woman, muse, colleague, and erotic companion for a number of famous and creative men including Rilke, Nietzsche, and Freud.[4]

Women as well as men need to be able to imagine that their Dream is possible, and have another person look at them and their dream with growth-enhancing Aphrodite consciousness. People speculate why there are so few famous women artists, or great chefs, or orchestra leaders, or noted philosophers—among the reasons given might be that women lack carriers of the Dream. Women have nurtured the Dream for men, while men in general haven't nurtured the Dream very well for the women in their lives.

This state of affairs is partially a result of stereotyped roles, which have limited the imagination as well as stifled opportunities for women. But tangible obstacles ("No woman need apply" difficulties) are decreasing, as are the lack of role models.

THE PYGMALION EFFECT

I think that the vision carrier—therapist, mentor, teacher, or parent with "a green thumb"—under whom others bloom and develop their gifts evokes what research psychologist Robert Rosenthal named the Pygmalion effect.[5] This term describes the power of positive expectations on the behavior of others. It is so called after Pygmalion, who fell in love with his own sculpture of the perfect woman, a statue that was brought to life by Aphrodite and became Galatea. (Similarly, in George Bernard Shaw's play *Pygmalion*, Henry Higgins turned a Cockney flower girl into an elegant lady—with whom he then fell in love. Shaw's play was the basis for Alan Jay Lerner's Broadway play *My Fair Lady*.)

Rosenthal found that students live up to—or down to—their teachers' expectations of them. He studied ghetto schoolchildren, whose academic performances deteriorate the longer they remain in school. These children tend to have teachers who are convinced that the children cannot learn. Rosenthal devised a research project to determine which came first: the expectation or the performance. He concluded that our expectations have an extraordinary influence on others, of which we are often oblivious.

As I read Rosenthal's study, I thought about my patient Jane, who came from a Spanish-speaking home and at first was thought of as slow in school. She entered fourth grade academically behind her classmates, as convinced as her previous teachers that she wasn't bright. But her fourth-grade teacher saw her in a different light, drew her out, and gave Jane challenges that she expected Jane to meet. The attention transformed the nine-year-old into a top student, who now spoke up in class and felt good about herself. Years later, Jane too became an inspirational teacher who saw and brought out the potential in her students.

Aphrodite's Pygmalion effect is also related to what I think of as her alchemy. In medieval Europe, alchemy was both a physical process in which substances were brought together in an effort to transform baser material into gold, and an esoteric psychological endeavor to transform the personality of the alchemist. We experience the alchemy of Aphrodite when we feel drawn toward another person and fall in love; we feel it when we are touched by her power of transformation and creativity; we know it when we appreciate the capacity we have to make what we focus on beautiful and valued because it is imbued with our love. Whatever is ordinary and undeveloped is the "baser" material of everyday life, which can be turned into "gold" through Aphrodite's creative, alchemical influence—in the same way that Pygmalion's statue of Galatea was turned into a real, live woman through love.

12.

Aphrodite:
Goddess of Love and Beauty,
Creative Woman and Lover

APHRODITE THE GODDESS

Aphrodite, Goddess of Love and Beauty, whom the Romans called Venus, was the most beautiful of the goddesses. Poets told of the beauty of her face and form, of her golden hair and her flashing eyes, soft skin, and beautiful breasts. To Homer, she was "a lover of laughter," filled with irresistible charm. She was a favorite subject for sculptors, who portrayed her in a state of undress or partial dress that revealed her graceful, sensual body—the Venus de Milo and the Aphrodite of Cnidos, known to us only through Roman copies, are the most famous of many.

"Golden" was the most frequent eptithet used by the Greeks to describe Aphrodite—it meant "beautiful" to the Greeks. And according to Paul Friedrich, noted scholar of Aphrodite, *gold / honey, gold / speech, gold / semen* are linguistically connected, symbolizing Aphrodite's deeper values of procreation and verbal creation.[1] She was associated with doves, those billing and cooing lovebirds, and swans, noted for their beauty and pairing; with flowers, especially roses, traditionally the gift of lovers; with sweet fragrances and fruits, especially golden apples and sensual, passion-red pomegranates (a symbol shared with Persephone).

GENEALOGY AND MYTHOLOGY

There are two versions of the mythological birth and origin of Aphrodite. Hesiod and Homer tell two contradictory stories.

In Homer's version, Aphrodite had a conventional birth. She was simply the daughter of Zeus and a sea nymph, Dione.

In Hesiod's version, Aphrodite was born as a consequence of a violent act. Cronos (who later became the ruler of the Titans and father of the first-generation Olympians) took a sickle, cut off the genitals of his father Uranus, and threw them into the sea. White foam spread around them as sperm and sea mixed, from which Aphrodite was born, emerging from her oceanic conception as a fully grown goddess.

The image of Aphrodite emerging from the sea was immortalized during the Renaissance by Botticelli in "The Birth of Venus"—sometimes referred to irreverently as "Venus on the Half-Shell." His painting shows a graceful and delicate nude figure standing on a seashell, being blown to the shore by flying wind gods amidst a shower of roses.

Aphrodite was said to have come ashore first either on the island of Cythera or on Cyprus. Then accompanied by Eros (Love) and Himeros (Desire), she was escorted into the assembly of the gods and received as one of them.

Many of the gods, struck by her beauty, vied for her hand in marriage. Unlike other goddesses who had not chosen either their mates nor their lovers (Persephone was abducted, Hera was seduced, Demeter was raped), Aphrodite was free to choose. She selected Hephaestus, the lame God of Craftsmen and God of the Fire of the Forge. Thus Hera's rejected son became Aphrodite's husband—and would often be cuckolded by her. Aphrodite and Hephaestus had no children. Their marriage may represent the union of beauty and craft, out of which art is born.

In her liaisons, Aphrodite was paired with second-generation Olympian male gods—the generation of the sons, rather than with the father-figure generation of Zeus, Poseidon, and Hades. Aphrodite was linked romantically with Ares, God of War, with whom she had a long-term affair and several children. Another lover was Hermes, Messenger of the Gods, who guided souls to the underworld and who was the patron god of travelers, athletes, thieves, and businessmen, as well as god of communication, inventor of musical instruments, and Olympian trickster.

She and Ares had three children: a daughter, Harmonia (Harmony), and two sons, Deimos (Terror) and Phobos (Fear), who accompanied their father in battle. Aphrodite and Ares represent the union of the two most uncontrollable passions—love and war, which, when in perfect balance, could produce Harmony.

The child of Aphrodite's union with Hermes was the bisexual god Hermaphroditus, who inherited the beauty of both parents, bore both of their names, and had the sexual characteristics of both. As a symbol, Hermaphroditus can represent bisexuality (erotic attraction toward both sexes) or androgyny (the existence, in one person, of qualities of abilities traditionally considered either masculine or feminine).

By some accounts, Eros, God of Love, was another of Aphrodite's sons. Like Aphrodite, the accounts of his mythological beginnings and time of appearance in the cosmos are contradictory. Hesiod says that Eros was a prime force in creation, present before the Titans and Olympians. Eros was also seen as a god who accompanied Aphrodite as she emerged from the sea. However, later myths describe him as a fatherless son of Aphrodite. The Greeks usually portrayed Eros as a virile young man, as did the Romans who called him Amor. With time, the Eros who mythologically began as a prime force became even further diminished, until today what is left of him is represented by the baby in diapers with a bow and a quiver of arrows, known as Cupid.

APHRODITE AND MORTALS

Aphrodite's relationships with mortal men were also important in her mythology. In some myths, she came to the aid of men who prayed to her for help. For example, Aphrodite responded to Hippomenes's prayers on the eve of his race with Atalanta. She gave him three golden apples and advice on how to use them, which saved his life and helped him win a wife he loved.

As noted earlier, Aphrodite also figured in the legend of Pygmalion, king of Cyprus. Pygmalion carved a statue of his ideal woman out of ivory—and the more he looked at it, the more he fell in love with his own creation. At a festival in honor of Aphrodite, he prayed to her for a wife like his statue. Later, as he kissed the ivory figure, the statue came alive. Now she was Galatea, whom he married—Aphrodite's answer to his prayers.

The Goddess of Love and Beauty also had many amorous liaisons with mortal men. For example, when Aphrodite saw Anchises grazing his cattle on a mountainside, she was seized by a desire for him (a mortal with a "body very much like a god," as Homer described him). Pretending to be a beautiful maiden, she stirred his passion with her words, and seduced him.

Later, when he fell asleep, she shed her mortal disguise and awakened her sleeping lover. She revealed that she would conceive their son, Aeneas, who would be famous as the legendary founder of Rome, and warned him not to reveal to anyone that she was the mother of his son. Anchises was said to later have drunk too much and boasted of his love affair with Aphrodite—whereupon he was struck by lightning and crippled.

Another famous mortal lover was Adonis, a handsome, youthful hunter. Aphrodite feared for his life and warned him to avoid ferocious beasts, but the thrill of the hunt and his fearlessness overpowered her advice. One day, while out hunting, his dogs flushed out a wild boar. Adonis wounded the animal with his spear, which provoked the pain-maddened beast to turn on him and savagely tear him to pieces.

After his death, Adonis was permitted to return from the underworld to Aphrodite for part of the year (Aphrodite shared him with Persephone). This myth cycle of death and return was the basis of the cult of Adonis. His annual return to Aphrodite symbolized the return of fertility.

Women were also powerfully affected by Aphrodite. Compelled to follow Aphrodite's dictates, unable to resist being drawn toward whomever Aphrodite decreed, a mortal woman could find herself in great jeopardy, as shown in the myth of Myrrha.

Daughter of a priest of Aphrodite, Myrrha fell passionately in love with her own father. According to various versions of this story, Aphrodite had caused this forbidden passion either because Myrrha's mother had boasted that her daughter was more beautiful than Aphrodite herself, or because Myrrha had neglected Aphrodite's worship. At any rate, she approached him in disguise and in darkness and became his secret lover. After several clandestine meetings, he discovered that this seductive woman was his own daughter. Filled with horror and disgust, driven by a need to punish her for what they had enjoyed together, he tried to kill her. She fled. Just as he was about to overtake her, she prayed to the gods to save her. Instantly, her prayer was answered: she was transformed into the fragrant myrrh tree.

Phaedra was another victim of Aphrodite's power. She was the ill-fated stepmother of Hippolytus, a handsome youth who had dedicated himself to Artemis and to a life of celibacy. Aphrodite used Phaedra as an instrument of her displeasure with Hippolytus, who refused to honor the Goddess of Love or her rites—Aphrodite caused Phaedra to fall hopelessly in love with her stepson.

In the myth, Phaedra tried to resist her passion, struggled against her illicit desire, and became sick. Finally, a handmaiden found out the cause of her misery, and approached the youth on her behalf. He was so outraged and horrified at the suggestion that he have a love affair with his stepmother, that—within earshot of Phaedra—he burst into a tirade against her.

Humiliated, she hanged herself, leaving a suicide note falsely accusing Hippolytus of raping her. When his father Theseus returned to find his dead wife and the note, he called on Poseidon, God of the Sea, to kill his son. As Hippolytus drove his chariot along the coast road, Poseidon sent huge waves and a sea monster to frighten his horses. The chariot overturned and Hippolytus was dragged to his death. Thus Aphrodite had her revenge—at Phaedra's expense.

Psyche and Atalanta were two mortal women who were transformed by Aphrodite's influence. In the myth of Eros and Psyche, Psyche had the misfortune to be so beautiful that men called her "a second Aphrodite." Thus they gave her the reverence and awe that were due the goddess, which offended Aphrodite.

In this myth, Psyche sought out the goddess whose wrath she had incurred. Aphrodite gave her four impossible tasks, each of which seemed initially beyond her abilities. In each instance, with help from unexpected quarters, Psyche was successful. Aphrodite acted as the transformative agent by providing the tasks through which Psyche—a mortal who had characteristics of the vulnerable goddesses—grew.

Aphrodite was also the transformative agent in the myth of Atalanta—a mortal who was compared to the virgin goddess Artemis. As noted earlier, Atalanta lost a footrace and gained a husband when she chose to pick up the three golden apples of Aphrodite.

APHRODITE THE ARCHETYPE

The Aphrodite archetype governs women's enjoyment of love and beauty, sexuality and sensuality. The realm of the lover exerts a powerful pull on many women; as a force with a woman's personality, Aphrodite can be as demanding as Hera and Demeter (the other two strong instinctual archetypes). Aphrodite impells women to fulfill both creative and procreative functions.

THE LOVER

Every woman who falls in love with someone who is also in love with her is at that moment a personification of the Aphrodite archetype. Transformed temporarily from an ordinary mortal into a goddess of love, she feels attractive and sensual, an archetypal lover.

When Aphrodite is present as the major archetype in a woman's personality, she falls in love often and easily. She has "it"—what the silent screen star Clara Bow was known for—namely sex appeal. She has a personal magnetism that draws others closer into an erotically charged field that enhances sexual awareness. The "voltage" goes up, and both feel attractive and vibrant as they are drawn toward each other.

When sensuality and sexuality in women are degraded—

as in Judeo-Christian, Moslem, and other patriarchal cultures, the woman who embodies Aphrodite the lover is considered a temptress or whore. Thus this archetype, if expressed, can put a woman at odds with standards of morality. Aphrodite women may be ostracized. For example, in Nathaniel Hawthorne's classic novel about Puritan New England, *The Scarlet Letter*, Hester Prynne was forced to wear a large red "A" for adultery. And the actress Ingrid Bergman was condemned by public opinion and forced into exile for her affair and subsequent marriage to Italian film director Roberto Rossellini. In biblical times, such women were stoned; and in contemporary Islamic countries death is still the penalty.

FALLING IN LOVE

When two people fall in love, each sees the other in a special, enhancing (Aphrodite-golden) light and is drawn toward the other's beauty. There is magic in the air; a state of enchantment or infatuation is evoked. Each feels beautiful, special, more godlike or goddesslike than their ordinary selves. The energy field between them becomes emotionally charged and erotic "electricity" is generated, which in turn creates a mutual magnetic attraction. In the "golden" space that surrounds them, sensory impressions are intensified: they hear music more clearly, fragrances are more distinct, the taste and touch of the lover are enhanced.

When a person falls in love with someone who does not return that love, however, she feels possessed by a cruel desire and unmet longings. She is repeatedly drawn to the loved one and repeatedly rebuffed. The intensity—which is wonderful when love is returned—now amplifies the pain instead.

ACTIVATION OF APHRODITE

Just as there are two mythic versions of the birth of Aphrodite, so also there are two ways in which this archetype comes into consciousness.

The first is a dramatic initiation, when Aphrodite emerges suddenly, full-blown and awesome, as a commanding presence from the waters of the unconscious. When sexuality feels like an instinctual response, having little to do with loving or even liking the man who arouses her, it is sexuality "cut off" from emotional closeness—metaphorically similar to Hesiod's version of Aphrodite's birth in the sea.

In their psychotherapy sessions, many women tell of the overwhelming impact of an unexpected, initial sexual response: "I was filled with desire I didn't even know I had. It was wonderful and scary at the same time." Once they have felt the power of Aphrodite, many young women find themselves drawn toward sexual intimacy. Others, now aware of what can happen, avoid exposure. Two women patients of mine provided examples of these contrasting responses. One sought more: "I look back on how I pretended to enjoy the date, when what I really wanted was the sex part of it." The other put up barriers: "I threw myself into studying, turned down dates, and insisted on going to an all-girls school. I figured I'd keep myself in some sort of mental convent until I was safely married. Meanwhile, I'd be better off untempted." After the first time, such a woman knows that she can be drawn toward sexual intimacy by a compelling wish to repeat the experience, once her body is aroused and her attention is drawn erotically toward a man. She then wants to merge with him, to be carried by passion toward orgasmic release, brought over the crest of heightened sexual arousal to a climax, where her individuality is submerged in the transpersonal orgasmic experience.

The second way that the archetype comes alive is in a relationship. It might be considered analogous to Homer's ordinary version of Aphrodite's birth and subsequent growth as a daughter of Zeus and a sea nymph Dione. Growth of trust and love, and a gradual reduction in inhibition precedes the evocation or "birth" of Aphrodite, heralded by the first orgasm in lovemaking and by a new desire for physical intimacy. One married woman who had several lovers prior to her marriage and two years of marriage before she became orgasmic, marveled, "It's as if my body now knows how."

PROCREATIVE INSTINCT

Aphrodite represents the drive to ensure the continuation of the species. As the archetype connected with the sex drive and the power of passion, Aphrodite can turn a woman into a vessel of procreation—if she does not practice birth control.

Unlike a woman under the influence of Demeter, who has sex because she wants a baby, an Aphrodite-influenced woman has a baby because of her desire for a man or her desire for the sexual or the romantic experience. Aphrodite whispers not to use birth control because it would detract from the passion of the moment or would make the first act of intercourse premeditated. To heed the goddess increases the risk of an unwanted pregnancy.

Coinciding with the procreative instinct, some women feel Aphrodite's influence most intensely at the time of ovulation, fourteen days before menstruation—when sex is most likely to lead to pregnancy. This is when they are more sexually responsive and have erotic dreams, when they most miss having sex if they are without sexual partners.

CREATIVITY

Aphrodite is a tremendous force for change. Through her flow attraction, union, fertilization, incubation, and birth of new life. When this process happens on a purely physical plane between a man and a woman, a baby is conceived. And the sequence is the same in all other creative processes as well: attraction, union, fertilization, incubation, a new creation. The creative product can be as abstract as an inspired union of two ideas that eventually gives birth to new theory.

Creative work comes out of an intense and passionate involvement—almost as if with a lover, as one (the artist) interacts with the "other" to bring something new into being. This "other" may be a painting, a dance form, a musical composition, a sculpture, a poem or a manuscript, a new theory or invention, that for a time is all-absorbing and fascinating. Creativity is also a "sensual" process for many people; it is an in-the-moment sensory experience involving touch, sound, imagery, movement, and sometimes even smell and taste. An artist engrossed in a creative process, like a lover, often finds that all her senses are heightened and that she receives perceptual impressions through many channels. As she works on a visual image, verbal phrase, or dance movement, multiple sense impressions may interact to create the result.

Just as Aphrodite the lover may proceed serially through many affairs of the heart, Aphrodite as a creative force may involve a woman in one intense creative effort after another. When one project ends, another possibility arises that fascinates her.

Sometimes both the creative and the romantic aspects of Aphrodite are present in the same woman. She then engages in intense relationships, moving from one to another as well as being engrossed in her creative work. Such a woman follows whatever and whoever fascinates her, and may lead an unconventional life, as did the dancer Isadora Duncan and the writer George Sand.

CULTIVATING APHRODITE

Aphrodite is the archetype most involved in sensual or sensory experience. Therefore, cultivating a keenness of perception and a here-and-now focus invites Aphrodite. Lovers are naturally attuned to each other's taste, fragrance, and beauty; music and tactile stimulation enhance their pleasure. Sex therapists teach "sensate focusing" or "pleasuring," methods that encourage a couple to be engrossed in the moment, to not become concerned about a goal, to learn how to enjoy pleasurable sensations.

Guilt and judgmental attitudes erect obstacles to enjoying either lovemaking or art making. Such obstacles arise when people feel a prohibition against pleasure, play, and other "nonproductive" activities, as well as against sex. Many people judge the pursuit of love and beauty as frivolous at best, and sinful at worst. For example, the Artemis and Athena archetypes focus on achieving goals, predisposing such women to devalue Aphrodite's enjoyment of the moment. And Aphrodite often threatens the priorities of the Hera and Demeter archetypes—monogamy or the maternal role—so the latter often have judgmental attitudes toward Aphrodite. And, finally, the introversion of the Persephone and Hestia archetypes make such women less responsive to "outer" attractions.

When women see the value of Aphrodite and seek to develop this aspect in themselves, they take a major mental step toward activating the archetype. Then they need to provide time and opportunity for Aphrodite to develop. A couple may need to take vacations away from their children, in a relaxed setting where they can enjoy themselves, talk, and make love. Or a woman may learn to give and receive a massage. Or she may take a belly-dancing class as a means of being at ease with and enjoying her body—a prerequisite for taking pleasure in lovemaking.

Cultivating an interest in art, poetry, dance, or music serves a similar purpose in the aesthetic sphere. One can develop the ability to become completely immersed in a visual, auditory, or kinesthetic experience. Once one is engrossed, then an interaction between oneself and the aesthetic medium can occur, out of which something new may emerge.

APHRODITE THE WOMAN

Ever since the goddess Aphrodite emerged from the sea in all her undressed glory, curvaceous, golden-haired, sexy women such as movie queens Jean Harlow, Lana Turner, and Marilyn Monroe have personified the Goddess of Love. Sometimes this goddess type runs true to form, blond hair and all, but more typically an Aphrodite woman is recognizable by her attractiveness rather than by her appearance alone. The Aphrodite archetype creates a personal charisma—a magnetism or electricity—that, combined with physical attributes, makes a woman "an Aphrodite."

When Aphrodite is an active part of a plain woman, that woman does not draw men to her from across the room. Those who come close, however, find her engaging and charming. Many rather ordinary-looking women with Aphrodite qualities attract others with the magnetic warmth of their personalities and their natural, unselfconscious sensuality. These "plain Janes" always seem to have men in their lives, while their more well-endowed, objectively pretty sisters may sit by the phone or sit out a dance, puzzling, "What does she have, that I don't?"

YOUNG APHRODITE

As a child, the little Aphrodite may have been an innocent little flirt. She may have had a way of responding to men, an interest in them, and an unconscious sensuality that made adults comment, "Wait until she grows up—she'll be a heart-breaker." She enjoys being the center of attention, likes wearing pretty clothes and being fussed over. She's usually not a shy child, and may have even been called "a little ham" for her impromptu performances and other attention-getting efforts, which charmed her audiences even then.

By eight or nine years old, many Aphrodite girls are in a hurry to grow up, dress up, and wear makeup. They have crushes on boys, are "teeny-bopper" fans of sexy male singers or rock groups. Some young Aphrodites are "nymphets": precociously aware of their sexuality, they enjoy the sense of power and attraction they have when older men respond to their teasing flirtatiousness.

PARENTS

Some parents groom their pretty daughters to be little Aphrodites. They emphasize their daughters' attractiveness, make them kiss the grownups, enter them in child beauty contests, and in general, focus on their feminine attractiveness over all other attributes and abilities.

But when the girl reaches puberty and the possibility of sexual activity, her parents may respond very differently. A common destructive pattern may arise: the parents give her covert encouragement to become sexually active, but then punish her. This situation allows parents to be both voyeurs and upholders of morals.

Fathers may react to the emerging sexuality of their Aphrodite daughters in a variety of ways. Many fathers respond to their daughters' growing attractiveness by inadvertently and/or unconsciously provoking noisy conflicts that create emotional and physical distance between the two. The daughters often seem to collaborate in the uproar, which protects both parties against becoming aware of their incestuous feelings. Some fathers become overly strict and refuse to let daughters date at all, or they become intrusive and controlling, "cross-examining" daughters about their dates and giving any male callers "the third degree." And yet other fathers are seductive.

Mothers have a range of reactions to Aphrodite daughters, too. Some mothers become strict and controlling, over-reacting to teenage music and dress styles, even when their daughters are behaving appropriately for their age group. Such mothers may impose their own "dress code," which emphasizes covering up and deemphasizes attractiveness, and may prohibit many activities. They may screen their daughters' friends of both sexes, or, as one woman ruefully observed, may treat either their daughters or boys or both as "potential sex maniacs." Like fathers, mothers too can develop a "jailer mentality" toward their Aphrodite daughters.

Intrusiveness may be more common in the mothers of Aphrodite daughters than in the fathers. Besides the intrusiveness motivated by the need to "keep on eye on" their attractive daughters, mothers sometimes live vicariously through daughters and want to hear every detail about their dates. To please such mothers, daughters need to be popular with boys.

Other mothers react competitively to the emerging Aphrodite in their daughters. Threatened by their daughters' attractiveness, and envious of their youth, the mothers depreciate the girls, make unfavorable comparisons, flirt with their daughters' boyfriends, and in many large and small ways undermine their daughters' budding womanhood. In her fairytale, Snow White's stepmother repeatedly asked, "Mirror, mirror on the wall, who is the fairest one of all?" This fairytale character represents the threatened (and therefore hostile) competitive mother.

The most helpful parents do not overvalue or overemphasize Aphrodite qualities and do not treat their daughters as pretty objects. Both parents affirm their daughters' attractiveness in the same positive way that they value other qualities such as intelligence, kindness, or talent for art. For the dating situation, they also provide guidance and limits appropriate for their daughters' age and maturity. Attractiveness to men is treated as a matter of fact that girls need to be aware of (not blamed for).

ADOLESCENCE AND EARLY ADULTHOOD

The adolescent and young adult years are crucial times for the Aphrodite woman, who may find herself caught between the stirrings of Aphrodite within her and the reaction of others. Given the double standard, the high school girl who has a desire for sexual experience every bit as strong as a sexually preoccupied young man, must weigh the consequences. A bad reputation, tarnished self-esteem, and a negative self-image may result if she acts on her urges. And "good girls" may avoid her, while young men with sex on their minds may flock around but not consider her "good enough" to be a steady, or a date for the prom.

There are other problems with an uncontrolled Aphrodite archetype, too. An unwanted pregnancy is one possibility. And an active Aphrodite risks exposure to sexually transmitted diseases. Another medical complication is a higher risk of cervical cancer later in life.

Young women are given little help with how to handle the insistent Aphrodite within. Sexual expression is a major choice with serious consequences. Some suppress their sexuality, although those who feel strong religious constraints may feel guilty anyway, blaming themselves for having "unacceptable" feelings. Others express sexuality within a steady relationship, a choice that works well if Hera is also a strong part of the personality, although an early marriage may be the result.

If Athena and Aphrodite are both strong elements in a young woman, she may use a combination of strategy and sexuality that is self-protective. One such women said, "Once I knew that I fell in and out of love easily, and had a strong sex drive to go along with it, I didn't take falling in love too seriously. What I did take seriously was birth control, who the guy was, and keeping this part of my life private."

When an Aphrodite women goes to college, social aspects will probably be the most important for her. She may choose a "party school"—a college noted more for social activities than academic studies.

She is not usually focused on long-range academic goals or on a career. Her budding interest in a professional career wanes at the prospect of taking difficult prerequisites that do not interest her. She is capable of plunging into college work only if she becomes fascinated with a subject—most often in a creative field involving interactions with people. She might be a drama major, for example, who goes from one role to another. Each time, she immerses herself in her role, tapping her own innate passion, and thus may turn out to be the most outstanding drama student in the school.

WORK

Work that does not involve an Aphrodite woman emotionally holds no interest for her. She likes variety and intensity; repetitious tasks such as housework, clerical, or laboratory work bore her. Only when she can be totally engrossed creatively does she do well. Thus, she is likely to be found in art, music, writing, dance, or drama, or with people who are special to her; for example, as a teacher, therapist, editor. As a consequence, she either hates her work and is probably doing a mediocre job, or loves it and thinks nothing of putting in extra time and effort. She almost always prefers a job that she finds interesting to a better-paying one with less appeal. She may achieve success as a result of doing what fascinates her but, unlike Athena or Artemis, she does not set out to achieve.

RELATIONSHIPS WITH MEN

Aphrodite women gravitate toward men who are not necessarily good for them or to them. Unless other goddesses have an influence, their choice of men is often similar to Aphrodite's own choices—creative, complex, moody or emotional men like Hephaestus, Ares, and Hermes. Such men do not aim for occupational pinnacles or positions of authority, and they don't want to head households or be husbands and fathers.

The introverted, intense Hephaestus type may have repressed anger that he sublimates into creative work. Like the God of the Forge, he may be both an artist and (in emotional terms) a cripple. His relationship with his parents may have been as bad as that of Hephaestus. He, too, may have been rejected by his mother when he didn't live up to her expectations, and may have been cut off from having a relationship with his father. Consequently, he may have a love/hate relationship with women, whom he resents for being both terribly important to him and untrustworthy. And he may feel very little closeness with men, whom he often feels estranged from and inferior to.

Often an intensely introverted man, the Hephaestus type is ill at ease in social situations, with no talent for small talk. Hence others don't linger in his company. The Aphrodite woman may be the exception. With her talent of focusing her total attention on the person she is meeting, she may draw him out and find him fascinating.

Feeling attractive and attracted to her, the Hephaestus man responds with his characteristic intensity, and a passionate connection is likely to flare up between them. She is attracted by the intensity of his feelings and responds in kind to his emotional fire, which may repel other women. She embraces his deeply felt erotic nature, which may lie dormant for periods of time—sublimated into his work along with his anger. When she evokes his passion, both lovers may be awed by the upsurge of his feeling. If he is a craftsman or an artist, she may also be drawn to the beautiful things he makes, and in doing so she may inspire his creativity.

The problems of loving a Hephaestus man are many, depending on the kind of feelings he keeps under wraps and on his psychological health. At one extreme, he may be a pent-up volcano, potentially paranoid—a loner whose work may not gain recognition because he is so solitary and hostile. In addition, feelings of anger, inferiority, and fear of loss are likely to be triggered in him by an Aphrodite woman's attractiveness or her attraction to others. If he is truly like Hephaestus, he may be able to keep his jealousy under control. Being around a Hephaestus man under these circumstances, however, feels like living on the side of an active volcano, wondering when an eruption might blow things sky high.

Some Hephaestus-Aphrodite combinations do work out very well. The Hephaestus man in this case is an introverted, creative man who feels a range of emotions (rather than mainly anger) in his characteristically intense and contained way. He expresses these emotions through his work and through a few important relationships. He loves her deeply and passionately, yet is not possessive. His intensity holds her emotionally, and his commitment to her provides a stability she needs.

Another man commonly attracted to an Aphrodite woman is volatile, like Ares (God of War, son of Hera and Zeus). The real-life history of this type of man may bear a close resemblance to Ares's mythological family configuration: raised by his bitter mother after his father left them. He is an emotional, passionate, blustering man, who has "supermacho" affectations. Lacking a real father as a role model and disciplinarian, and used to getting his way with his mother, he is impatient and has a low tolerance for frustration. He likes to be in charge, yet he may lose his head when pressured, which doesn't make him a good leader.

The Aphrodite-Ares combination is an inflammable mix. Both share a propensity to live in the here and now. Both are reactive rather than reflective; they are do-now, think-later people. Whenever they get together, erotic sparks or fiery tempers set off blazing interactions. They make both love and war. This combination invented fight-and-make-up lovers' quarrels.

Aphrodite and Ares are not the ingredients of a stable relationship. Besides the emotional flareups, his swagger-braggart machismo often causes a precarious economic situation. He is unable to think strategically or be prudent; in the heat of the moment, he may say or do something that costs him his job. If, in addition, the woman has Aphrodite's tendency for infidelity—or at the very least, her flirtatiousness—she further threatens his masculinity and triggers his possessiveness. Then he may become violent, and his outbursts may be brutal, creating terror and fear.

For all their fireworks, however, it is possible for some Ares-Aphrodite matches to endure and be relatively harmonious. In such a match, he has an Ares personality—impulsive, intensely emotional and combative by nature—but had a healthier family situation, and so isn't basically hostile. And she has enough Hera in her to develop an enduring bond with him.

A man who acts the eternal youth also attracts many Aphrodite women, who seem to have a penchant for immature, complex, subjectively focused men with creative potential. They resemble Hermes the Messenger God, youngest of the Olympians. She finds his facility with words intoxicating—especially when he is poetic—and is fascinated by his ability to move quickly from the heights to the depths (emotional or social). A Hermes type can be a trickster, a bit of the con man, who loves to outsmart "slower" minds. He's full of potential, often very talented though undisciplined, charismatic, and not committed to work or to her. Typically, he breezes in and out of her life. Pinning him down to anything is like trying to hold on to quicksilver. He talks in "maybes," and plays with the fantasy about living together or getting married. But she had better not count on it, because he's the last one to ever make a commitment. Sex with him is unpredictable and highly charged. He's a charming, sensitive lover, a playful Peter Pan who may never grow up.

Aphrodite-Hermes combinations suit some Aphrodite women very well, in that both share a here-and-now intensity and lack of commitment. However, if Aphrodite and Hera are both strong archetypes, this is a very painful match for her. Such a woman will bond deeply to him and be tormented by jealousy. Sexuality between them is intense. She is monogamous and wants to marry, but usually must settle for an arrangement that suits his need to come and go.

A mature Hermes man, however, is able to commit himself to work and to a relationship (as noted earlier, he may marry a Hestia woman); he's likely a business man or communicator rather than an elusive eternal youth. If so, the Aphrodite-Hermes match can be an excellent one. Their relationship can survive flirtations and even affairs, because neither are jealous or possessive people. Moreover, the relationship can endure because they enjoy each other's company and style. She keeps up with his on-the-move pace, which is compatible with her own. They can be intensely involved with each other one moment and independent the next, which suits them both.

MARRIAGE

If Aphrodite is one of several strong archetypes including Hera, then her presence enhances and vitalizes marriage with sexuality and passion. An enduring monogamous marriage, however, is often difficult for an Aphrodite woman to attain. Unless other goddesses are influential in containing Aphrodite within the marriage, or the marriage is a particularly fortuitous combination, she will probably follow a pattern of serial relationships. For example, actress Elizabeth Taylor, whose public image is that of a contemporary Aphrodite, has had a string of marriages.

RELATIONSHIPS WITH WOMEN: MISTRUSTED LADY

An Aphrodite woman may be mistrusted by other women, especially by Hera women. The less conscious or less responsible she is about her effect on men, the more disruptive an element she can be. For instance, she may go to a party and engage in intense, erotically charged conversations with the most interesting men there. Thus she stimulates jealousy, feelings of inadequacy, and fear of loss in many women who see their men reacting to her with increased animation, as the alchemy between them casts a golden aura around them both.

When women (especially a jealous or vindictive Hera) get angry with her, the Aphrodite woman is often shocked. She rarely bears other women ill-will, and since she is not possessive or jealous herself, she often has trouble fathoming the cause of the hostility toward her.

An Aphrodite woman often has a wide circle of women friends (none Hera women) and acquaintances who enjoy her spontaneity and attractiveness. Many of them share Aphrodite qualities with her. Others seem to function as her attendants, either enjoying her company or living vicariously through her amorous adventures. However, her friendships last only if her friends don't take personal offense when she treats casually the plans she has made with them.

A lesbian Aphrodite woman differs from a heterosexual one only in her sexual preference. She, too, brings Aphrodite consciousness to relationships and then, in turn, herself responds to the alchemy she generates. She becomes intensely involved in relationships, falls in love often, and as a consequence usually has a series of important relationships. Wanting to experience "everything life has to offer," she often has sexual relationships with men as well as women. Unconstrained by the need to live up to what men expect women to be, a lesbian Aphrodite—perhaps more than her heterosexual counterpart—exercises Aphrodite's prerogative to pick and choose her lovers. The alternative lifestyle that the lesbian community offers suits her lifelong unconventionality.

Lesbian women sometimes discover Aphrodite in themselves through a relationship with another woman, as suggested by Ruth Falk in her book, *Women Loving*.[2] She described looking at the beauty in another woman, and feeling beautiful herself; touching another woman and feeling as if she had been touched herself. In her view, each woman "mirrored" the other, allowing each to find her own feminine sensuality.

CHILDREN

Aphrodite women like children, and vice versa. A child senses that this woman looks at him or her with a nonjudgmental and appreciative eye. She draws out a child's feelings or abilities in such a way that the child feels beautiful and accepted. Often she instills a sense of specialness that may give the child confidence and help develop abilities and talents. She can get into the spirit of play and make-believe very easily. She seems to charm children into behaving well, and to inspire them with her infectious enthusiasm for whatever interests her. These are wonderful qualities in a mother. The children of Aphrodite women thrive and develop their individuality if Demeter qualities are also present.

An Aphrodite mother can captivate her children, who see her as beautiful and glamorous, but if (lacking Demeter) she doesn't consider their need for emotional security and constancy, she'll be inconsistent, which has negative consequences on them. Her children then revel in receiving her total attention one moment, and are desolated when her attention goes elsewhere the next moment. One of my patients had an Aphrodite mother who would leave her for long periods of time with a housekeeper. She described the homecomings that were so special: "Mother would swoop into the house, her arms outstretched to greet me. I felt as if I were the most important person in the world." Her mother brought "sunshine with her"; it was as if a goddess had returned. It didn't matter that she had resented her mother's absence and had even greeted news of her return with sullenness; all was forgiven as soon as she basked in her mother's charismatic Aphrodite glow. She grew up uncertain about her abilities (which were exceptional) and had to cope with feelings of worthlessness and depression, which paralleled her feeling when her mother was away.

When an Aphrodite mother's inconstant and intense attention is focused on a son, it affects his future relationships with women as well as his self-esteem and potential for depression. She creates a special intimacy between them that seduces the budding man in her son and draws him to her, and then she turns her attention somewhere else. A rival for her affection—often a new man, sometimes some other fascination—takes her away, leaving him feeling inadequate, devastated, powerless, angry, and sometimes humiliated as well. The son feels a personal rivalry, a competition he repeatedly loses with the men in his mother's life, which are feelings most daughters are spared. As a grown man, he yearns to have the intensity and the specialness he once felt with his mother, only this time he wants to be in control. Based on his childhood experience with his mother, he mistrusts a woman's fidelity, and may feel incapable of keeping her affection.

MIDDLE YEARS

The inevitability of aging may be a devastating reality for the Aphrodite woman if her attractiveness has been her chief source of gratification. Once she becomes self-conscious or anxious that her beauty is fading, her attention may shift, preventing her from total absorption in the other person. She may be unaware that this Aphrodite quality—even more than her physical beauty—was what drew people to her.

At midlife, an Aphrodite woman often also becomes unhappy with her choice of partners. She may notice how frequently she has been attracted to unconventional and sometimes unsuitable men. She may now want to settle down—a possibility she may have spurned before.

However, the middle years are not difficult for Aphrodite women who are engaged in creative work. Typically, such women retain their enthusiasm and still throw themselves into work that interests them. And now they have more experience to draw inspiration from, and more highly developed skills with which to express themselves.

LATER YEARS

Some Aphrodite women retain the capacity to see beauty in, and always be a little in love with, whatever or whomever they focus on. They grow old with grace and vitality. Their interest in others or involvement with creative work remains the most important part of their lives. They hold on to a youthful attitude as they move unselfconsciously from experience to experience, and person to person, fascinated with whatever comes next. Typically young at heart, they attract others to them and have friends of all ages. For example, Imogene Cunningham even in her nineties was a spritely photographer who continued to capture the beauty she saw on film, and in turn drew others to photograph her.

PSYCHOLOGICAL DIFFICULTIES

It is not easy to have Aphrodite as a compelling archetype. Women who follow Aphrodite's instinctive sexuality often get caught between, on the one hand, their own desire for sexual connection and their proclivity for generating erotic energy in others, and, on the other hand, a culture that considers a woman promiscuous if she acts on her desires and a tease if she does not.

IDENTIFYING WITH APHRODITE

A woman most closely identified with Aphrodite often is an extraverted woman with a lust for life and a fiery element in her personality. She likes men and draws them to her with her attractiveness and interest in them. Her attentiveness is seductive; she makes a man feel that he is special and sexy. This attention invites a reciprocal response in him, generating erotic attraction between them, which leads to a desire for sexual intimacy. If she identifies with Aphrodite, she will act on this desire without considering the consequences. But the consequences may be social condemnation, a series of shallow relationships, possible exploitation by men who seek sex with her and nothing more, and subsequent lowered self-esteem. She needs to know how to contain Aphrodite in some circumstances, and how to respond in others—how to choose wisely "when and with whom," and how not to be propelled by the archetype into destructive situations.

Her warm and attentive mode of relating may also be misread by men who mistakenly assume that she is especially interested in or sexually attracted to them. Then, when she rebuffs them, she may be thought of as a heartbreaker or tease, and blamed for leading men on. Such men may feel tricked and resentful, and may turn hostile and angry. As the object of unwanted infatuation and angry rejection, an Aphrodite woman may be hurt, may become angry herself, and may be confused about what she has done to evoke such responses. When an Aphrodite woman becomes aware of this pattern, she can learn to dampen the budding ardor of a man she doesn't want to encourage. She can indicate her unavailability to him or become more impersonal in manner.

DENYING APHRODITE

When an Aphrodite woman is raised in an atmosphere that condemns sexuality in women, she may attempt to stifle her interest in men, downplay her attractiveness, and consider herself bad for having sexual feelings. But guilt and conflict over expressing her Aphrodite nature lead to her feeling depressed and anxious. And if she acts the part so well that she splits off her sexuality and sensuality from her consciousness, she will lose touch with a major part of her real self, and thus lose her vitality and spontaneity.

DRAWBACKS OF LIVING IN THE PRESENT

Aphrodite women tend to live in the immediate present, taking life in as if it were nothing more than a sensory experience. In a grip of the moment, such a woman may respond as if there would be no future consequences to her actions, and/or no current loyalties that might conflict. This orientation goes beyond an impulsive affair that will be disruptive for all concerned. For example, she may buy beautiful things that she can't afford, or habitually "stand people up." She makes plans with great enthusiasm and every intention to carry them out. But when the appointed time comes, she may be engrossed in something or someone else.

Although the lessons are painful, experience is the best teacher for an Aphrodite woman. She learns that people get hurt and angry when she treats them as "out of sight, out of mind." When she doesn't think her financial situation through before impulsively buying what catches her eye, she finds that charge accounts get out of hand and dunning letters arrive. She repeats patterns that cause pain for herself and others, until she learns to resist the tyranny of the here-and-now, which has been leading her to live as if there were no tomorrow.

When an Aphrodite woman learns to reflect on the consequences before she acts, she will respond somewhat less impulsively and behave more responsibly. However, emotional priorities will continue to carry more weight than practical considerations. And she may still hurt others by her behavior, even when she deliberates on her course of action beforehand, because she ultimately follows her heart.

CASUALTIES OF LOVE

Men may become casualties when an Aphrodite woman "loves them and leaves them." She falls in love very easily, each time sincerely convinced that she has found the perfect man. In the magic of the moment, he may feel himself a god in love with a goddess, only to be dropped and replaced. As a consequence, she leaves in her wake a series of wounded, rejected, depressed, or angry men who feel used and discarded.

An Aphrodite woman may go through a series of intense love affairs, swept up each time by the magic (or archetypal experience) of being in love. To end this pattern, she must learn to love someone "warts and all"—someone who is an imperfect human rather than a god. First she must become disenchanted with facile infatuations; usually only experience can bring about such disillusionment. Only then can she stay in a relationship long enough to accept the human flaws in her partner and herself and to discover the human dimensions of love.

The "Curse" of Love

The goddess Aphrodite's power to make others love could be destructive. For example, she sometimes compelled a woman to love someone who did not or could not return her love. Or she created passion that was shameful or illicit, would lead to conflict or humiliation, and would eventually destroy the woman or her positive qualities. Myrrha, Phaedra, and Medea were three mythological women who were so cursed. As a result, they became "sick" with love. And when Aphrodite was angry at Psyche, she planned to have her fall in love "with the vilest of men." The goddess was quite aware that love could cause suffering.

Women who are unhappily bound by their love may be contemporary victims of Aphrodite. Some seek psychiatric help for their misery. Two typical patterns have emerged in my practice. In the first, the woman is in love with a man who treats her badly or who minimizes her. She subordinates everything else in her life for the "crumbs" of attention she occasionally gets from him. Her involvement may be of short duration or may have stretched over decades. Characteristically, she is tormented by the relationship and by her efforts to convince herself that he really loves her, in spite of evidence to the contrary. She is depressed and unhappy, yet highly ambivalent about changing her situation. But to feel better she would have to give up the destructive relationship, which has an addictive hold on her.

The second pattern appears even more hopeless. Here the woman is in love with a man who makes it clear that he wants nothing to do with her. He avoids her when he can and feels cursed by her unrequited love. Again, her obsessive involvement with him may span years, effectively preventing the possibility of any other relationship. In pursuit of him, she may have followed him to another city (as one of my patients did) or may have been arrested for trespassing or forcibly ejected from his house.

To free oneself from this curse of Aphrodite is difficult. In order to change, the woman must see the destructiveness of this attachment and want to let the relationship go. It takes a tremendous effort to avoid the temptation to see him and become reengaged with him. But she must do so before she can invest her emotions elsewhere.

WAYS TO GROW

Knowledge about her archetypal pattern is helpful information for all types of women, especially for Aphrodite women. It helps them to know that it is their "goddess-given" nature to fall in love easily, to experience erotic attractions, and to have a strong sexual drive that many other women do not. Such knowledge helps free Aphrodite women from guilt for being who they are. At the same time, they must become aware that they must look out for their own best interests, because the goddess does not.

Although other goddess archetypes may not be prominent in an Aphrodite woman, they usually are present at least in latent form. With certain life experiences, they can grow in influence, offsetting or modifying Aphrodite's power in a woman's psyche. If an Aphrodite woman develops skills or acquires an education, Artemis and Athena are likely to grow in importance. If she marries and has a child, Hera and Demeter may have a stabilizing influence. If she develops Hestia through meditation, she may more easily resist the extraverted pull of erotic attraction. And cultivating Persephone's introversion may allow an Aphrodite woman to live out a sexual experience in fantasy rather than in reality.

When an Aphrodite woman becomes conscious of her pattern, and decides to modify it so that she or others she loves will not be hurt, a major shift occurs. Making choices and shaping consequences becomes possible, once she can sort out her priorities and act on them. The Psyche myth describes a developmental path she can follow.

THE PSYCHE MYTH: A METAPHOR FOR PSYCHOLOGICAL GROWTH

The myth of Eros (Amor) and Psyche has been used as an analogy for the psychology of the feminine by several Jungian analysts—most notably, Erich Neumann in his book *Amor and*

Psyche, and Robert Johnson in *She*. Psyche is a pregnant mortal woman who seeks to be reunited with her husband, Eros, God of Love and Aphrodite's son. Psyche realizes that she must submit herself to an angry and antagonistic Aphrodite if she is ever to be reconciled with Eros, so she presents herself to the goddess. To test her, Aphrodite gives her four tasks.

The four tasks of Aphrodite have important symbolic meanings. Each one represents a capability that women need to develop. Each time Psyche masters a task, she acquires an ability she did not have before—an ability equated in Jungian psychology with the animus or masculine aspect of a woman's personality. Although these abilities often feel "masculine" to women who, like Psyche, need to make an effort to develop them, they are natural attributes of Artemis and Athena women.

As a mythological figure, Psyche is a lover (like Aphrodite), a wife (like Hera), and a pregnant mother (Demeter). Moreover, in the course of her myth she also goes to the underworld and returns (and so resembles Persephone as well). Women who put relationships first and react instinctively or emotionally to others need to develop the abilities symbolized by each task. Only then can they assess their options and act decisively in their best interests.

Task 1: Sorting the Seeds. Aphrodite leads Psyche into a room and shows her an enormous pile of seeds jumbled together—corn, barley, millet, poppy, chick peas, lentils, and beans—and tells her that she must sort each kind of seed or grain into its own pile before evening. The task seems impossible until a host of lowly ants come to her aid, placing each kind, grain by grain, in its own mound.

Similarly, when a woman must make a crucial decision, she often must first sort out a jumble of conflicted feelings and competing loyalties. The situation is often especially confusing when Aphrodite has a hand in the situation. "Sorting the seeds" is, then, an inward task, requiring that a woman look honestly within, sift through her feelings, values, and motives, and separate what is truly important from what is insignificant.

When a woman learns to stay with a confused situation and not act until clarity emerges, she has learned to trust "the ants." These insects are analogous to an intuitive process, the workings of which are beyond conscious control. Or clarity can come through her conscious efforts to systematically or logically assess and assign priority to the many elements involved in a decision.

Task 2: Acquiring Some Golden Fleece. Aphrodite next orders Psyche to acquire some golden fleece from the terrible rams of the sun. They are huge, aggressive, horned beasts who are in a field, butting against each other. If Psyche were to go among them and try to take their wool, she would surely be trampled or crushed. Once again the task seems impossible until a green reed comes to her aid and advises her to wait until sundown, when the rams disperse and retire. Then she can safely pick strands of golden fleece off the brambles against which the rams had brushed.

Symbolically, the golden fleece represents power, which a woman needs to acquire without being destroyed in the attempt to attain some. When an Aphrodite woman (or a vulnerable goddess type) goes out into the competitive world where others battle aggressively for power and position, she may be hurt or disillusioned if she does not recognize the dangers. She may become hardened and cynical; her caring and trusting self may become a casualty, "trampled underfoot." An armored Athena can be in the midst of a battlefield, directly involved in strategy and politics, but a woman who is like Psyche does better observing, waiting, and gradually acquiring power indirectly.

Acquiring the golden fleece without destroying Psyche is a metaphor for the task of gaining power and remaining a compassionate person. In my psychiatric practice, I find that keeping this task in mind is very helpful to every woman who is learning to assert herself. Otherwise, by focusing only on expressing her needs or anger, her conversations become alienating confrontations that do not help her achieve what she wants and that present her in a harsh, destructive light.

Task 3: Filling the Crystal Flask. For the third task, Aphrodite places a small crystal flask in Psyche's hand and tells her she must fill it with water from a forbidding stream. This stream cascades from a spring at the summit of the highest cliff to the lowest depth of the underworld, before being drawn up through the earth to emerge once more from the spring. Metaphorically, this stream represents the circular flow of life, into which Psyche must dip to fill her flask.

As she gazes at the icy stream, which is etched deeply into a jagged cliff and guarded by dragons, the task of filling her flask seems impossible. This time, an eagle comes to her aid. The eagle symbolizes the ability to see the landscape from a distant perspective and swoop down to grasp what is needed. This is not the usual perceptive mode for a woman, such as Psyche, who is so personally involved that she "cannot see the forest for the trees."

It is especially important for Aphrodite women to get some emotional distance on her relationships, in order to see overall patterns and pick out important details that will enable her to grasp what is significant. Then she can assimilate experience and shape the form her life can take.

Task 4: Learning to Say No. For her fourth and final task, Aphrodite orders Psyche to descend into the underworld with a small box for Persephone to fill with beauty ointment. Psyche equates the task with death. Now it is a far-seeing tower's turn to give advice to her.

This task is more than the traditional hero's test of courage and determination, for Aphrodite has made it particularly difficult. Psyche is told that she will encounter pathetic people who will ask her for help, and three times she will have to "harden her heart to compassion," ignore their pleas, and continue on. If she does not, she will stay forever in the underworld.

To set a goal and keep to it in the face of requests for help is especially difficult for all except virgin goddess women. Maternal Demeter women and obliging Persephone women are the most responsive to the needs of others, while Hera and Aphrodite women are somewhere in between.

The task Psyche accomplishes when she says no, three times, is to exercise choice. Many women allow themselves to be imposed on and diverted from doing something for themselves. They cannot accomplish whatever they set out to do, or what is best for them, until they learn to say no. Whether it is a person who needs their company or comfort, or the attraction of an erotically charged relationship, until a woman can say no to her particular susceptibility, she cannot determine her own life course.

Through the four tasks, Psyche evolves. She develops capabilities and strengths as her courage and determination are tested. Yet, despite all she acquires, her basic nature and priorities remain unchanged: she values a love relationship, risks everything for it, and wins.

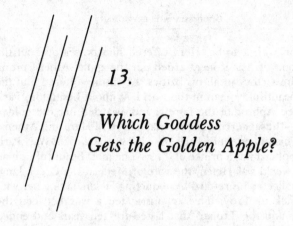

13.

Which Goddess
Gets the Golden Apple?

Competition, conflicts and alliance among the goddesses occur within a woman's psyche—as they once did on Mt. Olympus. Which one does a woman heed? Which one does she ignore? How much choice does she exercise? These inner figures representing powerful archetypal patterns compete for expression, as Greek goddesses themselves once vied for the golden apple—the prize decided by the judgment of Paris.

THE JUDGMENT OF PARIS

All the Olympians except Eris, Goddess of Strife and Discord (a minor goddess), were invited to the wedding of Peleus, King of Thessaly, to the beautiful sea nymph Thetis. Eris came to the great occasion uninvited, and got her revenge for the slight. She disrupted the festivities by tossing a golden apple inscribed "For the Fairest" among the assembled guests. It rolled across the floor and was immediately claimed by Hera, Athena, and Aphrodite. Each felt it was rightfully and deservedly hers. They could not, of course, decide among themselves who was the most beautiful, so they appealed to Zeus for a decision. He declined to make the choice, instead directing them to find the shepherd Paris, a mortal with an eye for beautiful women, who would be the judge.

The three goddesses found Paris living the bucolic life with a mountain nymph on the slopes of Mt. Ida. In turn, each of the three beautiful goddesses attempted to influence his decision with a bribe. Hera offered him power over all the kingdoms of Asia if he awarded her the apple. Athena promised him victory in all his battles. Aphrodite offered him the most beautiful woman in the world. Without hesitation, Paris declared Aphrodite the fairest, and awarded her the golden apple—thus incurring the eternal hatred of Hera and Athena.

This Judgment of Paris later led to the Trojan War. Paris the shepherd was a prince of Troy. The most beautiful woman in the world was Helen, the wife of Menelaus, a Greek king. Paris collected his reward by abducting Helen, taking her with him back to Troy. This act instigated a war between the Greeks and the Trojans that lasted for ten years and ended with the destruction of Troy.

Five Olympians arrayed themselves on the side of the Greeks: Hera and Athena (whose partisanship for the Greek heroes was colored by their animosity toward Paris), joined by Poseidon, Hermes, and Hephaestus. Four gods and goddesses took the side of the Trojans: Aphrodite, Apollo, Ares, and Artemis.

The Judgment of Paris also inspired some of the greatest literature and drama in Western civilization. The events set in motion by that decision were immortalized in the *Iliad*, the *Odyssey*, and the *Aeneid* (the three great classical epics), as well as in the tragedies of Aeschylus, Sophocles, and Euripides.

UPDATING THE JUDGMENT OF PARIS

Each contemporary woman faces her own personal Judgment of Paris. The questions are the same ones presented to the Olympian guests: "Which goddess gets the golden apple?" and "Who is to judge?"

WHICH GODDESS GETS THE GOLDEN APPLE?

In the myth, only three of the goddesses present claimed the apple for themselves. The three were Hera, Athena, and Aphrodite. In an individual woman's psyche, however, the competitors may differ. Maybe only two are vying for the apple, or three, or four—any combination of the seven goddesses may be in conflict with each other. Within each woman, activated archetypes often vie for supremacy, or compete for dominance.

Given the original myth, what does it mean to choose "the fairest"—with Hera, Athena, and Aphrodite vying for preeminence over the other two? Looking at what these three goddesses symbolize, I was struck by the realization that they can represent the three major directions that a woman's life can take—aspects within a woman that often are in conflict. Hera puts marriage first; so would the woman who identifies with Hera's goals. Athena values the use of intellect to achieve mastery, a woman who honors her as the fairest would consider her career primary. Aphrodite favors beauty, love and passion, and creativity as the ultimate values, and the woman who agrees will place the vitality of her subjective life above enduring relationships and achievements.

These choices are fundamentally different, because each of these three goddesses is in a different category. Hera is a vulnerable goddess, Athena a virgin goddess, and Aphrodite is the alchemical goddess. In the lives of women, one of the three styles represented by these categories usually predominates.

WHO IS TO JUDGE? WHO DECIDES WHICH GODDESS GETS THE GOLDEN APPLE?

In the myth, a mortal man made the decision. In patriarchal cultures, mortal men do. And, of course, if men decide what women's place should be, then the choice is limited to what suits men. For example, the 3 K's—Kinder, Küche, Kirche (children, kitchen, and church)—once defined the boundaries of most German women's lives.

On a personal level, the question "Which goddess gets the golden apple?" describes an ongoing competition. Beginning with her parents and relatives, extending to teachers and classmates, friends, dates, husbands, and even children—the Judgment of Paris goes on and on, with everyone handing out or withholding "golden apples," rewarding her with approval for what pleases them. For example, the little girl who has a quiet, solitary aspect to her personality (thanks to Hestia), as well as being a competitive tennis player (which may be either Artemis or Athena's influence), and whose motherly (Demeter) qualities come out with her little cousins will find that she gets approval more for some things than others. Does her father praise her for playing a good game of tennis or for being a good little mother? What does her mother value? Is this an introverted family, that expects its members to spend quiet time on their own? Or is this an extraverted family that thinks anyone who wants to be alone is peculiar? Is a girl supposed to hold back, not show what a good backhand she has, and always let a man beat her? Given the expectations of others, what does she do?

If a woman lets others decide what is important to her, then she will live out her parents' expectations and will conform to her social class assumptions of what she should do. In her life, which goddess will be honored will be determined by others.

If a woman decides for herself "which goddess gets the golden apple," basing that decision on the strength of the goddess in her, then whatever she decides will be meaningful to her. It may or may not be supported by her family and culture, but it will feel authentic.

GODDESSES IN CONFLICT: THE COMMITTEE AS METAPHOR

Within a woman, the goddesses may vie among themselves, or one may rule. Each time the woman must make a major decision, there may be a contest among the goddesses for the golden apple. If so, does the woman decide among competing priorities, instincts, and patterns? Or is the course she takes determined for her—by the goddess?

Joseph Wheelwright, a Jungian analyst and a mentor of mine, says that what goes on in our heads can be thought of as being like a committee, with various aspects of our personalities sitting around the table—male as well as female, young and old, some noisy and demanding, others quiet and cut off. If we are fortunate, a healthy ego sits at the head of the table, chairing the committee, deciding when and who should have a turn or take the floor. A chairperson keeps order by being an observant participant and an effective executive—qualities shared with a well-functioning ego. When the ego functions well, appropriate behavior results.

Chairing the committee is not an easy task, especially when there are goddesses in every woman, demanding and claiming power, at times in conflict with each other. When a woman's ego cannot keep order, one goddess archetype may intervene and take over the personality. Metaphorically, then, that goddess rules the mortal. Or an inner equivalent of an Olympian war can occur when equally strong archetypal elements are in conflict.

When a person is in inner conflict, the outcome depends on how the "members" of that particular person's "committee" work together. Like all committees, the functioning of the group depends on the chairperson and the members—who they are, how strong their viewpoints are, how cooperative or how contentious the group process is, and how much order the chair maintains.

ORDERLY PROCESS: THE EGO FUNCTIONS WELL AS CHAIR, AND ALL GODDESSES HAVE THE OPPORTUNITY TO BE HEARD

The first possibility is that there is an orderly process, presided over by an observing ego who can make clear choices based on adequate information. The ego is aware of the constituents and their different needs and motivations All relevant aspects of the personality are heard, reality is considered, and tension is tolerated. Since each goddess speaks for a particular instinct, value, or aspect of a woman's psyche (the totality of her personality), the amount of say that any one goddess has depends on how strong that particular archetype is, how involved it may be in that particular agenda item, and how much of the floor the ego (as chairperson) allows the goddess to have.

For example, a woman's decision may be what to do on Sunday. Hestia favors solitude and proposes a quiet day at home. Hera feels she has obligation to visit her husband's relatives. Athena reminds her that she has some unfinished work to do on funding a proposal. Artemis advocates going to a women's conference.

Or a woman's decision may concern what to do with the second half of her life. Here, every aspect of the personality, each goddess, may have a vested interest in the outcome. For example, is this the time, "now that the children are grown," to end an unsatisfactory marriage? Here Demeter may tip the scales. She had allied herself with Hera to stay in an unhappy situation "because of the children." Now will she join forces with Artemis and favor independence?

Or is this the time to go back to school or make a career change, thus heeding Athena or Artemis?

Or is it finally Demeter or Hera's turn to be heard? Has the woman focused all her energies on developing her career or becoming professionally proficient, and now at midlife—having arrived either at her destination or at a plateau—does she now feel an upsurge of maternal instinct, thanks to Demeter? Or does she know that she is lonely, look with envy at couples, and want to be married—having, up to now, refused to heed Hera?

Or is the missing goddess the quietest one of all—is it Hestia's turn to come up, as midlife brings with it a need for reflection and a search for spiritual values?

Midlife may bring a new configuration of goddesses, or the new prominence of one goddess. This potential shift happens at every major new stage of life—adolescence, adulthood, retirement, menopause, as well as midlife. When a time of transition comes, if the ego is in charge of an orderly, reflective, conscious process, then the woman considers priorities, loyalties, values, and reality factors. She does not force resolution of conflicting choices; resolution comes after the issues have become clear. This process may take five minutes, when she's deciding what to do on Sunday. Or it may take five years, when she is contemplating a major life change.

For example, I've seen women struggle for years to resolve "the baby question." Such a woman wonders what to do with her maternal instinct, what to do with her career. And what should she do if her husband and she disagree—if one wants a child and the other does not? What should she do now that she is in her thirties and motherhood is a time-limited possibility?

All these questions plagued the artist Georgia O'Keeffe, who never had a child. From Laura Lisle's biography, we know that O'Keeffe had since childhood felt an inner drive to be an artist. We know, too, that when she was in her mid-twenties she confided to a friend, "I've just got to have a baby—if I don't, my life just won't be complete."[1] When "the baby question" was a major issue, she was also deeply in love with Alfred Stieglitz, whom she first lived with and then married. He was one of the most influential forces in modern art. His gallery and his opinion of art and artists made artists' reputations. Stieglitz was convinced that O'Keeffe should not become a mother because it would divert her from painting. Thirty years older than O'Keeffe, and already a father with grown children, Stieglitz also did not want to become a father again.

The conflict within her and with him over the baby question, which began in 1918, went on for five years, apparently resolved only after two events tipped the scales. In 1923, a hundred of her paintings were exhibited. For perhaps the first time, she had outer confirmation that fulfilling the dream of being a successful artist was possible. That same year, Stieglitz's daughter gave birth to a son and then went into a severe postpartum depression, from which she was never to fully recover.

Concern for Stieglitz, for their relationship, and for her career as an artist aligned many parts of O'Keeffe against a strong maternal instinct. Hera, Aphrodite, Artemis, and Athena all sided against Demeter.

Although this alignment of the goddesses plus circumstance weighed the decision against having a child, O'Keeffe needed to let go of the possibility of being a mother without feeling resentful; otherwise this issue (or any issue) isn't fully resolved. When a person feels that she didn't have a choice and was forced to give up something important by outer circumstance, or inner compulsion, she feels angry, impotent, and depressed. Resentment saps her vitality and prevents her from concentrating fully on whatever she is doing, however meaningful the task may be. For O'Keeffe (or any woman) to be able to experience the loss of something important, and then plunge into creative work—her ego had to be more than a passive observer that tallies up the voting strength of archetypes. She had to actively endorse the outcome. To do this, a woman must be able to say, "I see who I am and what the circumstances are. I affirm these qualities as me, I accept reality as it is." Only then can the energy bound up in an issue be freed for other use.

SEE-SAW AMBIVALENCE: THE EGO IS INEFFECTUAL, AS COMPETING GODDESSES STRUGGLE FOR DOMINATION

While an orderly process is the best resolution, it is unfortunately not the only way in which internal conflict may be handled. If the ego passively goes along with whichever side is temporarily in power, then a see-saw pattern results, as first one side "wins" and gets its way, and then the other.

For example, a married woman may be strongly indecisive about ending an affair (knowing if she does not end the affair, that it will end her marriage). The conflict within her may feel as unresolvable and unending as the Trojan War once seemed. A woman with an ineffectual ego repeatedly ends the affair, only to be drawn back into it again and again.

The Trojan War is an apt metaphor for this situation. Helen, the fought-over prize, was like a passive ego in the midst of a marriage-or-affair conflict. A passive ego is held hostage, a possession of first one side and then the other.

The Greek forces were intent on returning Helen to her husband. On their side were the upholders of marriage. Foremost of them was Hera, Goddess of Marriage, who insisted that the struggle continue until Troy was destroyed and Helen returned to her husband, Menelaus. Also aiding the Greeks was Hephaestus, God of the Forge, who made armor for Achilles. Hephaestus's sympathy for the Greek position is understandable, since he was Aphrodite's cuckold husband. Another Greek ally was Poseidon, the patriarchal god who lived under the sea. And Athena, upholder of the rights of the patriarchy, naturally sided with the lawful husband.

These Olympians represent attitudes within a woman

that would act on her to preserve the marriage. They saw marriage as a sacred vow and as a lawful institution, believed that a wife is the possession of the husband, and felt sympathy for the husband.

Aphrodite, Goddess of Love and winner of the golden apple, was, of course, on the side of Troy. Interestingly, so were Artemis and Apollo, the androgynous twins—who may symbolize nonstereotyped roles for men and women, allowable only when the power of the patriarchy is challenged. The fourth Olympian on the side of Troy was Ares, God of War, who (like Paris) made love to the wife of another man. Ares was Aphrodite's lover.

These four Olympians speak for elements or attitudes in a woman's psyche that are often drawn together in an affair. They speak for sexual passion and love. They speak for autonomy—an insistence that her sexuality belongs to her and is not a possession of either the marriage or her husband. These four rebel against traditional roles, and are impulsive. Thus they join forces in an affair that can be seen as a declaration of war against her husband.

If a woman's ego passively goes along with the current winner of the inner conflict and the outer competition for her, she will see-saw back and forth between the two men in the triangle. This ambivalence damages both relationships, and all concerned.

COMMITTEE CHAOS: THE EGO BECOMES OVERWHELMED BY THE CONFLICTING GODDESSES

When fierce conflicts arise in a woman's psyche and the ego cannot maintain order, then an orderly process cannot even begin. Many voices are raised, and a cacophony of internal noise results—as if the goddesses were screaming their concerns, each trying to drown out the others. The woman's ego cannot sort out what the voices in her are saying, while a great pressure builds up inside. The woman in whom such chaos is going on feels confused and pressured to do something, at a time when she cannot keep her thoughts straight.

I once had a patient in her mid-forties in whom this "committee chaos" was precipitated as she was about to leave her husband. There was no other man, and it was a twenty-year marriage that others idealized. As long as she only contemplated this separation, she could hear the many competing points of view, more or less rationally. But when she told her husband what she was considering, and left to think things through, internal chaos erupted. She said it felt like "having a washing machine going on in my head" or "being in a washing machine." Aspects of herself were reacting with fear and alarm to what was an authentic decision, although full of risks.

For a while she was immobilized—her ego was temporarily overwhelmed. But rather than give up and go back, she held on to her need to sort things out, and stayed with friends until she achieved some clarity. Gradually her ego regained its usual position, and she heard and considered the voices of alarm and fear. In the end, she left her husband. And a year later, she was finally certain that it had been the right decision.

In such a situation, it is helpful to talk to someone else about the conflicting fears and impulses, or to write them out, in order to begin the process of sorting out the competing issues. When a mass of problems is broken down into separate concerns, the ego may no longer feel overwhelmed.

"Committee chaos" is often temporary, a short lapse following an initial chaotic reaction to something perceived as new and threatening. The ego shortly afterward restores order. If the ego does not restore order, however, the mental chaos can lead to a breakdown. The mind remains full of competing emotions, thoughts, and images; it becomes impossible to think logically; and the person stops functioning.

FAVORED AND CENSORED COMMITTEE MEMBERS: THE BIASED CHAIR FAVORS SOME GODDESSES AND REFUSES TO RECOGNIZE OTHERS

As chairperson, a biased ego recognizes only certain favored committee members. It silences others who express needs, feelings, or viewpoints that it considers unacceptable by calling them out of order. It censors whatever it doesn't want to look at or hear about, so that on the surface there appears to be no conflict. "Favored goddess status" is sometimes held by a few or even one goddess, whose views dominate. These are the goddesses with whom the ego identifies.

Meanwhile, the perspective and priorities of out-of-favor goddesses are suppressed or repressed. They may be mute or may not even appear to be present on the committee. Instead, their influence is felt "outside the committee room"—or outside consciousness. Actions, psychosomatic symptoms, and moods may be expressions of these censored goddesses.

"Acting out" is unconsciously motivated behavior that reduces tension created by conflicting feelings. For example, a married woman, Barbara, feels resentful that her husband's sister Susan always assumes that she, Susan, can always get a ride with Barbara. Barbara can't say no without feeling selfish and guilty, and she can't get angry because anger is unacceptable. Thus her ego as chair sides with Hera and Demeter, the goddesses who insist that she be the good wife who looks out for her husband's relatives and be a nurturing, caretaking person. Her ego represses the virgin goddesses who resent taking care of others. Inward tension builds up, which she discharges by "acting out." Barbara "forgets" the appointment to pick up Susan. Deliberately standing Susan up would have been very hostile—something Artemis or Athena might even advocate doing on purpose. By "forgetting," however, Barbara "acts out" the hostility and discourages Susan's habit. But Barbara is still "innocent" of her own anger and her assertion of independence.

Another, more significant example of acting out was provided by a patient of mine. She was due to audition for a supporting role in an important movie. The casting director had seen her and thought she might be perfect for the part, so he had asked her to try out. It was her big chance. The thirty-year-old actress was a member of a small repertory theater, and lived with the director of the theater. They had had an on-again, off-again relationship for three years.

Some part of her knew that he could not tolerate her having more success than he. But she had repressed this knowledge—along with a number of other insights that protected her from seeing him as he really was. When the movie opportunity came along, she prepared for the audition, rehearsed until the last minute, and became so absorbed that she "lost track of the time." She missed the appointment.

Thus, she "acted out" her ambivalence—although she wanted the role and consciously threw her efforts into it. Artemis gave her ambition, and Aphrodite helped her express her talent. But she was unconsciously afraid to get the role and test the relationship: Hera put the relationship first, and Demeter protected the man from feeling threatened or inadequate. Her decision not to try out for the role was made outside of consciousness.

Psychosomatic symptoms may be expressions of censored goddesses. For example, the independent woman with Athena qualities, who never asks for help and never seems to need anyone, may develop asthma attacks, or ulcers. Perhaps this is the only way her ego can allow dependent Persephone to get some maternal nurturing. Or the giving, Earth Mother type may turn out to have labile hypertension. Her blood pressure skyrockets from normal to high, often when she seems especially selfless. Although she may not have enough Artemis to stay focused on her own priorities, she feels tension and resentment when she so readily puts the needs of others first.

Moods can also reflect censored goddesses. That far-off, distant mood that a happily married woman gets into when she hears about friends who took different paths may represent the stirrings of virgin goddesses. That vague dissatisfaction felt by the career woman when she gets her period could be an unsatisfied Demeter.

Shifting Gears: When Several Goddesses "Take Turns"

Women often describe themselves as being "more than one person," when several goddesses take turns being the dominant influence. For example, Carolyn sells over a million dollars of insurance a year; she stays on top of a myriad of details and aggressively goes after clients. At work, she's an effective mixture of Athena and Artemis. At home, the business tiger turns into a solitary pussycat, who pads contentedly around her house and garden, as an introverted Hestia taking pleasure in solitude.

Leslie is the idea person in her advertising agency. Her presentations sparkle. Her creativity and her ability to be persuasive make her very effective. She's a dynamic mix of Artemis and Aphrodite, who easily slips into being a compliant Persephone with her husband.

Both women are aware that they behave like two different people, as they shift gears and go from one facet of their personalities to another; the daily changes are perfectly natural to them. In each situation they feel that they are being true to themselves—or to the goddesses that "take turns" being expressed in them.

Knowing about the shifts in their personalities, the "either-or" choices of psychological type tests confuse or amuse many women, who are well aware that the answers depend on how they feel. Whether they describe the reactions of their work self or their private self, the mother or the artist in them, how they react when they are by themselves or when they are in a couple, will affect their answers. The answers and thus the personality profile so often seems to depend on "which goddess" in the woman is taking the test. As one woman psychologist remarked, "I'm very extraverted at a party, and its not just a persona or party face I put on, it's me having a good time! Yet catch me doing my research and I'm a very different person." She's a bubbling Aphrodite in one setting; extraverted, emotionally responsive, and sensual. In the other, she's a careful Athena, meticulously carrying out a project she has thought through and now must gather evidence to verify.

When there is one major goddess archetype that dominates a woman's personality, her psychological type tests usually conform to Jungian theory. She will be consistently either extraverted (reacting directly to outer events and people) or introverted (responding to inner impressions she has); she will use either thinking (weighing rational considerations) or feeling (which weighs values) to evaluate people and situations; and either trust information obtained through the five senses, or through intuition. Sometimes only one of the four functions (thinking, feeling, sensation, intuition) is well-developed.

When there are two or more dominant goddess archetypes, a woman doesn't necessarily conform to one psychological type. She may be both introverted and extraverted, depending on the circumstances—and the prevailing goddess: an extraverted Artemis or Demeter may "have the golden apple" in one situation, but pass it to introverted Hestia or Persephone in another.

According to Jungian theory, thinking and feeling are the assessing functions, sensation and intuition the perceptive ones. When one of these four is the most developed, its opposite (the other one in the pair) is theoretically the least conscious one. Theory holds when one goddess pattern underlies the whole personality: while an Athena woman thinks with great clarity, her ability to assess feeling values is characteristically almost nonexistent. But such may not be the case when there is more than one important goddess. For example, if Artemis joins Athena as an activated archetype, then feeling as well as thinking may be equal or near-equally developed, contrary to theory.

Under these circumstances—when the goddesses cooperate and take turns being expressed within a woman—"which goddess gets the golden apple" depends on the circumstances and the task at hand.

CONSCIOUSNESS AND CHOICE

Once a woman (through her observing ego) becomes aware of the goddess archetypes and develops an appreciation of the committee as a metaphor for inner process, she has two very useful insight tools. She can listen with a sensitive ear to the voices within herself, recognize "who" is speaking, and become aware of the goddesses that influence her. When they represent conflicting aspects of herself that she must resolve, she can tune into the needs and concerns of each goddess, and then decide for herself what is most important.

If some goddesses are inarticulate and difficult to recognize—their presence only surmised through an acting-out episode, a psychosomatic symptom, or a mood—she may need time and attention to perceive who they are. Having an idea of the archetypal patterns and knowing the range of goddesses may help her identify those who need recognition.

Since all the goddesses are innate patterns in every woman, an individual woman may realize the need to become better acquainted with a particular goddess. In this case, efforts to develop or strengthen the influence of a particular goddess may be successful. For example, when Dana was working on her thesis it was often hard for her to muster the effort to do library research. But imagining herself as Artemis on a hunt gave her the impetus to get to the library and seek the articles she needed. The image of herself as Artemis activated the energy she needed for the task.

Actively imagining goddesses can help a woman know the archetypes active in her psyche. She might visualize a goddess, and then, once she has a vivid image in her mind, see if she can have a conversation with the visualized figure. Using "active imagination"—as this process that was discovered by Jung—is called, she may find that she can ask questions and get answers. If she is receptively attuned to hear an answer that she does not consciously invent, a woman using active imagination often finds herself as if in a real conversation, which increases her knowledge about an archetypal figure that is a part of herself.

Once a woman can tune in to the different parts of herself and can listen, observe, or feel her differing priorities and competing loyalties, she can then sort them out and measure their importance to her. She then can make conscious choices: when conflicts arise, she decides what priorities to place above others, and what course of action she will take. As a result, her decisions resolve inner conflicts instead of instigating internal wars. Step by step, she thus becomes a conscious choicemaker who repeatedly decides for herself which goddess gets the golden apple.

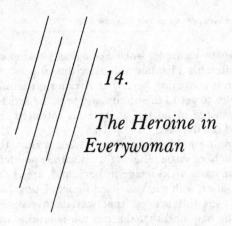

14.

The Heroine in Everywoman

There is a potential heroine in everywoman. She is the leading lady in her own life story on a journey that begins at her birth and continues through her lifetime. As she travels on her particular path, she will undoubtedly encounter suffering; feel loneliness, vulnerability, uncertainty; and know limitations. She also may find meaning, develop character, experience love and grace, and learn wisdom.

She is shaped by her choices, by her capacity for faith and love, by her ability to learn from experience and make commitments. When difficulties arise, if she assesses what she can do, decides what she will do, and behaves in ways consistent with her values and feelings, she is acting as the heroine-protagonist of her own myth.

Although life is full of unchosen circumstances, there are always moments of decision, nodal points that decide events or alter character. To be a heroine on her own heroic journey, a woman must begin with the attitude (or even at first act "as if") that her choices do matter. In the process of living from this premise, something happens: a woman becomes a choice-maker, a heroine who shapes who she will become. She either grows or is diminished by what she does or does not do and by the attitudes she holds.

My patients have taught me that it is not just what happened to them that shaped who they are, but what happened in them that made the difference. What they felt and how they reacted inwardly and outwardly determined who they became, much more than the degree of adversity they encountered. For example, I have met people who survived childhoods full of deprivation, cruelty, beatings, or sexual abuse. Moreover, they did not become (as might be expected) like the adults who abused them. Despite all the bad they experienced, they felt compassion for others, both then as well as now. Traumatic experience left its mark; they were not unscathed, yet an essence of trust, a capacity to love and hope, a sense of self survived. As I surmised why, I began to understand the difference between heroine and victim.

As children, each of these people somehow saw themselves as protagonists in a terrible drama. Each had an inner myth, a fantasy life, or imaginary companions. A daughter who was beaten and humiliated by her abusive father, and was not protected by her depressed mother, recalled telling herself when she was child that she was not related to this uneducated, backwoods family, that she was really a princess who was being tested by these ordeals. Another beaten and sexually molested child, who as an adult did not fit into the mold (that battered children eventually batter *their* children), escaped into a vivid fantasy life where life was far different. A third thought of herself as a warrior. These children thought ahead and planned how they could escape their families when they were old enough. They chose how they would react in the meantime. One said, "I would never let anyone see me cry" (instead, she would walk into the foothills and, out of sight, weep). Another said, "I think my mind left my body. I'd go somewhere else whenever he started to touch me."

These children were heroines and choicemakers. They maintained a sense of themselves apart from how they were treated. They assessed the situation, decided how they would react in the present, and made plans for the future.

As heroines, they were not strong and powerful demigods like Achilles or Heracles, who in Greek mythology were stronger and more protected than mere mortals (like comic book superheroes or John Wayne characters). These children, as precocious human heroines, were more like Hansel and Gretel, who had to use their wits when they were abandoned in the forest, or when the witch fattened Hansel for dinner. These children were like the rabbits who followed a vision to a new home in Richard Adams's novel *Watership Down:* they were small and powerless, sustained by an inner myth that if they endured and kept on, they would make it to a better place later.

Ayla, whose heroic journey takes her through Jean M. Auel's novels *The Clan of the Cave Bear* and *The Valley of Horses,* is a mythic heroine in prehistoric Ice Age Europe. The time and details are different and dramatic, yet the themes are remarkably similar to those faced by contemporary human heroines. Repeatedly, Ayla must decide what she will do in the face of opposition, or danger. She is a Neolithic orphan raised in a Cro-Magnon culture that devalues her and limits what she can do because she is a woman. Her appearance, capacity for communicating and crying, her courage and ability to think, all count against her in the culture. But her courage rises in response to circumstances that are not of her own choosing. What evolves into an odyssey in *The Valley of Horses* did not start out as a heroic quest (as is typical of journeys undertaken by human heroes), but as a journey to find others like herself. Similarly, in real-life stories of human women, as in myths of heroines, emotional or affiliative bonds to others are key elements. A woman heroine is one who loves or learns to love. She either travels with another or others or seeks union or reunion on her quest.

THE PATH

There are crucial forks in every road, where a decision needs to be made. Which path to take? Which direction to follow? To continue on a course consistent with one's principles, or go along with others? To be honest, or cheat? To go to college, or work? To have the baby, or an abortion? To leave a relationship, or stay? To marry, or say no to a particular man? To go immediately for medical help on discovering a lump in your breast, or put it off? To quit school or job, and see something else? To have an affair and risk the marriage? To give up or persevere? Which choice? Which path? What cost?

I recall the one vivid lesson from a college course in economics that I have over the years found applicable in psychiatry: the true cost of anything is what we give up in order to have it. It is the path not taken. To take the responsibility of making the choice is crucial and not always easy. What defines the heroine is that she does it.

The nonheroine woman, in contrast, goes along with someone else's choice. Rather than actively deciding if this is what she wants to do, she half-heartedly acquiesces. What often results is a self-made victim who says (after the fact), "I didn't really want to do this. It was your idea" ("It's all your fault that we got into this mess, or moved here, or that I am unhappy"). Or she may feel victimized and accuse, "We are always doing what you want to do!" without acknowledging that she never took a position or stood her ground. From the simplest question, "What do you want to do tonight?"—to which she replies, "Whatever you want to do"—her habit of deference can grow until what she does with her life is out of her hands.

There is also another nonheroine pattern. It is lived out by the woman who stays at a crossroads, unclear about how she feels, or uncomfortable as choicemaker, or unwilling to make a choice because she doesn't want to give up any options. She is often a bright, talented, attractive woman who is playing at life, backing away from relationships that turn too serious for her or from careers that require too much time or effort. Her not-deciding stance is, of course, in reality a choice of nonaction. She may spend ten years waiting at the crossroads, before she becomes aware that life is passing her by.

So women need to become choicemaker-heroines instead of being passive, or victim-martyrs, or pawns moved around by other people or circumstance. Becoming a heroine is an enlightening new possibility for women who have been inwardly ruled by vulnerable goddess archetypes. Asserting themselves is a heroic task for women who have been as compliant as Persephone; or who have put their men first, as would Hera; or who have looked out for everyone else's needs, as does Demeter. To do so goes against how they were raised, as well.

Moreover, the need to become a choicemaker-heroine is a jolt to many women who mistakenly assumed that they already were. As virgin goddess women, they may have been as psychologically "armored" as Athena, as independent of men's opinions as Artemis, or as self-sufficient and solitary as Hestia. Their heroic tasks are to risk intimacy or to become vulnerable emotionally. For them, the choice that requires courage is to trust someone else, or need someone else, or be responsible for someone else. Speaking up or taking risks in the world may be easy for such women. For them, marriage and motherhood require courage.

The heroine-choicemaker must repeat Psyche's first task of "sorting the seeds" whenever she is at a crossroads, and must decide what to do now. She must pause to sort out her priorities and motives, and the potentialities in the situation. She needs to see what the choices are, what the emotional cost could be, where the decisions will lead her, what intuitively matters most to her. On the basis of who she is and what she knows, she must make a decision about which path to take.

Here I touch once more on a theme I developed in my first book, *The Tao of Psychology:* the necessity for choosing a "path with heart." I feel that one must deliberate and then act, must scan every life choice with rational thinking but then base the decision on whether one's heart will be in it. No other person can tell you if your heart is involved, and logic cannot provide an answer.

Often when a woman faces those either/or choices that will greatly affect her life, someone else is pressuring her to make up her mind: "Get married!" "Have a child!" "Sell the house!" "Change jobs!" "Quit!" "Move!" "Say yes!" "Say no!" Very often a woman has to make up her mind and her heart in a pressure cooker created by someone else's impatience. To be a choicemaker, she needs to insist on making decisions in her own time, knowing that it is her life and she who will live with the consequences.

In order for clarity to develop, she also needs to resist inner pressure to decide precipitously. Initially, Artemis or Aphrodite, Hera or Demeter, may dominate with their characteristic intensity or instinctive response. They may try to crowd out Hestia's feelings, Persephone's introspection, or Athena's cool thinking. But these latter goddesses, when attended to, provide a fuller picture and allow a woman to make decisions that take all aspects of herself into consideration.

THE JOURNEY

As a woman proceeds on a heroine's journey, she confronts tasks, obstacles, and dangers. How she responds and what she does will change her. Along the way, she will find what matters to her and whether she has the courage to act on what she knows. Her character and compassion will be tested. She will encounter the dark, shadowy aspects of her personality, sometimes at the same time that her strengths become more evident and her self-confidence grows, or when fear overtakes her. Grief will probably be known to her, as she experiences loss, limitations, or defeat. The heroine's trip is a journey of discovery and development, of integrating aspects of herself into a whole, yet complex personality.

RECLAIMING THE POWER OF THE SNAKE

Every heroine must reclaim the power of the snake. To understand the nature of the task, we need to go back to the goddesses, and to women's dreams.

Many statues of Hera show snakes entwined in her robes, while Athena was portrayed with snakes wreathed around her shield. Snakes had been symbols of the pre-Greek Great Goddess of old Europe, and serve as symbolic reminders (or remnants) of the power once held by the female deity. One famous early representation of a deity (Crete 2000–1800 B.C.) was a female goddess with breasts bared, arms outstretched, and a snake in each hand.

The snake often appears in women's dreams as an unknown, an awesome symbol that the dreamer warily approaches when she begins to sense that she can assert her own power over her life. For example, the dream of a thirty-year-old married woman, soon to be separated and on her own: "I am on a trail, when I look ahead and see that the path I am on will pass under a large tree. A huge, female snake is coiled peacefully around the lowest branch. I know it is not poisonous, and I'm not repulsed—in fact, it is beautiful, but I hesitate." Many dreams like this come to mind, where the dreamer is awed or aware of the power of a snake rather than fearful of it as dangerous: "There is a snake coiled up under my desk . . . ,"

"I see a snake coiled on the porch . . . ," "Three snakes are in the room. . . . "

Whenever women begin to claim their own authority, or make decisions, or become aware of having a new sense of their own political or psychic or personal power, snake dreams are common. The snake seems to represent this new strength. As a symbol, it represents power once held by goddesses, as well as phallic or masculine power, representative of animus qualities. Often the dreamer senses whether it is a male or female snake, which helps to clarify the kind of power the snake symbolizes.

Coinciding with these dreams, in waking life the dreamer may be coping with questions raised after she took on a new role in a position of authority or autonomy; for example, "Can I be effective?" "How will the role change me?" "If I am strong, will people still like me?" and "Will this role threaten my most important relationships?" The dreams of women who never before have had a sense of their own potency seem to say that such women must approach power warily, as they would an unknown snake.

I think of women who gain a sense of their own power and authority as "reclaiming the power of the snake," which was lost by feminine deities and human women when the patriarchal religions stripped the goddesses of their power and influence, cast the snake as the evil element in the Garden of Eden and made women the lesser sex. Then I think of an image that represents for me the possibility that women will reemerge with power, beauty, and nurturing abilities. The image is a terra cotta of a beautiful woman or goddess (thought to represent Demeter, in the Terme Museum, Rome) rising from the earth, holding a sheaf of wheat, flowers, and a snake in each hand.

RESISTING THE POWER OF THE BEAR

The heroine-choicemaker, unlike her male counterpart, can be threatened by the overpowering pull of maternal instinct. A woman may become pregnant at an inopportune time or in adverse circumstances, if she cannot resist Aphrodite and/or Demeter. When this happens, she may be diverted from a chosen path—the choice-maker as a captive of her instinct.

For example, a woman graduate student I knew almost lost sight of her own goals as she felt herself caught up by the urge to become pregnant. She was married and working toward a doctoral degree when she became obsessed with the idea of having a baby. During this time, she had a dream. In it, a large female bear held the woman's arm between her teeth and wouldn't let go. The woman tried unsuccessfully to get free herself. Then she appealed to some men for help, but they were of no use. In the dream she wandered until she came on a statue of a mother bear and her cubs—reminiscent of a Bufano statue at the San Francisco Medical Center. When she put her hand on the statue, the bear let her go.

When she thought about the dream, she felt the bear symbolized the maternal instinct. Real bears are superb mothers, nurturing and fiercely protective of their vulnerable young. Then when it is time for the now-grown cubs to be on their own, the bear mother toughly insists that her reluctant cubs leave her and go out into the world to fend for themselves. This symbol of maternity had gotten a grip on the dreamer, and would not let her go until she touched an image of a maternal bear.

To the dreamer, the message of the dream was clear. If she could promise to hold on to the intent to have a child when she finished her degree (only two years longer), then maybe her obsession to get pregnant now would go away. And sure enough, after she and her husband had decided to have a child, and she had made an inner commitment to get pregnant as soon as she finished the degree, the obsession disappeared. Once again she could concentrate on her studies, uninterrupted by thoughts about pregnancy. As long as she held the image, the instinct lost its grip. She knew that if she were ever to have both career and family, she had to resist the power of the bear long enough to get her doctoral degree.

Archetypes exist outside of time, unconcerned with the realities of a woman's life or her needs. When goddesses exert an influence, the woman as heroine must say yes, or no, or "not now" to the demands. If she does not exercise conscious choice, then an instinctual or an archetypal pattern will take over. A woman needs to "resist the power of the bear" and yet honor its importance to her, if she is caught in the grip of the maternal instinct.

FENDING OFF DEATH AND DESTRUCTION

In heroic myths, every protagonist invariably comes up against something destructive or dangerous in her path that could destroy her. This is also a very common theme in women's dreams.

For example, a woman lawyer dreamed that, just as she had stepped outside of her childhood church, she was attacked by two savage black dogs. They jumped at her, trying to bite her neck—"It felt as if they were going for the jugular." As she raised her arm to ward off the attack, she awoke from the nightmare.

Now, since she had begun work at an agency, she had become increasingly bitter at the way she was treated. Men often assumed she was only a secretary. Even when they knew who she was, she often felt slighted or discounted. In turn, she became critical and hostile.

At first, the dream seemed to her to be an exaggerated statement of how she felt—"under attack" all the time. Then she considered whether there was anything in her that was like the savage dogs. She thought about what was happening to her at this job, and was startled and distressed by her own insight: "I'm turning into a hostile bitch!" She recalled the charitable attitude and happier times she associated with her childhood church, and knew that she had "stepped out" of that place. The dream made an impact. The dreamer's personality was in real danger of being destroyed by the hostility she felt and that she directed at others. She was becoming cynical and hostile. In reality as in the dream, *she* was in danger, not the people she directed her bitterness toward.

Similarly, the negative aspects or shadow of a goddess can be destructive. The jealous, vindictive, or resentful side of Hera can be poisonous. A woman who becomes possessed by these feelings, and knows it, fluctuates between being vindictive and being appalled by what she has felt and done. As the heroine in her struggles with the goddess, she may have dreams in which she is being attacked by snakes (indicating that the power they represent is dangerous to the dreamer). In one such dream, a poisonous snake darted at the dreamer's heart; in another, a snake sank its fangs into the dreamer's leg and wouldn't let go. In real life, both women were trying to get over a betrayal ("snake in the grass" behavior) and faced the danger of becoming overcome by venomous feelings (like the dream of the savage dogs, this dream had two levels of meaning; it was a metaphor about what was happening to her and in her).

When the danger to the dreamer comes in human form, as attacking or ominous men or women, the danger often is from hostile criticism or a destructive role (while animals often seem to represent feelings or instincts). For example, a woman had returned to college once her children were in elementary school; she dreamed that "a large prison matron" woman barred her way. The figure she had to get by seemed to personify her mother's negative judgments about her, as well as the mother role she identified with; the dream commented that this identification was imprisoning.

Hostile judgments from inner figures are often destructive; for example, "You can't do that because you are (bad, homely, incompetent, dumb, untalented)." Whatever the particular litany, they say, "You have no right to aspire for more," and are messages that can defeat a woman and stifle her confidence or good intentions. Such attacking critics are often pictured in dreams as threatening men. The inner criticism usually parallels the opposition or hostility that the woman encountered in her environment; the critics are parroting the messages of her family or her culture.

Looked at psychologically, every enemy or demon faced by a heroine in dream or myth represents something destructive, primitive, undeveloped, distorted, or evil in the human psyche that seeks to overpower and defeat her. The women who dreamed of savage dogs and dangerous snakes saw that as they were struggling with hurtful or hostile acts done *to* them by others, that they were also equally threatened by what was happening *inside* of them. The enemy or demon may be a negative part of her own psyche, a shadow element that threatens to defeat what is compassionate and competent in her; the enemy or demon may be in the psyche of other individuals who want to hurt, dominate, humiliate, or control her; or as is often the case, she may be endangered by both.

For example, in *The Clan of the Cave Bear*, Ayla's capabilities stir up the animosity of Broud, a brutal and proud clan leader, who humiliates her and rapes her. In *Watership Down*, the pioneer rabbits had to face the General, a power-mad, fascist, one-eyed rabbit. And the courageous furry-footed, child-sized hobbits in *The Fellowship of the Ring* were up against the evil power of Sauron of Mordor and his hideous Ringwraiths.

SURVIVING LOSS AND GRIEF

Loss and grieving is another theme in women's lives and in heroine myths. Somewhere along the way someone dies or must be left behind. Loss of a relationship plays a significant part in women's lives because most women define themselves by their relationships and not by their accomplishments. When someone dies, leaves them, moves away, or becomes estranged, it is consequently a double loss: the loss of the relationship itself, and the loss of the relationship as a source of identity.

Many a woman who has been the dependent partner in a relationship finds herself on the heroine's path only after suffering a loss. Pregnant Psyche, for example, was deserted by her husband Eros. In her quest for reunion, she undertook the tasks through which she evolved. Divorced and widowed women of any age may have to make choices and be on their own for the first time in their lives. For example, the death of a lover-companion prompted Atalanta to return to her father's kingdom, where the famous footrace was held. This parallels the course of women who begin a career after the loss of a relationship. And Ayla was forced to leave the Clan of the Cave Bear without her son Durc, carrying only her memories and her grief.

Metaphorically, a psychological death occurs whenever we are forced to let go of something or someone and must grieve for the loss. The death may be an aspect of ourselves, an old role, a former position, or beauty or other youthful qualities that are now gone and must be mourned; or a dream that is no more. Or it may be a relationship, ended by death or distance, that leaves us grieving.

Will the heroine in the woman emerge or survive the loss? Can she grieve and go on? Or will she give up, become bitter, or overcome by depression, will she stop her journey at this point? If she goes on, she will be choosing the path of the heroine.

GETTING THROUGH THE DARK AND NARROW PASSAGE

Most heroic journeys involve going through a dark place—through mountain caverns, the underworld, or labyrinthine passages to emerge, finally, into the light. Or they may involve traveling through a desolate wasteland or desert to a green land. This journey is analogous to passing through a depression. In the myths as in life, the traveler needs to keep on moving, to keep on functioning, to do what has to be done, to stay in touch with her companions or manage alone, to not stop and give up (even when she feels lost), to maintain hope in darkness.

The darkness may represent those dark, repressed feelings (of anger, despair, resentment, blame, vengeance, betrayal, fear, and guilt) through which people must pass if they are to get out of a depression. It is a dark night of the soul, when in the absence of light or love life seems meaningless, a cosmic joke. Grieving and forgiving is usually the way out. Thereafter, vitality and light may return

It helps to realize that death and rebirth, in myth and dreams, are metaphors for loss, depression, and recovery. In retrospect, many such dark periods turn out to be rites of passage, a time of suffering through which a woman has learned something of value, and has grown. Or she may have been, for a while, like Persephone in the underworld, a temporary captive who later becomes a guide for others.

EVOKING THE TRANSCENDENT FUNCTION

In standard heroic myths, after setting out on the quest, encountering and overcoming dangers, dragons, and darkness, the protagonist invariably gets stuck, unable to go forward or back. There may be impossible barriers in either direction. Or she may need to solve a riddle before a way will open. What should she do now, when what she consciously knows is not enough? Or when her ambivalence in the situation is so strong that a decision seems impossible? When she is caught between the rock and the hard place?

When the heroine-choicemaker finds herself in an unclear situation, where every route or choice seems potentially disastrous, or at best a dead-end, the first trial she faces is to stay herself. In every crisis, a woman is tempted to become the victim instead of staying the heroine. If she stays true to the heroine in herself, she knows that she is in a hard place and may be defeated, but she holds on to the possibility that something may change. If she turns into a victim, she will blame others or curse fate, drink or take drugs, attack herself with demeaning criticism, or give up completely, or even think of suicide. Or she may abdicate as heroine by becoming immobilized, or by becoming hysterical or panic stricken, acting impulsively or irrationally until someone else takes over.

Whether in myth or life, when a heroine is in a dilemma, all she can do is be herself, true to her principles and loyalties, until something unexpectedly comes to her aid. To stay with the situation, with the expectation that an answer will come, sets the inner stage for what Jung called "the transcendent function." By this he means something that arises from the unconscious to solve the problem or show the way to an ego (or heroine) who needs help from something beyond itself (or in herself).

For example, in the myth of Eros and Psyche, Aphrodite gave Psyche four tasks that required more of Psyche than Psyche knew how to do. Each time, she was initially overwhelmed, and then help or advice came—via ants, a green reed, an eagle, and a tower. Similarly, Hippomenes knew that he must compete in the race to win Atalanta's hand because he loved her. But he knew he couldn't run fast enough to win and so would lose his life trying. On the eve of the race, he prayed for help to Aphrodite, who helped him win the race and Atalanta. And when the brave rabbits in *Watership Down* got in a tight spot, Kehaar, the noisy gull, arrived in the nick of time—as Gandalf the Magician did for the hobbits. All these stories are variants of the same plot as the classic Western, when the brave but outnumbered group suddenly hears the bugle and knows that the cavalry is coming to rescue them.

These something-will-come-to-the-rescue plots are archetypal situations. The theme of rescue speaks to a human truth, which a woman as heroine needs to heed. When she is in an inner crisis and doesn't know what to do, she must not give up or act out of fear. To hold the dilemma in consciousness, wait for new insight or changed circumstance, and meditate or pray for clarity all invite a solution from the unconscious that can transcend the impasse.

For example, the woman who had the bear dream was in a personal crisis, and in the midst of her doctoral work, when her urge to have a baby arose. The maternal instinct gripped her with the compelling intensity of something previously repressed and now demanding its due. Before the dream, she was caught in an either/or, and neither satisfactory, situation. The solution needed to be felt, not logically arrived at, in order to change the situation. Only when the dream made an impression on her at an archetypal level, and she absolutely knew that she would hold on to her intent to have a baby, could she comfortably defer pregnancy. The dream was an answer to her dilemma from her unconscious, which came to the rescue. The conflict disappeared when this symbolic experience deepened her understanding and provided her with an intuitively felt insight.

The transcendent function can also be expressed through synchronistic events, those meaningful coincidences between an inner psychological situation and an outer event. When synchronicity happens, it can feel like a miracle, sending tingles up the spine. For example, several years ago a patient of mine started a self-help program for women. If she raised a specific amount of money by a certain deadline, she would get matching funds from a foundation, which would thus guarantee the program's existence. As the deadline approached, she still did not have the necessary amount. Yet she knew her project was needed, so she didn't give up. Then, in the mail, came a check for the exact amount she needed. It was an unexpected payment, with interest, of a long-forgotten loan that she had written off as a bad debt two years before.

Most synchronistic events do not provide such tangible answers to a dilemma. Instead, they usually help resolve a problem by providing emotional clarity or symbolic insight. For example, I was pressured by a previous publisher to have this book rewritten by a specific person whose task would be to shorten the book considerably and express the ideas in a more popular style. The "it's not good enough" message that I had been receiving for two years had been psychologically battering, and I was weary. Part of me (that felt like a compliant Persephone) was ready to let someone else do it, just so it would get done. And I was being influenced by wishful thinking that it would turn out well. During a crucial week—after which the book would have been turned over to the writer—a synchronistic event came to my aid. A visiting author from England, whose book had been rewritten by this very same writer under similar circumstances happened to speak to a friend of mine about the experience that very week. He voiced what I had never put in words, and yet intuitively knew would happen: "the soul was taken out of my book." When I heard these words, I felt that I had been given a gift of insight. He symbolized what would happen to my book, which cut through my ambivalency and freed me to act decisively. I hired my own copy editor and proceeded to finish the book myself.

I heard the message of that synchronistic event loud and clear. Events providing further insight or help then fell into place. Grateful for the lesson I had been provided, I remembered the ancient Chinese saying that expresses faith in synchronicity and transcendent function, "When the pupil is ready, the teacher will come."

The function of creative insight is also similar to the transcendent function. In a creative process, when there is as yet no known solution to a problem, the artist-inventor-problem solver has faith that an answer exists, and stays with the situation until the solution comes. The creator is often in a state of heightened tension. Everything that can be done or thought of, has been done. The person then trusts a process of incubation, out of which something new can emerge. The classic example is the chemist Kekulé, who discovered the structure of the benzene molecule. He wrestled with the problem but could not figure it out until he dreamed of a snake holding its tail in its mouth. He intuitively knew that this provided the answer—the carbon atoms took a ring formation. He then tested and proved this hypothesis true.

FROM VICTIM TO HEROINE

In thinking about the heroine's journey, I have been struck by how the Alcoholics Anonymous organization (AA) transforms an alcoholic from victim to heroine or hero. AA evokes the transcendent function, and, in effect, provides lessons in how to become a choicemaker.

The alcoholic begins by accepting that she is in a desperate dilemma: she cannot continue to drink, and she cannot stop. At this point, in despair, she joins a fellowship in which people on the same journey help each other. She is told that she must call on a power greater than herself to get her out of this crisis.

AA emphasizes the need to accept what cannot be changed, to change what can be, and know the difference. In teaching the person to take one day at a time, the AA principles show what is needed when a person is in a precarious emotional state and cannot see the way clearly. Gradually, one step at a time, the alcoholic becomes a choicemaker. She discovers that help is available from a power greater than the ego. She finds that people can help each other and forgive each other. And she discovers that she can be competent and have compassion for others.

Similarly, the heroine's journey is an individuation quest. Traveling this path, the heroine may find, lose, and rediscover what has meaning to her, until she holds on to these values in all kinds of circumstances that test her. She may repeatedly encounter whatever threatens to overcome her, until finally the danger of losing her selfhood is over.

In my office, I have a painting of the interior of a chambered nautilus shell that I painted many years ago. It emphasizes the shell's spiral pattern, and serves as a reminder that the path we take is so often spiral in shape. We cycle through patterns that bring us repeatedly back in the vicinity of whatever our nemesis is that we must meet and master. Often it is the negative aspect of a goddess that can take us over: a susceptibility to fall into Demeter or Persephone depressions, a problem with Hera's jealously and mistrust, a temptation to be a promiscuous Aphrodite, or an unscrupulous Athena or a ruthless Artemis. Life presents us with repeated opportunities to face what we fear, what we need to become conscious of, or what we need to master. Each time we cycle around the spiral path to the place that gives us difficulty, hopefully, we gain more consciousness and can respond more wisely the next time; until we can finally pass through that nemesis place at peace and in harmony with our deepest values, and not be negatively affected at all.

THE END OF THE JOURNEY

What happens at the end of the myth? Eros and Psyche are reunited, their marriage is honored on Mt. Olympus, and Psyche bears a daughter named Joy. Atalanta chooses the apples, loses the footrace, and marries Hippomenes. Ayla journeys across the steppes of Europe to find others like herself; she ends this part of her saga in the Valley of Horses, with Jondalar as her mate and with the smiling promise of acceptance by others. Note that after proving her courage and competency, the heroine does not go riding off into the sunset by herself, like the archetypal cowboy hero. Nor is she cast in the mold of the conquering hero. Union, reunion, and home are where her journey ends.

The individuation journey—the psychological quest for wholeness—ends in the union of opposites; in the inner marriage of "masculine" and "feminine" aspects of the personality that can be symbolized by the Eastern image of yin and yang contained within a circle. Said more abstractly and without assigning gender, the journey toward wholeness results in having the ability to be both active and receptive, autonomous and intimate, to work and to love. These are parts of ourselves that we can come to know through life experiences, parts that are inherent in all of us. This is the human potential with which we start.

In the final chapters of *The Fellowship of the Ring*, the last temptations to wear the ring were overcome and the ring of power was destroyed forever. This round with evil won, their heroic task completed, the hobbits returned home to the Shire. The rabbits of *Watership Down* also survived their heroic journey to come home, to their new peaceful community. T. S. Eliot, in *The Four Quartets*, writes,

> We shall not cease from exploration
> And the end of all our exploring
> Will be to arrive where we started
> And know the place for the first time.

All seem rather unspectacular endings—paralleling real life. The recovered alcoholic may have gone to hell and back now to reappear an ordinary sober person. The heroine who fended off hostile attacks, reclaimed her power, and struggled with goddesses may seem similarly ordinary—at peace with herself. Like the hobbit at home in the Shire, however, she does not know if or when a new adventure that will once more test her very being will announce itself.

When it comes time for me to say goodbye to patients when the work we have done together is finished, I think of myself as someone who has accompanied them on a difficult and significant part of their journey. Now it is time for them to continue on their own. Maybe I joined them when they were between a rock and a hard place. Maybe I helped them to find the path they had lost. Maybe I stayed for a time in a dark passage with them. Mostly, I helped them to see with more clarity and make their own choices.

As I finish writing, and reach the end of this book, I hope that I may have been your companion for a while, sharing what I have learned with you, helping you to be a choice-maker on your own particular journey.

Love to you.

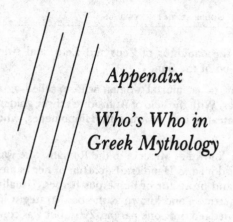

Appendix

*Who's Who in
Greek Mythology*

CAST OF CHARACTERS

Achilles (a kil′ ēz), Greek hero in the Trojan War, who was favored by Athena.

Aphrodite (af ro dī′ tē), the Goddess of Love and Beauty, known as Venus to the Romans. The unfaithful wife of Hephaestus, the lame God of the Forge, she had many affairs, and many offspring from her numerous liaisons. Ares, the God of War; Hermes, the Messenger God; and Anchises, who fathered Aeneas (from whom the Romans claimed their descent) were some of the most noteworthy of her lovers. The alchemical goddess.

Apollo (a pol′ ō), also called Apollo by the Romans, the handsome God of the Sun and god of fine arts, medicine, and music. He was one of the twelve Olympians, son of Zeus and Leto, and twin brother of Artemis. Sometimes also referred to as Helios.

Ares (a′ rēs), or Mars, as he was called by the Romans, was the bellicose God of War. One of the twelve Olympians, Ares was the son of Zeus and Hera. According to Homer, he was despised by his father for taking after his mother. Ares was a lover of Aphrodite, with whom he had three children.

Artemis (ar′ te mis), whom the Romans called Diana, was Goddess of the Hunt and Moon. She was one of the three virgin goddesses, the daughter of Zeus and Leto, and twin sister of Apollo, God of the Sun.

Atalanta (at a lan' ta), a mortal woman who excelled as a hunter and a runner. With the help of Aphrodite's three golden apples, she was defeated in a footrace by Hippomenes, who won her as his wife.

Athena (a thē' na), known as Minerva to the Romans. She was the Goddess of Wisdom and Handicrafts, patron of her namesake city Athens, and protector of numerous heroes. Usually portrayed wearing armor, and known as the best strategist in battle. She acknowledged only one parent, Zeus, but was considered also the daughter of wise Metis, the first consort of Zeus. A virgin goddess.

Cronos (krō' nos), or Saturn (Roman). A Titan and the youngest son of Gaea and Uranus, who emasculated his father and became the chief god. Husband of Rhea and the father of six of the Olympians (Hestia, Demeter, Hera, Hades, Poseidon, Zeus) who swallowed them when they were born. He in turn was overpowered by his youngest son Zeus.

Demeter (de mē' ter), known as Ceres to the Romans. Demeter is the Goddess of Grain or agriculture. In her most important myth, the emphasis is on her role as mother of Persephone. A vulnerable goddess.

Dionysus (dī o nī' sus), known as Bacchus to the Romans, the God of Wine and Ecstasy, whose women worshippers annually sought communion with him in the mountains through revels or orgies.

Eros (er' os), God of Love, also known as Amor to the Romans; husband of Psyche.

Gaea or Gaia (jē' a or gī a), the Goddess Earth. Mother and wife of Uranus (sky), and parents of the Titans.

Hades (hā' dēz) or Pluto, ruler of the Underworld, a son of Rhea and Cronos, abductor-husband of Persephone, and one of the twelve Olympians.

Hecate (hek' a tē) was the Goddess of the Crossroads, who looked in three directions. She was associated with the uncanny and the mysterious, and was a personification of the wise witch. Hecate was associated with Persephone, whom she accompanied when the maiden was returned from the underworld, and with the moon goddess Artemis.

Hephaestus (he fes' tus), known as Vulcan by the Romans, is God of the Forge and patron of artisans. He was the cuckolded husband of Aphrodite, and the lame or club-footed rejected son of Hera.

Hera (her' a), also known as Juno to the Romans. Hera was the Goddess of Marriage. As official consort and wife of Zeus, she was the highest-ranking goddess on Mt. Olympus. A daughter of Cronos and Rhea, she was also the sister of Zeus and the other first-generation Olympians; portrayed by Homer as a jealous shrew, and revered in her worship as the Goddess of Marriage. One of three vulnerable goddesses, she personifies the archetype of the wife.

Hermes (hur' mēz), better known by his Roman name Mercury: the Messenger of the Gods, the patron god of trade, communication, travelers, and thieves. He conducted souls to Hades, was sent by Zeus to bring Persephone back to Demeter. He had an affair with Aphrodite, and was linked in household and temple religious rituals with Hestia.

Hestia (hes' ti a), also known as the Roman goddess Vesta; the virgin Goddess of the Hearth and least known of the Olympians. Her fire made home and temple sacred. Personifies the archetype of the Self.

Paris (par' is), Prince of Troy, awarded the golden apple inscribed "for the fairest" to Aphrodite, who offered him Helen, the most beautiful woman in the world as a bribe. Paris took Helen with him to Troy, thus instigating the Trojan War for she was already married to Menelaus, a Greek king.

Persephone (per sef' ō nē), also referred to by the Greeks as the Kore (kō' rē) or the Maiden, and called Proserpina by the Romans. The abducted daughter of Demeter who became Queen of the Underworld.

Poseidon (pō sī' don), God of the Sea. An Olympian more commonly known by his Roman name Neptune. Raped Demeter while she was searching for her abducted daughter Persephone.

Psyche (sī′ kē), a mortal heroine, who completed the four tasks of Aphrodite, and was reunited with her husband Eros.

Rhea (rē′ a), daughter of Gaea and Uranus, sister and wife of Cronos. Mother of Hestia, Demeter, Hera, Hades, Poseidon, and Zeus.

Uranus (ū rā′ nus), also known as the sky, father sky, or the heavens. Fathered the Titans with Gaea, and was emasculated by his son, Cronos, who threw his genitals into the sea; from which Aphrodite was (according to one version) born.

Zeus (zūs) called Jupiter or Jove by the Romans, ruler of the heavens and earth, and chief god of the Olympians; youngest son of Rhea and Cronos, who overthrew the Titans and established the supremacy of the Olympians as rulers of the universe. Philandering husband of Hera, who had many wives, many affairs, and numerous offspring from these liaisons— many of whom were the second-generation Olympians, or heroes of Greek mythology.

GODDESS CHART

Goddess	Category	Archetypal Roles	Significant Others
Artemis (Diana) Goddess of the Hunt and Moon	Virgin Goddess	Sister Competitor Feminist	Sister Companions (nymphs) Mother (Leto) Brother (Apollo)
Athena (Minerva) Goddess of Wisdom and Crafts	Virgin Goddess	Father's Daughter Strategist	Father (Zeus) Chosen Heroes
Hestia (Vesta) Goddess of the Hearth and Temple	Virgin Goddess	Maiden Aunt Wise Woman	None
Hera (Juno) Goddess of Marriage	Vulnerable Goddess	Wife Commitment Maker	Husband (Zeus)
Demeter (Ceres) Goddess of Grain	Vulnerable Goddess	Mother Nurturer	Daughter (Persephone) or children
Persephone (Proserpina) Maiden and Queen of the Under-world	Vulnerable Goddess	Mother's Daughter Receptive Woman	Mother (Demeter) Husband (Hades/Dionysus)
Aphrodite (Venus) Goddess of Love and Beauty	Alchemical Goddess	Lover (Sensual Woman) Creative Woman	Lovers (Ares, Hermes) Husband (Hephaestus)

GODDESS CHART (CONTINUED)

Goddess	Jungian Psychological Type	Psychological Difficulties	Strengths
Artemis	Usually Extraverted Usually Intuitive Usually Feeling	Emotional distance, ruthlessness, rage	Ability to set own goals and reach them, independence, autonomy; friendships with women
Athena	Usually Extraverted Definitely Thinking Usually Sensation	Emotional distance, craftiness, lack of empathy	Ability to think well, to solve practical problems and strategize; form strong alliances with men
Hestia	Definitely Introverted Usually Feeling Usually Intuitive	Emotional distance, Lack of social persona	Ability to enjoy solitude; to have a sense of spiritual meaning
Hera	Usually Extraverted Usually Feeling Usually Sensation	Jealousy, vindictiveness, rage; inability to leave destructive relationship	Ability to make a lifetime commitment; fidelity
Demeter	Usually Extraverted Usually Feeling	Depression, burnout, fostering dependency, unplanned pregnancy	Ability to be maternal and nurturing of others; generosity
Persephone	Usually Introverted Usually Sensation	Depression, manipulation, withdrawal into unreality	Ability to be receptive; to appreciate imagination and dreams; potential psychic abilities
Aphrodite	Definitely Extraverted Definitely Sensation	Serial relationships, promiscuity; difficulty considering consequences	Ability to enjoy pleasure and beauty; to be sensual and creative

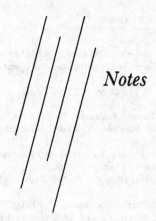

Notes

The primary sources for each chapter are listed first, followed by foot-noted references.

All references to Jung's Collected Works (abbreviated *CW*) are taken from *Collected Works of C. G. Jung*, edited by Sir Herbert Read, Michael Fordham, and Gerhard Adler; translated by R. F. C. Hull; Executive Editor, William McGuire; Bollingen Series 20 (Princeton, N.J.: Princeton University Press).

INTRODUCTION: THERE ARE GODDESSES IN EVERYWOMAN

Lerner, Harriet E. "Early Origins of Envy and Devaluation of Women: Implications for Sex Role Stereotypes." *Bulletin of the Menninger Clinic* 38, no. 6 (1974):538–553.

Loomis, Mary, and Singer, June. "Testing the Biopolarity Assumption in Jung's Typology." *Journal of Analytic Psychology* 24, no. 4 (1980).

Miller, Jean Baker. *Toward a New Psychology of Women.* Boston: Beacon Press, 1976.

Neumann, Erich. *Amor and Psyche: The Psychic Development of the Feminine.* Translated by Ralph Manheim, Bollingen Series 54. New York: Pantheon Books, 1956.

1. Betty Friedan, *The Feminine Mystique* (New York: Dell, 1963), p. 69.
2. Joseph Campbell, *The Hero with a Thousand Faces*, 2nd ed., (Bollingen Series 17 Princeton, N.J.: Princeton University Press, 1968), p. 19.

CHAPTER 1: GODDESSES AS INNER IMAGES

Jung, C. G. "Archetypes of the Collective Unconscious" (1954). *CW*, vol. 9, part 1 (1968), pp. 3–41.

Jung, C. G. "The Concept of the Collective Unconscious." *CW*, vol. 9, part 1, pp. 42–53.

Marohn, Stephanie. "The Goddess Resurrected." *Womenews* (published by the Friends of the San Francisco Commission on the Status of Women) 8, no. 1 (June 1983).

Mayerson, Philip. *Classical Mythology in Literature, Art, and Music.* New York: Wiley, 1971.

Spretnak, Charlene, ed. *The Politics of Women's Spirituality: Essays on the Rise of Spiritual Power Within the Feminist Movement.* New York: Doubleday, 1982.

Stone, Merlin. *When God Was a Woman.* New York: Harvest/Harcourt Brace Jovanovich, by arrangement with Dial Press, 1978.

1. Anthony Stevens, *Archetypes: A Natural History of the Self* (New York: Morrow, 1982), pp. 1–5.
2. C. G. Jung, "The Concept of the Collective Unconscious" (1936), *CW*, vol. 9, part 1 (1968), p. 44, and "Archetypes of the Collective Unconscious" (1954), *CW*, vol. 9, part 1 (1968), pp. 3–4.
3. Hesiod, *Theogony*, in *Hesiod*, trans. Richard Lattimore (Ann Arbor, Mich.: The University of Michigan Press, 1959).
4. Marija Gimbutas, "Women and Culture in Goddess-Oriented Old Europe," in *The Politics of Women's Spirituality: Essays on the Rise of Spiritual Power Within the Women's Movement*, ed. Charlene Spretnak (New York: Doubleday, 1982), pp. 22–31.
5. Robert Graves, *The Greek Myths*, vol. 1 (New York: Penguin, 1982), p. 13.
6. Jane Ellen Harrison, *Mythology* (New York: Harcourt Brace Jovanovich, 1963 [originally published 1924]), p. 49.
7. Merlin Stone, *When God Was a Woman* (New York: Harvest/Harcourt Brace Jovanovich, by arrangement with the Dial Press, 1978), p. 228.

CHAPTER 2: ACTIVATING THE GODDESSES

1. C. G. Jung, "Psychological Aspects of the Mother Archetype" (1954), *CW*, vol. 9, part 1 (1968), p. 79.
2. Maxine Hong Kingston, *The Woman Warrior* (New York: Vintage Books/Random House, 1977).
3. This shift in goddess archetypes during menstrual cycles is based on clinical observations from my psychiatric practice. For research support documenting a shift from independent and active (or aggressive) to dependent and passive attitudes correlated with menstrual cycles, see Therese Benedek, "The Correlations Between Ovarian Activity and Psychodynamic Processes," in Therese Benedek, ed., *Psychoanalytic Investigation* (New York: Quadrangle/New York Times Book Co., 1973), pp. 129–223.

CHAPTER 3: THE VIRGIN GODDESSES

Gustaitis, Rasa. "Moving Freely through Nighttime Streets." *Pacific News Service*, 1981. Syndicated article (found, for example, in *City on a Hill*

Press, University of California, Santa Cruz, April 9, 1981).

Harding, M. Esther. "The Virgin Goddess." In *Women's Mysteries*. New York: Bantam Books, published by arrangement with Putnam's, 1973, pp. 115–149.

Kotschnig, Elined Prys. "Womanhood in Myth and Life." *Inward Light* 31, no. 74 (1968).

Kotschnig, Elined Prys. "Womanhood in Myth and Life, Part 2." *Inward Light* 32, no. 75 (1969).

1. M. Esther Harding, "The Virgin Goddess," in *Women's Mysteries* (New York: Bantam Books, published by arrangement with Putnam's, 1973), p. 147.

2. "Focused consciousness," as described by Irene Claremont de Castillejo, is considered an attribute of the animus or of men: "The power to focus is man's greatest gift but not man's prerogative; the animus plays this role for a woman." "It is only when she needs a focused kind of consciousness that the help of the animus is needed." From Claremont de Castillejo, *Knowing Woman*, Chapter 5, "The Animus—Friend or Foe" (New York: Putnam's, for the C. G. Jung Foundation for Analytic Psychology, 1973), pp. 77–78. I am using her terminology, but disagree with her assumption, based on Jung's model of women's psychology, that focused consciousness is always a masculine attribute.

3. Marty Olmstead, "The Midas Touch of Danielle Steel," *United* (United Airlines Flight Publication), March 1982, p. 89.

4. This summary of psychoanalytic theory of women's psychology is based on the following works of Sigmund Freud from *The Standard Edition of the Psychological Works of Sigmund Freud*, ed. J. Strachey (London: Hogarth Press), hereafter referred to as *Standard Edition:*

Sigmund Freud, "Three Essays on the Theory of Sexuality" (1905), *Standard Edition*, vol. 7 (1953), pp. 135–243.

Sigmund Freud, "Some Psychological Consequences of the Anatomical Distinction Between the Sexes" (1925), *Standard Edition*, vol. 19 (1961), pp. 248–258.

Sigmund Freud, "Female Sexuality" (1931), *Standard Edition*, vol. 21 (1961), pp. 225–243.

5. This summary of Jung's theory of women's psychology is based on the following works:

C. G. Jung, "Animus and Anima" (1934), *CW*, vol. 7 (1966), pp. 188–211.

C. G. Jung, "The Syzygy: Anima and Animus," (1950), *CW*, vol. 9, part 2 (1959), pp. 11–22.

C. G. Jung, "Women in Europe" (1927), *CW*, vol. 10 (1964), pp. 113–133.

6. C. G. Jung, *CW*, vol. 7, p. 209.

7. C. G. Jung, *CW*, vol. 10, p. 117.

CHAPTER 4: ARTEMIS

Guthrie, W. K. C. "Artemis." In *The Greeks and Their Gods.* Boston: Beacon Press, 1950, pp. 99–106.

Kerènyi, C. "Leto, Apollon and Artemis." In *The Gods of the Greeks.* Translated by Norman Cameron. New York: Thames & Hudson, 1979. (Originally published 1951.)

Kerènyi, Karl. "A Mythological Image of Girlhood: Artemis." In *Facing the Gods,* edited by James Hillman. Irving, Texas: Spring, 1980, pp. 39–45.

Mayerson, Philip. "Artemis." In *Classical Mythology in Literature, Art, and Music.* New York: Wiley, 1971, pp. 150–169.

Moore, Tom. "Artemis and the Puer." In *Puer Papers.* Irving, Texas: Spring, 1979, pp. 169–204.

Malamud, René. "The Amazon Problem." *Spring* (1971), pp. 1–21.

Otto, Walter F. "Artemis." In *The Homeric Gods.* Translated from the German by Moses Hadas. New York: Thames & Hudson, published by arrangement with Pantheon Books, 1979, pp. 80–90.

Schmidt, Lynda. "The Brother-Sister Relationship in Marriage." *Journal of Analytical Psychology* 25, no. 4 (1980): 17–35.

Zabriskie, Philip T. "Goddesses in Our Midst." *Quadrant* (Fall 1974), pp. 41–42.

1. Walter F. Otto, "Artemis." In *The Homeric Gods,* trans. Moses Hadas (New York: Thames & Hudson, 1979), pp. 86–87.

2. Callimachus, "To Artemis," in *Hymns and Epigrams,* trans. A. W. Mair (Cambridge, Mass.: Harvard University Press, 1969), p. 63.

3. Lynn Thomas, *The Backpacking Woman* (New York: Doubleday, 1980), p. 227.

4. China Galland, *Women in the Wilderness* (New York: Harper & Row, 1980), p. 5.

5. Frances Horn, *I Want One Thing* (Marina del Rey, Calif.: DeVorss), 1979.

6. Laurie Lisle, *Portrait of an Artist: A Biography of Georgia O'Keeffe* (New York: Washington Square Press/Pocket Books/Simon & Schuster, published by arrangement with Seaview Books, 1981), p. 436.

7. Lisle, p. 430.

8. M. Esther Harding, *Woman's Mysteries* (New York: Bantam, 1973), p. 140.

9. "Meleager and Atalanta," in *Bullfinch's Mythology* (Middlesex, England: Hamlyn, 1964), p. 101.

10. This section was suggested by Walter F. Otto's description of Artemis, 1979.

11. I have used Bernard Evslin's retelling of this myth from "Atalanta," in *Heroes, Gods and Monsters of the Greek Myths* (Toronto: Bantam Pathfinder, published by arrangement with Four Winds Press, 1975), p. 173–190.

CHAPTER 5: ATHENA

Downing, Christine. "Dear Grey Eyes: A Revaluation of Pallas Athene." In *The Goddess.* New York: Crossroad, 1981, pp. 99–130.

Elias-Button, Karen. "Athene and Medusa." *Anima* 5, no. 2 (Spring Equinox, 1979): 118–124.

Hillman, James. "On the Necessity of Abnormal Psychology: Ananke and Athene." In *Facing the Gods.* Edited by James Hillman. Irving, Texas: Spring, 1980, pp. 1–38.

Kerènyi, C. "Metis and Pallas Athene." In *The Gods of the Greeks.* Translated by Norman Cameron. New York: Thames & Hudson, 1979, pp. 118–129. (Originally published 1951.)

Kerènyi, Karl. *Athene: Virgin and Mother.* Translated by Murray Stein. Irving, Texas: Spring, 1978.

Mayerson, Philip. "Athena." In *Classical Mythology in Literature, Art, and Music.* New York: Wiley, 1971, pp. 169–175; pp. 431–433.

Otto, Walter F. "Athena." In *The Homeric Gods.* Translated by Moses Hadas. New York: Thames & Hudson, by arrangement with Pantheon Books, 1979, pp. 43–60.

Rupprecht, Carol Schreier. "The Martial Maid and the Challenge of Androgyny." *Spring* (1974), pp. 269–293.

Stein, Murray. "Translator's Afterthoughts." In Kerènyi, Karl, *Athene: Virgin and Mother.* Translated by Murray Stein. Irving, Texas: Spring, 1978, pp. 71–79.

1. Hesiod, *Theogony,* in *Hesiod,* trans. Richard Lattimore (Ann Arbor, Mich.: The University of Michigan Press, 1959), p. 177.
2. Wilfred Sheed, *Clare Booth Luce* (New York: Dutton, 1982).
3. Carol Felsenthal, *The Sweetheart of the Silent Majority: The Biography of Phyllis Schlafly* (New York: Doubleday, 1981).
4. Walter F. Otto, "Athena," in *The Homeric Gods,* trans. Moses Hadas (New York: Thame & Hudson, by arrangement with Pantheon Books, 1979), p. 60.
5. For example, the twenty-five successful corporate women (all of whom held positions as presidents or divisional vice-presidents of nationally recognized firms) studied by Henning and Jardim fit an Athena pattern. They were father's daughters—daughters who shared interests and activities with their successful fathers. Paralleling Metis, who was swallowed by Zeus, their mothers were women whose education either equalled or surpassed their husbands; yet twenty-four of twenty-five mothers were housewives, the twenty-fifth was a teacher. The father-daughter relationship was recalled vividly as the significant one; recollection of the mother-daughter relationship was vague and generalized. Margaret Henning and Anne Jardim, "Childhood," In *The Managerial Woman* (New York: Pocket Books/Simon & Schuster, 1978), pp. 99–117.
6. Christine Downing, "Dear Grey Eyes: A Revaluation of Pallas Athene," in *The Goddess* (New York: Crossroad, 1981), p. 117.

Chapter 6: Hestia

Bradway, Katherine. "Hestia and Athena in the Analysis of Women." *Inward Light* 151 (1978), no. 91: 28–42.

Demetrakopoulos, Stephanie. "Hestia, Goddess of the Hearth." *Spring* (1979), pp. 55–75. This article was my major source for the mythology and rituals of Hestia.

"The Hymn to Hestia" and "The Second Hymn to Hestia." In *Homeric Hymns.* Translated by Charles Boer. Rev. ed. Irving, Texas: Spring, 1979, pp. 140–141.

Jung, C. G. "The Spirit Mercurius: Part 2: no. 3, Mercurius as Fire." *CW*, vol. 13, pp. 209–210.

Jung, C. G. "The Spirit Mercurius: Part 2: no. 8, Mercurius and Hermes." *CW*, vol. 13, pp. 230–234.

Kirksey, Barbara. "Hestia: A Background of Psychological Focusing." In *Facing the Gods.* Edited by James Hillman. Irving, Texas: Spring, 1980, pp. 101–113.

Koltuv, Barbara Black. "Hestia/Vesta." *Quadrant* 10 (Winter 1977), pp. 58–65.

Luke, Helen M. "Goddess of the Hearth." In *Woman: Earth and Spirit* (New York: Crossroad, 1981), pp. 41–50.

Mayerson, Philip. "Hestia (Vesta)." In *Classical Mythology in Literature, Art, and Music.* New York: Wiley, 1971, pp. 115–116.

Mayerson, Philip. "Hermes (Mercury)." In *Classical Mythology in Literature, Art, and Music* (New York: Wiley, 1971), pp. 210–226.

1. "The Hymn to Aphrodite I," In *Homeric Hymns*, trans. Charles Boer, rev. ed. (Irving, Texas: Spring, 1979), p. 70.
2. "The Hymn to Aphrodite I," p. 70.
3. Stephanie Demetrakopoulos, "Hestia, Goddess of the Hearth," *Spring* (1979), pp. 55–75.
4. T. S. Eliot, *Four Quartets* (New York: Harcourt Brace Jovanovich [no date], originally published 1943), p. 16.
5. C. G. Jung, "Concerning Mandala Symbolism," *CW*, vol. 9, part 1, p. 35.
6. May Sarton, *Journal of a Solitude* (New York: Norton, 1973), pp. 44–45.
7. Ardis Whitman, "Secret Joys of Solitude," *Reader's Digest* 122, no. 732 (April 1983): 132.

Chapter 7 The Vulnerable Goddesses

1. Irene Claremont de Castillejo. *Knowing Woman* (New York: Putnam's, for the C. G. Jung Foundation for Analytical Psychology, 1973), p. 15.

CHAPTER 8: HERA

Downing, Christine. "Coming to Terms with Hera," *Quadrant* 12, no. 2 (Winter 1979).

Kerènyi, C. "Zeus and Hera" and "Hera, Ares and Hephaistos." In *The Gods of the Greeks.* Translated by Norman Cameron. New York: Thames & Hudson, 1979, pp. 95–98, 150–160. (Originally published 1951).

Kerènyi, C. *Zeus and Hera: Archetypal Image of Father, Husband and Wife.* Translated by Christopher Holme. Bollingen Series 65. Princeton, N.J.: Princeton University Press, 1975.

Kerènyi, Karl. "The Murderess—Medea." In *Goddesses of Sun and Moon.* Irving, Texas: Spring, 1979, pp. 20–40.

Mayerson, Philip. "Hera (Juno)." In *Classical Mythology in Literature, Art, and Music.* New York: Wiley, 1971, pp. 94–98.

Mayerson, Philip. "Medea." In *Classical Mythology in Literature, Art, and Music.* New York: Wiley, 1971, pp. 346–352.

Stein, Murray. "Hera: Bound and Unbound." *Spring* (1977), pp. 105–119. This article was my most important source for the archetype of Hera. Stein's article associates the mating instinct with Hera, and describes her three phases.

Zabriskie, Philip. "Goddesses in Our Midst," *Quadrant* (Fall 1974), pp. 37–39.

1. Murray Stein, "Hera: Bound and Unbound." *Spring* (1977), p. 108.

2. Nancy Reagan, *Quest* (1982). Similar sentiments by Nancy Reagan in *Nancy,* with Bill Libby (New York: Berkley, 1981).

3. Diana Trilling, *Mrs. Harris: The Death of the Scarsdale Diet Doctor* (New York: Harcourt Brace Jovanovich, 1981).

CHAPTER 9: DEMETER

Demetrakopoulos, Stephanie. "Life Stage Theory, Gerontological Research, and the Mythology of the Older Woman: Independence, Autonomy, and Strength." *Anima* 8, no. 2 (Spring Equinox 1982): 84–97.

Friedrich, Paul. "The Fifth Queen: The Meaning of Demeter" and "The Homeric Hymn to Demeter." In *The Meaning of Aphrodite,* Chicago: University of Chicago Press, 1978, pp. 149–180.

"The Hymn to Demeter." In *The Homeric Hymns,* translated by Charles Boer. 2nd ed., rev. Irving, Texas: Spring, 1979, pp. 89–135.

Jung, C. G. "Psychological Aspects of the Mother Archetype" (1954). *CW,* vol. 9, part 1 (1968), pp. 75–110.

Kerènyi, C. *Eleusis: Archetypal Image of Mother and Daughter.* Translated by Ralph Manheim. New York: Schocken Books, published by arrangement with Princeton University Press, 1977. Previously printed in the Bollingen Series (1967).

Luke, Helen M. "Mother and Daughter Mysteries." In *Woman: Earth and Spirit.* New York: Crossroad, 1981, pp. 51–71.

Zabriskie, Philip. "Goddesses in Our Midst." *Quadrant* (Fall 1979), pp. 40–41.

1. "Hymn to Demeter," in *The Homeric Hymns,* trans. Charles Boer, 2nd ed., rev. (Irving, Texas: Spring, 1979), p. 89.

2. C. Kerènyi, *Eleusis, Archetypal Image of Mother and daughter,* trans. Ralph Manheim (New York: Schocken Books, published by arrangement with Princeton University Press, 1977). Previously printed in the Bollinger Series (1967).

3. Susan Issacs, "Baby Savior," *Parents Magazine* (September 1981), pp. 81–85.

4. Pauline Bart, "Mother Portnoy's Complaints," *Trans-Action* (November-December 1970), pp. 69–74.

CHAPTER 10: PERSEPHONE

Dowling, Colette. *The Cinderella Complex: Women's Hidden Fear of Independence.* New York: Summit Books, 1981. The Cinderella Complex describes a Persephone pattern. The book provides an excellent understanding of how family and culture reinforce this archetype with "apprehensive oversolicitude" and inhibition of assertiveness and independence.

Downing, Christine. "Persephone in Hades." *Anima* (1977) no 1., (Fall Equinox): 22–29.

"The Hymn to Demeter" (the Abduction of Persephone). In *The Homeric Hymns,* translated by Charles Boer. 2nd ed., rev. Irving, Texas: Spring, 1979, pp. 89–135.

Kerènyi, C. *Eleusis: Archetypal Image of Mother and Daughter,* translated by Ralph Manheim. New York: Schocken Books, reprinted by arrangement with Princeton University Press, 1977. Previously printed in The Bollingen Series (1967).

1. M. Esther Harding, "All Things to All Men," in *The Way of All Women* (New York: Putnam's, for the C. G. Jung Foundation for Analytic Psychology, 1970), p. 4.

2. Harding, p. 16.

3. Hannah Green, *I Never Promised You a Rose Garden* (New York: Signet Books/New American Library, by arrangement with Holt, Rinehart, and Winston, 1964).

4. Walter F. Otto, *Dionysus: Myth and Cult,* trans. with an Introd. by Robert B. Palmer (Bloomington: Indiana University Press, 1965), p. 116.

5. *Autobiography of a Schizophrenic Girl,* with analytic interpretation by Marguerite Sechehaye. Translated by Grace Rubin-Rabson (New York: Signet Books/New American Library, published by arrangement with Grune & Stratton, 1970).

CHAPTER 11: THE ALCHEMICAL GODDESS

Tennov, Dorothy. *Love and Limerence: The Experience of Being in Love.* New York: Stein & Day, 1979.
1. C. G. Jung, "Problems of Modern Psychotherapy" (1931), *CW*, vol. 16 (1966), p. 71.
2. Daniel J. Levinson, *The Seasons of a Man's Life* (New York: Ballantine Books, published by arrangement with Alfred A. Knopf, 1979), p. 109.
3. Toni Wolff, "A Few Thoughts on the Process of Individuation in Women," *Spring* (1941), pp. 91–93.
4. H. Peters, *My Sister, My Spouse: A Biography of Lou Andreas-Salome* (New York: Norton, 1962).
5. Robert Rosenthal, "The Pygmalion Effect Lives," *Psychology Today* (September 1973), pp. 56–62. (Definitive text: Robert Rosenthal and Lenore Jacobson. *Pygmalion in the Classroom: Teacher Expectation and Pupil's Intellectual Development* (New York: Holt, Rinehart, & Winston, 1968).

CHAPTER 12: APHRODITE

Friedrich, Paul. *The Meaning of Aphrodite.* Chicago: University of Chicago Press, 1978. This was my chief source for the mythology and symbolism of Aphrodite.
Kerènyi, Karl. "The Golden One—Aphrodite." In *Goddesses of the Sun and Moon.* Translated by Murray Stein. Irving, Texas: Spring, 1979, pp. 41–60.
"The Hymn to Aphrodite," "The Second Hymn to Aphrodite," and "The Third Hymn to Aphrodite." In *The Homeric Hymns,* Translated by Charles Boer. 2nd ed., rev. Irving, Texas: Spring, 1979, pp. 69–83.
Johnson, Robert. *She: Understanding Feminine Psychology.* New York: Harper & Row, 1977. (Originally published 1976.)
Mayerson, Philip. "Aphrodite (Venus)." In *Classical Mythology in Literature, Art, and Music.* New York: Wiley, 1971, pp. 182–210.
Neumann, Erich. *Amor and Psyche: The Psychic Development of the Feminine.* Translated by Ralph Manheim. (Bollingen Series 54) New York: Pantheon, 1956.
Otto, Walter F. "Aphrodite." In *The Homeric Gods,* translated by Moses Hadas. New York: Thames & Hudson, published by arrangement with Pantheon Books, 1979, pp. 91–103.
Zabriskie, Philip. "Goddesses in Our Midst." *Quadrant* (Fall 1979), pp. 36–37.
1. Paul Friedrich, *The Meaning of Aphrodite* (Chicago: University of Chicago Press, 1978), p. 79.
2. Ruth Falk, *Women Loving* (New York: Random House; and Berkeley: Bookworks, 1975).

CHAPTER 13: WHICH GODDESS GETS THE GOLDEN APPLE?

Jung, C. G. "Psychological Types." *CW*, vol. 6.
Mayerson, Philip. "The Trojan War." In *Classical Mythology in Literature, Art, and Music.* New York: Wiley, 1971, pp. 375–422.
1. Lisle, Laura. *Portrait of an Artist: A Biography of Georgia O'Keeffe* (New York: Washington Square Press/Simon & Schuster, by arrangement with Seaview Books, 1981), p. 143.

CHAPTER 14: THE HEROINE IN EVERYWOMAN

Adams, Richard. *Watership Down.* New York: Avon Books, published by arrangement with Macmillan, 1975.
Auel, Jean M. *The Clan of the Cave Bear.* New York: Bantam Books, by arrangement with Crown Publishers, 1981.
Auel, Jean M. *The Valley of Horses.* New York: Crown Publishers, 1982.
Tolkien, J. R. R. *The Fellowship of the Ring Trilogy.* New York: Ballantine Books, by arrangement with Houghton Mifflin, 1965.
1. T. S. Eliot. *Four Quartets* (New York: Harcourt Brace Jovanovich, no date), p. 59.

APPENDIX: WHO'S WHO IN GREEK MYTHOLOGY

Zimmerman, J. E. *Dictionary of Classical Mythology.* New York: Bantam Books, by arrangement with Harper & Row, 1964. Source for pronunciation of names.

Bibliography

This bibliography is divided into four sections: 1, Mythology; 2, Archetypal Psychology (Jungian Analytical Psychology); 3, Psychology of Women (other than Jungian); and 4, General Psychology (relevant to this book).

1. MYTHOLOGY

Bullfinch's Mythology. Middlesex, England: Hamlyn, 1964.

Bullfinch's Mythology: The Greek and Roman Fables Illustrated. Compiled by Bryan Holme, with an Introduction by Joseph Campbell. New York: Viking Press, 1979.

Callimachus. "To Artemis." In *Hymns and Epigrams.* Translated by A. W. Mair. Cambridge, Mass.: Harvard University Press, 1969.

Campbell, Joseph. *The Hero with a Thousand Faces.* 2nd ed. Bollingen Series 17. Princeton, N.J.: Princeton University Press, 1968.

Campbell, Joseph. "Joseph Campbell on the Great Goddess." *Parabola* 5, no. 4 (1980).

Evslin, Bernard. "Atalanta." In *Heroes, Gods and Monsters of the Greek Myths.* New York: Bantam Pathfinder, published by arrangement with *Scholastic* Magazine, 1975. (Originally published 1966.)

Friedrich, Paul. *The Meaning of Aphrodite.* Chicago: University of Chicago Press, 1978.

Garnell, L. R. [Lewis Richard]. *The Cults of the Greek States.* New Rochelle, N.Y.: Caratzas Brothers, 1977. vol. 1, chaps. 7, 8, 9 (Hera); vol. 1, chaps. 10, 11, 12 (Athena); vol. 2, chaps. 13, 17, 18 (Artemis); vol. 2, chaps. 21, 22, 23 (Aphrodite); vol. 3, chaps. 2, 3, 4 (Demeter-Kore); vol. 5, chaps. 8 (Hestia). (Originally written between 1895 and 1909.)

Gimbutas, Marija. *The Goddesses and Gods of Old Europe: 6500–3500, Myths and Cult Images.* Berkeley and Los Angeles: University of California Press, 1982.

Graves, Robert. *The Greek Myths.* 2 vols. New York: Penguin, 1979, 1982. (Originally published 1955.)

Graves, Robert. *The White Goddess.* New York: Farrar, Straus & Giroux, 1980. (Originally published 1948.)

Guthrie, W. K. C. *The Greeks and Their Gods.* Boston: Beacon Press, 1950.

Hadas, Moses, ed. *Greek Drama.* New York: Bantam, 1982. (Originally published 1965.)

Hamilton, Edith. *Mythology.* Boston: Little, Brown, 1942.

Harrison, Jane Ellen. *Mythology.* New York: Harcourt Brace Jovanovich, 1963. (Originally published 1924.)

Hesiod. *Theogony.* In *Hesiod,* translated by Richard Lattimore. Ann Arbor, Michigan: The University of Michigan Press, 1959.

Homer. *The Iliad.* Translated by Richard Lattimore. Chicago: University of Chicago Press, 1951.

The Homeric Hymns. Translated by Charles Boer. Irving, Texas: Spring, 1979.

James, E. O. [Edwin Oliver]. *The Cult of the Mother Goddess.* London, England: Thames & Hudson, 1959.

Kerènyi, C. *The Heroes of the Greeks.* London: Thames & Hudson, 1959.

Kerènyi, C. *The Gods of the Greeks.* Translated by Norman Cameron. New York: Thames & Hudson, 1979. (Originally published 1951.)

Kerènyi, Karl. *Athene: Virgin and Mother.* Translated by Murray Stein. Zurich, Switzerland: Spring, 1978.

Kerènyi, Karl. *Goddesses of the Sun and Moon.* Translated by Murray Stein. Irving, Texas: Spring, 1979.

Mayerson, Philip. *Classical Mythology in Literature, Art, and Music.* New York: Wiley, 1979.

Monaghan, Patricia. *The Book of Goddesses and Heroines.* New York: Dutton, 1981.

Otto, Walter F. *The Homeric Gods.* New York: Thames & Hudson, 1979. (Originally published 1954.)

Spretnak, Charlene. *Lost Goddesses of Early Greece: A Collection of Pre-Hellenic Mythology* Boston: Beacon Press, 1981. (Originally published 1978.)

Walker, Barbara G. *The Woman's Encyclopedia of Myths and Secrets.* San Francisco: Harper & Row, 1983.

Zimmerman, J. E. *Dictionary of Classical Mythology.* New York: Bantam Books, 1978. (Originally published 1964.)

2. ARCHETYPAL PSYCHOLOGY (JUNGIAN ANALYTICAL PSYCHOLOGY)

Berry, Patricia. "The Rape of Demeter/Persephone and Neurosis." *Spring* (1975).

Bradway, Katherine. "Hestia and Athena in the Analysis of Women." *Inward Light* 41, no. 91 (1978).

Claremont de Castillejo, Irene. *Knowing Woman.* New York: Putnam's Sons, 1973. Published for the C. G. Jung Foundation for Analytic Psychology.

Demetrakopoulos, Stephanie A. "Hestia, Goddess of the Hearth: Notes on an Oppressed Archetype." *Spring* (1979).

Demetrakopoulos, Stephanie A. "Life Stage Theory, Gerontological Research, and the Mythology of the Older Woman: Independence, Autonomy, and Strength." *Anima* 8, no. 2 (1982).

Downing, Christine. "Persephone in Hades." *Anima* 4, no. 1 (1977).

Downing, Christine. "Coming to Terms with Hera. *Quadrant* 12, no. 2 (1979)

Downing, Christine. *Goddess: Mythological Images of the Feminine.* New York: Crossroad, 1981.

Downing, Christine. "Goddess Sent Madness." *Psychological Perspectives* 12, no. 2 (1981).

Downing, Christine. "Come Celebrate with Me." *Anima* 9, no. 1 (1982).

Elias-Button, Karen. "Athena and Medusa: A Woman's Myth." *Anima* 5, no. 2 (1979).

Goldenberg, Naomi R. "Archetypal Theory after Jung." *Spring* (1975).

Hall, Nor. *The Moon and the Virgin: Reflections on the Archetypal Feminine.* New York: Harper & Row, 1980.

Harding, M. Esther. *The Way of All Women.* New York: Putman's, 1973. Published for the C. G. Jung Foundation for Analytical Psychology.

Harding, M. Esther. *Woman's Mysteries: Ancient and Modern.* New York: Bantam, 1973. (Originally published 1971.)

Harding, M. Esther. "The Value and Meaning of Depression." *Psychological Perspectives* 12, no. 2 (1981).

Heisler, Verda. "Individuation through Marriage." *Psychological Perspectives* 1, no. 2 (1970).

Hillman, James. "Anima." *Spring* (1973).

Hillman, James. "Anima II." *Spring* (1974).

Hillman, James. *The Dream and the Underworld.* New York: Harper & Row, 1979.

Hillman, James. "Ananke and Athene." In *Facing the Gods*, edited by James Hillman. Irving, Texas: Spring, 1980.

Hillman, James, ed. *Facing the Gods.* Irving, Texas: Spring, 1980.

Johnson, Robert. *She: Understanding Feminine Psychology.* New York: Harper & Row, 1977. (Originally published 1976.)

Jung, Emma. *Animus and Anima.* New York: Spring, 1969. (Originally published 1957.)

Jung, C. G. All references to Jung's Collected Works are taken from Collected Works of C. G. Jung, edited by Sir Herbert Read, Michael Fordham, and Gerald Adler; translated by R. F. C. Hull, Executive Editor, William McGuire, Bollingen Series 20, (Princeton, N.J.: Princeton University Press).

Jung, C. G. *The Practice of Psychotherapy.* In *Collected Works of C. G. Jung*, vol. 16. 1966.

Jung, C. G. *Two Essays on Analytic Psychology.* In *Collected Works of C. G. Jung*, vol. 7. 1966.

Jung, C. G. *Alchemical Studies.* In *Collected Works of C. G. Jung*, vol. 13. 1967.

Jung, C. G. *Archetypes of the Collective Unconscious.* In *Collective Works of C. G. Jung,* vol. 9, part 1. 1968.

Jung, C. G. *Psychological Types.* In *Collected Works of C. G. Jung,* vol. 6. 1971.

Jung, C. G., and Kerènyi, C. *Essays on a Science of Mythology: The Myths of the Divine Child and the Divine Maiden.* Translated by R. F. C. Hull. Bollingen Series 22. New York: Harper & Row, 1963. (Originally published 1949.)

Kerènyi, C. *Zeus and Hera: Archetypal Image of Father, Husband and Wife.* Bollingen Series 65. Princeton, N.J.: Princeton University Press, 1975.

Kerènyi, C. *Eleusis: Archetypal Image of Mother and Daughter.* New York: Schocken, 1977. (Originally published 1967.)

Kerènyi, Karl. "A Mythological Image of Childhood: Artemis." In *Facing the Gods,* edited by James Hillman. Irving, Texas: Spring, 1980.

Kirksey, Barbara. "Hestia: A Background of Psychological Focusing." In *Facing the Gods,* edited by James Hillman. Irving, Texas: Spring, 1980.

Koltuv, Barbara Black. "Hestia/Vesta." *Quadrant* 10, no. 2 (1977).

Kotschnig, Elined Prys. "Womanhood in Myth and Life." *Inward Light* 31, no. 74 (1968).

Kotschnig, Elined Prys. "Womanhood in Myth and Life, Part 2." *Inward Light* 32, no. 75 (1969).

Laub-Novak, Karen. "Reflections on Art and Mysticism." *Anima* 2, no. 2 (1976).

Leonard, Linda Schierse. *The Wounded Woman. Healing the Father-Daughter Relationship.* Boulder, Colo.: Shambhala Publications, 1983. (Originally published 1981.)

Lockhart, Russell A. "Eros in Language, Myth, and Dream." *Quadrant* 11, no. 1 (1978).

Loomis, Mary. "A New Perspective for Jung's Typology: The Singer-Loomis Inventory of Personality." *Journal of Analytical Psychology* 27, no. 1 (1982).

Loomis, Mary, and Singer, June. "Testing the Bipolarity Assumption in Jung's Typology." *Journal of Analytical Psychology* 25, no. 4 (1980).

Luke, Helen M. "The Perennial Feminine." *Parabola* 5, no. 4 (1978).

Luke, Helen M. *Woman, Earth and Spirit.* New York: Crossroad, 1981.

Malamud, René. "The Amazon Problem." *Spring* (1971).

Mattoon, Mary Ann. *Jungian Psychology in Perspective.* New York: Free Press/Macmillan, 1981.

Moore, Tom. "Artemis and the Puer." In *Puer Papers.* Irving, Texas: Spring, 1979.

Neumann, Erich. *The Great Mother: An Analysis of the Archetype.* Translated by Ralph Manheim. London: Routledge & Kegan Paul, 1955.

Neumann, Erich. *Amor and Psyche: The Psychic Development of the Feminine.* Translated by Ralph Manheim. Bollingen Series 54. New York: Pantheon Books, 1956.

Neumann, Erich. "The Psychological Stages of Feminine Development."
    Spring (1959).
Perera, Sylvia Brinton. *Descent to the Goddess: A Way of Initiation for Women.*
    Toronto: Inner City Books, 1981.
Rupprecht, Carol. "The Martial Maid and the Challenge of Androgyny
    (Notes on an Unbefriended Archetype)." *Spring* (1974).
Schmidt, Lynda. "The Brother-Sister Relationship in Marriage." *Journal of*
    Analytical Psychology 25, no. 1 (1980).
Singer, June. *Androgyny.* New York: Doubleday, 1976.
Singer, June. "Rise of the Androgyny Phenomena." *Anima* 3, no. 2 (1977).
Spretnak, Charlene. "Problems with Jungian Uses of Greek Goddess
    Mythology." *Anima* 6, no. 1 (1979).
Stein, Murray. "Hera: Bound and Unbound." *Spring* (1977).
Stein, Murray. "Translator's Afterthoughts." In Karl Kerènyi, *Athene: Vir-*
    gin and Mother. Translated by Murray Stein. Zurich: Spring, 1978.
Stevens, Anthony. *Archetypes: A Natural History of the Self.* New York: Mor-
    row, 1982.
Ulanov, Ann Belford. "Archetypes of the Feminine." In *The Feminine in*
    Jungian Psychology and Christian Theology. Evanston, Ill.: Northwestern
    University Press, 1971.
Wheelwright, Jane. *Women and Men.* San Francisco: C. G. Jung Institute of
    San Francisco, 1978.
Wolf, Toni. "A Few Thoughts on Individuation in Women." *Spring*
    (1941).
Zabriskie, Philip. "Goddesses in Our Midst." *Quadrant* 17, (1974).

3. PSYCHOLOGY OF WOMEN (PERSPECTIVES OTHER THAN JUNGIAN)

Applegarth, Adrienne. "Some Observations on Work Inhibitions in
    Women." *Journal of the American Psychoanalytic Association* 24, no. 5
    (1976).
Bart, Pauline B. "Portnoy's Mother's Complaint." *Trans-Action* (Novem-
    ber–December 1970).
Bart, Pauline B. "Depression in Middle-Aged Women." In *Women in Sexist*
    Society, edited by Vivian Gornick and Barbara K. Moran. New York:
    Basic Books, 1971.
Benedek, Therese, and Rubinstein, Boris B. "The Sexual Cycle in Women:
    The Relationship Between Ovarian function and Psychodynamic
    Processes." *Psychosomatic Medicine Monographs* 3, nos. 1, 2 (1942). Ed-
    ited for inclusion in Therese Benedek, *Psychoanalytic Investigations:*
    Selected Papers, "The Correlation Between Ovarian Activity and Psy-
    chodynamic Process." New York: Quadrangle, 1973.
Bernardez-Bonesatti, Teresa. "Women and Anger: Conflicts with Aggres-
    sion in Contemporary Women." *Journal of the American Medical Wom-*
    en's Association 33, no. 5 (1978).

Besdine, Matthew. "Mrs. Oedipus." *Psychology Today* (March 1971).

Carmen, Elaine; Russo, Nancy F.; and Miller, Jean B. "Inequality and Women's Mental Health: An Overview." *American Journal of Psychiatry* 138, no. 11 (1981).

Chernin, Kim. *The Obsession: Reflections on the Tyranny of Slenderness.* New York: Harper & Row, 1981.

Chesler, Phyllis. *Women & Madness.* New York: Doubleday, 1972.

Chicago, Judy. *Through the Flower.* New York: Doubleday, 1977.

Dowling, Colette. *The Cinderella Complex: Women's Hidden Fear of Independence.* New York: Summit Books, 1981.

Erikson, Erik. "Inner and Outer Space: Reflections on Womanhood." *Daedalus* (1964).

Freeman, Jo, ed., *Women: A Feminist Perspective,* 2nd ed. New York: Basic Books, 1979.

The Female Experience. From the editors of *Psychology Today.* Del Mar, Calif.: CRM, 1973.

Field, Joanna. *A Life of One's Own.* Los Angeles: Tarcher, 1981.

Friedan, Betty. *The Feminine Mystique.* New York: Dell, 1964.

Galland, China. *Women in the Wilderness.* New York: Harper & Row, 1980.

Gilligan, Carol. *In a Different Voice: Psychological Theory and Women's Development.* Cambridge, Mass.: Harvard University Press, 1982.

Gornick, Vivian, and Moran, Barbara K., eds. *Women in Sexist Society.* New York: Basic Books, 1971.

Gray, Elizabeth Dodson. *Why the Green Nigger: Re-mything Genesis.* Wellesley, Mass.: Roundtable Press, 1979.

Greer, Germaine. *The Female Eunuch.* New York: McGraw-Hill, 1971.

Griffin, Susan. *Rape: The Power of Consciousness.* New York: Harper & Row, 1979.

Heilbrun, Carolyn G. *Toward a Recognition of Androgyny.* New York: Harper & Row, 1974.

Heilbrun, Carolyn G. *Reinventing Womanhood.* New York: Norton, 1979.

Hennig, Margaret, and Jardim, Anne. *The Managerial Woman.* New York: Simon & Schuster, 1978.

Horner, Matina. "Why Bright Women Fear Success." In *The Female Experience,* from the editors of *Psychology Today.* Del Mar, Calif.: CRM, 1973.

Howell, Elizabeth, and Bayes, Marjorie, eds. *Women and Mental Health.* New York: Basic Books, 1981.

Koedt, Ann; Levine, Ellen; and Rapone, Anita, eds. *Radical Feminism.* New York: Quadrangle, 1973.

Kolbenschlag, Madonna. *Kiss Sleeping Beauty Good-Bye: Breaking the Spell of Feminine Myths and Models.* New York: Doubleday, 1979.

Lakoff, Robin, *Language and Woman's Place.* New York: Harper & Row, 1975.

Lederer, Wolfgang. *The Fear of Women.* New York: Harcourt Brace Jovanovich, 1968.

Lerner, Harriet E. "Early Origins of Envy and Devaluation of Women: Implications for Sex Role Stereotypes." *Bulletin of the Menninger Clinic* 38, no. 6 (1974).

Martin, Del. *Battered Wives.* New York: Simon & Schuster, 1977.

Miller, Jean Baker. *Psychoanalysis and Women.* New York: Brunner/Mazel, 1973. (Paperback edition, Baltimore: Penguin, 1979.)

Miller, Jean Baker. *Toward a New Psychology of Women.* Boston: Beacon Press, 1976.

Nadelson, Carol C., and Notman, Malkah T. *The Woman Patient. Vol. 2: Concepts of Femininity and the Life Cycle.* New York: Plenum Press, 1982.

Notman, Malkah T., and Nadelson, Carol C. "The Rape Victim: Psychodynamic Considerations." *American Journal of Psychiatry* 133, no. 4 (1976).

Ochs, Carol. *Behind the Sex of God: Toward a New Consciousness—Transcending Matriarchy and Patriarchy.* Boston: Beacon Press, 1977.

Person, Ethel Spector. "Women Working: Fears of Failure, Deviance and Success." *Journal of the American Academy of Psychoanalysis* 10, no. 1 (1982).

Rohrbaugh, Joanna Bunker, ed. *Women: Psychology's Puzzle.* New York: Basic Books, 1979.

Rossi, Alice S. "Life-Span Theories and Women's Lives." *Signs* 6, no. 1 (1980).

Rubin, Lillian B. *Women of a Certain Age: The Midlife Search for Self.* New York: Harper & Row, 1979.

Scarf, Maggie. *Unfinished Business: Pressure Points in the Lives of Women.* New York: Ballantine Books, 1981.

Seiden, Anne M. "Overview: Research on the Psychology of Women. Part 2. Women and Families, Work, and Psychotherapy." *American Journal of Psychiatry* 133, no. 10 (1976).

Seidenberg, Robert. "The Trauma of Eventlessness." In *Psychoanalysis and Women,* edited by Jean Baker Miller. Baltimore: Penguin, 1973.

Spretnak, Charlene, ed. *The Politics of Women's Spirituality: Essays on the Rise of Spiritual Power Within the Feminist Movement.* New York: Doubleday, 1982.

Staines, Graham; Tarvis, Carol; and Jayaratne, T. E. "The Queen Bee Syndrome." In *The Female Experience,* from the editors of *Psychology Today.* Del Mar, Calif.: CRM, 1973.

Steinem, Gloria. *Outrageous Acts and Everyday Rebellions.* New York: Holt, Rinehart, & Winston, 1983.

Stone, Merlin. *When God Was a Woman.* New York: Harcourt Brace Jovanovich, 1976.

Symonds, Alexandria. "Violence Against Women: The Myth of Masochism." *American Journal of Psychotherapy* 33, no. 2 (1979).

Thomas, Lynn. *The Backpacking Woman.* New York: Doubleday, 1980.

Weissman, Myrna M., and Kaplan, Gerald L. "Sex Differences and the

Epidemiology of Depression." In *Gender and Disordered Behavior,* edited by E. S. Gomberg and V. Franks. New York: Brunner/Mazel, 1979.

Weisstein, Naomi. "Psychology Constructs the Female." In *Radical Feminism,* edited by Anne Koedt, Ellen Levine, and Anita Rapone. New York: Quadrangle, 1973. (Also published in *Woman in Sexist Society,* edited by Vivian Gornick and Barbara K. Moran. New York: Basic Books, 1971.)

4. General Psychology (References Relevant to This Book)

Erikson, Erik. *Childhood and Society.* 2nd ed. New York: Norton, 1963.

Feinstein, A. David. "Personal Mythology as a Paradigm for a Holistic Public Psychology." *American Journal of Orthopsychiatry* 49, no. 2 (1979).

Freud, Sigmund. *The Standard Edition of the Psychological Works of Sigmund Freud,* ed. J. Strachey. London: Hogarth Press.

Gardner, Earl R., and Hall, Richard C. W. "The Professional Stress Syndrome." *Psychosomatics* 22, no. 8 (1981).

Gendlin, Eugene T. *Focusing.* New York: Bantam Books, 1981. (Originally published 1978.)

Harris, Mark. "Teaching Is a Form of Loving." *Psychology Today* (September 1973).

Jaynes, Julian. *The Origin of Consciousness in the Breakdown of the Bicameral Mind.* Boston: Houghton Mifflin, 1976.

Levinson, Daniel. *The Seasons of a Man's Life.* New York: Ballantine, 1979.

Neugarten, Bernice L., ed. *Middle Age and Aging: A Reader in Social Psychology.* Chicago: University of Chicago Press, 1968.

Metzner, Ralph. *Know Your Type.* New York: Doubleday, 1979.

Rosenthal, Robert. "The Pygmalion Effect Lives." *Psychology Today* (September 1973).

Rosenthal, Robert, and Jacobson, Lenore. *Pygmalion in the Classroom: Teacher Expectation and Pupil's Intellectual Development.* New York: Holt, Rinehart, & Winston, 1968.

Richards, M. C. (Mary Caroline). *Centering in Pottery, Poetry, and the Person.* Middleton, Conn.: Wesleyan University Press, 1975. (Originally printed 1961.)

Safan-Gerard, Desy. "How to Unblock." *Psychology Today* (January 1978).

Sheehy, Gail. *Passages: Predictable Crises of Adult Life.* New York: Dutton, 1977.

Tennov, Dorothy. *Love and Limerence: The Experience of Being in Love.* Briarcliff Manor, New York: Stein & Day, 1979.

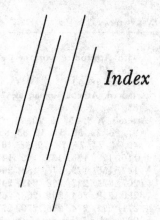

Index

Hephaestus, 15, 19, 76, 141, 165–
166, 234, 264, 270; genealogy,
299; man, with Aphrodite woman, 247–248
Hera, 7–8, 15, 16, 18, 19, 21, 25,
28, 29, 30, 31, 33, 39, 42, 43,
47, 53, 60, 62, 67, 68, 78, 93,
94, 101, 113, 119, 122, 123,
125, 132–167, 168, 171, 174,
176, 177, 178, 179, 180, 184,
204, 212, 215, 216, 224, 234,
238, 242, 246, 248, 250, 251,
258, 259, 261, 263–264, 265,
268, 269, 270, 273, 274, 281,
282, 283, 286, 294; adolescence
and early adulthood, 149–150;
archetypal roles, 301; capacity
for commitment, 144–145; children, 156–157; cultivating, 147–
148; description of archetype,
142–148; description of goddess,
139–142; description of Hera
woman, 8–9, 148–158; disappointed expectations, 159–160;
early years, 148–149; genealogy
and mythology, 140–142, 299;
identifying with, 158–159; invoking, 33; Jungian psychological type, 302; later years, 158;
marriage, 145–146, 154–156;
Medea Syndrome, 161–163;
middle years, 157; as mother,
14, 156–157; negative pattern,
146–147; oppressed and oppres-
sor, 160–161; parents, 149; psychological difficulties, 158–163,
302; relationships with men,
152–153; relationships with
women, 151–152; relative power
of, 22; sexuality, 153–154; significant others, 301; strengths,
302; as vulnerable goddess, 132–
138; ways to grow, 163–167; as
wife, 142–144; work, 150–151
Heracles, 77, 198–199, 279
Heraclitus, 221

Hercules. *See* Heracles
Hermaphroditus, 235
Hermes, 19, 170, 192, 198, 234–
235, 264; genealogy, 299; as
god, relation to Hestia, 109,
114–115, 129–130; man, with
Aphrodite woman, 247, 249–
250; man, with Hestia woman,
123–124, 250
Heroine, becoming a, 278–295;
end of the journey, 294–295;
evoking the transcendent function, 289–293; fending off death
and destruction, 286–288; getting through the dark and nar-
row passage, 289; the path, 280–
282; reclaiming the power of the
snake, 283–284; resisting the
power of the bear, 284–286; surviving loss and grief, 288–289;
from victim to heroine, 293–294
Hesiod, 17–18, 76, 234, 235, 240
Hestia, 11, 15, 16, 18, 19, 25, 29,
30, 31, 34, 35–45, 79, 99, 107–
131, 137, 224, 225, 242, 250,
258, 267, 268, 274, 276, 282;
adolescence and early adulthood, 120; archetypal roles, 301;
children, 124–125; cultivating,
116–117; description of archetype, 110–117; description of
goddess, 107–109; description of
Hestia woman, 9, 117–126; devaluation of, 127; early years,
118; genealogy and mythology,
107–108, 299; as hearthkeeper,
111–112; and Hermes, 109,
114–115, 129–130; identifying
with, 126–127; invoking, 33; as
inward-focused, 110–111, 113–
114; Jungian psychological type,
302; later years, 125–126; marriage, 122–123; middle years,
125; as mother, 14, 124–125;
parents, 118–120; psychological
difficulties, 126–127, 302; rela-

scription of goddess, 197–199; description of Persephone woman, 205–215; early years, 205–206; genealogy and mythology, 169–171, 197–199, 299; as guide to underworld, 202–204; identifying with, 215–217; invoking, 33; Jungian psychological type, 302; as the Kore, 199–200; later years, 214–215; marriage, 212–213; middle years, 214; as mother, 14, 213–214; as mother's daughter, 200; parents, 206–207; psychological difficulties, 215–219, 302; relationships with men, 209–211; relationships with women, 209; relative power of, 23; sexuality, 211; significant others, 301; strengths, 302; susceptibility to psychological illness, 218–219; as symbol of spring, 204; as vulnerable goddess, 132–138; ways to grow, 220–223; work, 208–209

Perseus, 77

Persistence, in Demeter woman, 173–174

Persona, in Hestia woman: fashioning, 127–128; lack of, 119, 126

Phaedra, 257; myth of, 237

Phobos, 235

Plath, Sylvia, 203

Playboy magazine, 201

Pluto. *See* Hades

Poseidon, 15, 18, 19, 47, 108, 130, 131, 234, 237, 264, 270; genealogy, 299–300

Postmenopausal period, and goddess shift, 34. *See also* Later life

"Post menopausal zest," 30

Power of bear, resisting, 284–286

Power of snake, reclaiming, 283–284

Predisposition to a goddess archetype, 26–27

Pregnancy, 73, 172–173, 176,

178–179, 187, 189–190, 240–241, 246, 268–270, 284–286 (*see also* Children); and goddess activation, 29–30

Pretty Baby, 201

Previn, Doree, 203

Procreative instinct, Aphrodite archetype as, 240–241

Prophecy, God of. *See* Apollo

Proserpina. *See* Persephone

Provider, Demeter woman as, 173

Psyche, 257; and Eros, myth of, 5–6, 7, 198, 237–238, 258–262, 282, 288, 290, 294; genealogy, 300

Psychic, Persephone woman as, 222

Psychological difficulties: Aphrodite woman, 254–258, 302; Artemis woman, 66–71, 302; Athena woman, 99–104, 302; Demeter woman, 188–193, 302; Hera woman, 158–163, 302; Hestia woman, 126–127, 302; Persephone woman, 215–219, 302

Psychosis, in Persephone woman, 219

Puberty, and goddess activation, 29. *See also* Adolescence and early adulthood; Parents

Pygmalion, 231

Pygmalion, 224, 232, 236

Pygmalion effect, of alchemical goddess, 231–232

Quality of consciousness: alchemical goddess, 226–227; virgin goddesses, 37–38; vulnerable goddesses, 133–135

Queen of Underworld, Persephone as, 197, 198–199, 202–204

Rage: in Artemis woman, 68–69; in Hera woman, 146–147, 161–163; transforming into work, 165–166

A Note on *Gods in Everyman*

The archetypes of both genders exist within each of us. While the goddesses are most dominant in women, the gods are most dominant in men. However, most women will find at least one of the male archetypes active within them and recognize this as a missing piece of the puzzle that completes their identity.

Gods in Everyman can take us beyond self-recognition to help women realize which archetypes are active within their fathers, lovers, spouses, and sons. Like *Goddesses in Everywoman*, *Gods in Everyman* describes the effects of stereotypes or expectations on men. Realizing that some archetypes are favored over others by the dominant culture will bring about a compassionate understanding of the social pressures on men; this can only lead to a greater understanding of the men in your life. Identifying the god and goddess archetypes at work within each of us will help us tap their power and become better heroes and heroines in our own life stories.

ALSO BY JEAN SHINODA BOLEN

GODDESSES IN EVERYWOMAN
Powerful Archetypes in Women's Lives

Available in Paperback and Ebook

"*Goddesses in Everywoman* supplies powerful concrete images that can be used effectively to produce self-understanding and change. Highly recommended." —*Booklist*

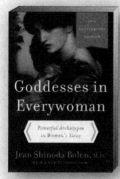

GODDESSES IN OLDER WOMEN
Archetypes in Women Over Fifty

Available in Paperback and Ebook

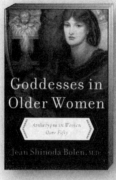

"For those who celebrate their maturity, Bolen's thoughtful mytho-psychology will be an inspiration."—*Publishers Weekly*

GODS IN EVERYMAN
Archetypes That Shape Men's Lives

Available in Paperback and Ebook

"A fascinating book. . . . Novel, visionary, and helpful." —*San Francisco Chronicle*

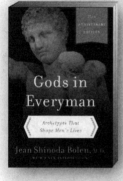

THE TAO OF PSYCHOLOGY
Synchronicity and the Self

Available in Paperback

Understanding the moments that touch and transform our lives.

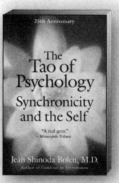

CROSSING TO AVALON
A Woman's Midlife Quest for the Sacred Feminine

Available in Paperback

"[Bolen] charts a path that will lead many readers to the heart of their own emotional and spiritual pilgrimages." —*San Francisco Chronicle Book Review*

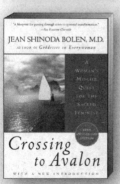